No other way

101 704 416 3

MANCHESTER
UNIVERSITY PRESS

Derek Paget

No other way to tell it

DRAMADOC/DOCUDRAMA ON TELEVISION

Manchester University Press

Manchester and New York

Distributed exclusively in the USA by St. Martin's Press

The right of Derek Paget to be identified as the author of this work has been asserted by him in accordance with the Copyright, Designs and Patents Act 1988.

Published by Manchester University Press
Oxford Road, Manchester M13 9NR, UK
and Room 400, 175 Fifth Avenue, New York, NY 10010, USA

Distributed exclusively in the USA by
St. Martin's Press, Inc., 175 Fifth Avenue, New York,
NY 10010, USA

Distributed exclusively in Canada by
UBC Press, University of British Columbia, 6344 Memorial Road,
Vancouver, BC, Canada V6T 1Z2

British Library Cataloguing-in-Publication Data
A catalogue record for this book is available from the British Library

Library of Congress Cataloging-in-Publication Data applied for

ISBN   0 7190 4532 0 *hardback*
        0 7190 4533 9 *paperback*

First published 1998
02 01 00 99 98   10 9 8 7 6 5 4 3 2 1

Typeset by Special Edition Pre-press Services, London
Printed in Great Britain by Bell and Bain Ltd, Glasgow

Contents

Acknowledgements

I try in this book to bridge what is often seen as a gap between the academy and the entertainment industry; people from both worlds have been helpful to me in my attempt to combine theory and practice.

From television, my thanks to Ray Fitzwalter, Tony Garnett, Ian McBride, Martin McKeand, Alasdair Palmer, Jeremy Sandford, Sita Williams and Leslie Woodhead. All, variously, talked to me, loaned me scripts, treatments, tapes and papers, and offered their time and hospitality. I must single out two people: Ian McBride, for his additional ready granting of access to the working processes at Granada; and his colleague Sita Williams, for her unfailing willingness to consider ideas, offer perspectives, organise assistance, and cheerfully to deal with so many questions and requests for help. The casts and crews involved in the work I invaded at Granada were always both welcoming and willing to share their experience.

From the academy, I have enjoyed the collaborative assistance of Ted Braun, John Corner, Richard Kilborn, Nicola Shaughnessy, Robert Shaughnessy and Gareth Palmer. John Corner's published work, and discussions with him about dramadoc/docudrama, have been a great stimulus. Also, the editors of the academic journals *Studies in Theatre Production* and *Continuum* kindly made early space for material now reworked in Chapters 1 and 8.

Pitched between the academy and the industry, and operating energetically in both, are David Edgar and Alan Rosenthal. Both contributed a great deal to the book; both have long-standing interests in the subject and have helped over the years to establish its cultural importance. The 'Reality Time' conference in 1996 at Birmingham University, which David Edgar organised, was central to the whole process of writing. It was here I met the media lawyers Patrick Swaffer and Oliver Goodenough, who helped me to understand their work. The former kindly commented on Chapter 2 in draft.

My thanks also to Manchester University Press (Matthew Frost, Anita Roy, and Stephanie Sloan were exemplary in their helpfulness throughout), and to University College Worcester, who, in making me a Reader in 1992, gave me time away from teaching to research and to write.

Finally, I want – as ever – to thank Jessica Paget, for all her help.

Introduction

This book is about a type of television programme that has attracted, and will probably continue to attract, more than its fair share of controversy and comment. Television dramadoc/docudrama has frequently found a direct line into all sorts of public debates but has also itself classically been the source of complicated and confused debate. It is of course not simply the appellations 'dramadoc' or 'docudrama' that have been at issue, but a documentary mode that has considerable cultural importance in the twentieth century. Documentary's historic claim to be a truth-teller in its representation of the real can provoke a difficult situation whenever there is a suspicion that some kind of lie has been told. This can lead to dire consequences for the perpetrator.

A case in Germany will illustrate what I mean. Michael Born, a respected director of upwards of thirty programmes for Stern TV, was recently jailed for four years as a common criminal for having allegedly passed off fiction as fact. The documentary films he made seemed to be factual and were accepted as such for a long time, but Born had used actors to fake documentaries, hoodwinking both audiences and (so they claim) his employers. It is hard to avoid the thought that the somewhat draconian punishment meted out to him is a reflection of documentary's cultural status as a kind of faith. It was Born's bad faith – his apostasy – which ultimately constituted his biggest crime. Thomas Frickel, another German film maker, remarked: 'Born was imprisoned for religious reasons.'[1]

Dramadoc/docudrama is problematical because it openly proclaims both a documentary and a dramatic provenance. This 'both/and' claim is often met with a critical refusal, an 'either/or' counter-claim. The suspicion that you cannot have 'both/and' in this case is ever present. Mixing drama and documentary is sometimes seen as a fake and bogus exercise. The essential problems are:

(a) the nature and status of the factual material used in the programme,

(b) the kinds of dramatic representation the programme employs,
(c) the overarching worry that 'dramatic licence' might mean that liberties are taken, and gross simplifications made, by programme makers.

In recent years there has been a further worry about the effects on the form of a sensationalising tendency in all television – indeed in all media. This might be termed the 'tabloid tendency', with its perceived preference for melodramatic and emotive treatments of important and unimportant issues alike.[2]

Dramadoc/docudrama is a great provoker of headlines that reflect these concerns. On both sides of the Atlantic, newspaper sub-editors signal cultural anxiety through inventive headlines. The increasingly popular idea that the boundary between fact and fiction is becoming dangerously blurred and that fact and fiction are now harder than ever to distinguish is at the heart of such phrase-making as: 'Blurring the boundaries', 'The "truth" of fiction is stranger than the facts', 'Friction over faction', 'Dubious drama', 'Drama out of suffering', 'Fact or fiction?', 'True to the facts?', 'An unsuitable case for television treatment?', 'Making a documentary drama out of a crisis'. All these, and more, reflect in their coinages, scare quotes and question marks the doubt and suspicion surrounding a form of programme that is in many ways unique to television. In a previous book I also succumbed to the typographical and linguistic neurosis (by calling it *True Stories?*). 'Making (documentary) drama out of a crisis' has become something of a cliché, but I thought of using it as the title for the present book; like all clichés, it contains a valuable nugget of truth.

In common with many important abstract concepts, the boundary between fact and fiction is both abundantly clear and impossibly muddled. Rather like a rainbow, it is perceptible enough on one level; it is possible to agree that it is 'there' and even to describe it in some detail, but as one attempts to approach it practically, it recedes and teases thought. Finding the foot of this rainbow is not as doomed an enterprise as it might seem, especially when exploration has been going on for thirty years or more. I hope that the many examples of practice that I shall quote, the thoughts of production staff working on dramadoc/docudrama and important writings on the subject (see the Bibliography) will help map the course of the form's development and also inform a discussion of its worth and significance.

Popular enough with audiences, the dramadoc/docudrama is often critically reviled as flawed and tainted – and its value is questioned thereby. Its secure place in popular culture makes it more significant than habitual criticism allows, however. Frequently portrayed as bad documentary, bad drama, or both these things simultaneously, dramadoc/docudrama is best understood first of all as itself – a form in its own right rather than some kind of 'mongrel', 'hybrid' or even 'bastard' form (as it has been labelled in the past). That, at any rate, is the principal thesis of this book: only by understanding dramadoc/docudrama in and for itself can it be known properly. There are, of course, some poor examples (as there are of any form), but the best have something to offer that no other form can achieve, uniting within one text television's historic popular mission both to inform and to entertain.

The present influence of American practices throughout television has contributed to the debate about tabloid tendencies with their alleged 'dumbing down' of popular culture. The widespread existence of co-production intensifies this allegation in the case of the modern dramadoc/docudrama. But this end-of-century critical notion seems to me part of what Jib Fowles has called 'TV priggery', or the holier-than-thou élitist response of intellectuals content to rubbish the output of network television by day while secretly watching (and enjoying) a good deal of it by night (1992: ix). 'Dumbing down' may well be going on, as programme makers accede to the virtually unrestrained demands of the marketplace – as evidenced by ratings. But this is not the whole picture; the continuing high profile of dramadoc/docudrama programmes in public debates about a range of issues is one assurance of this.

The project of the book

I hope this book will tap into wider debates about the nature of television's representations of public and private worlds as we move towards a new century. The discussion will frequently touch upon macro-issues proposed in, for example, John Corner's *The Art of Record* (1996) and Richard Kilborn and John Izod's *An Introduction to Television Documentary* (1997). Both works make important recent contributions to the complex theoretical arguments that have raged, and that I believe will continue to rage, around film and television representations of the real. The dramadoc and the docudrama are micro-features of this macro-debate, and this is the first time that a book-length enquiry has been solely devoted to the dual British and American traditions of practice. The subject is more usually approached in books via accounts of documentary proper in which dramadoc/docudrama appears as a relatively minor element.[3]

To begin with, therefore, I give an account of the production processes that obtain in the 1990s by examining two recent films. The 1992 film *Hostages* will feature later in this Introduction (and elsewhere in the book); the controversy that surrounded its transmission in Britain and the nature of the dispute with its real-world protagonists determine its centrality as case-study material. Chapter 1 looks in detail at the actual filming of the 1996–97 *Goodbye My Love*, offering a perspective on the problems of a form that is inexorably drawn towards the compelling 'personal story'. The effect of the disciplines of the filming process on both the documentary and the drama inputs involved are considered here.

The legal and regulatory frameworks that govern broadcast television are under considerable pressure from the personalised narratives of recent practice, especially when they trespass on the lives of individuals. In Chapter 2 the problems caused by this shift to a tabloid-tendency journalism of the 'first resort' are highlighted by a consideration of the work of the media lawyer – a little-understood aspect of the genesis of these programmes.[4] The lawyer, unlike the postmodern cultural theorist, has no room for the excess in meaning; his or her job is to be able at a moment's notice to demonstrate that meanings transmitted clearly correspond to what is permissible in both legal and regulatory senses. As such, their work contrasts with the more open seeking of nuanced meaning that is the proper project of the student and the critic. Chapter 2, then, considers how meanings on television are 'supervised' by other social institutions, and questions whether the supervision is heavier for this form in particular, and for television in general, than it is for other media (television executives certainly feel that it is).

From this basis in existing practice, Chapter 3 will move on to examine the codes and conventions of the form as they are now articulated. It will offer a taxonomy of codes and conventions that are useful in accounting for modern practice and in making comparisons with historical precedents. There will be a direct link between the methodologies of the television studio and location that are examined in Chapter 2 (heavily filmic and dramatic) and the factual elements that are present in some conventions (especially those which ground the form as partly documentary). I offer some provisional definitions of my own that try to explain what makes the form so characteristically different from either 'drama' or 'documentary'.

Making definitions through the perspective of present practice determined the material covered in Chapter 4. The terms 'drama' and 'documentary' and 'fact' and 'fiction' are unavoidable in definitions and descriptions of the form. They are often presented as binary oppositions (the 'either/or' argument); this is at the very heart of the dramadoc/docudrama debate. By examining the complex cultural histories behind the principal terms that are used to define and describe the form I hope to show that cultural relativities are necessarily already embedded in any discussion of current practice. My 'wordsearch' is not intended to relativise the key terms out of existence; it is more to show the richness of an essentially transgressive form and to illustrate that this territory, if it does exist in a border country, is much more interesting than simple accusations of blurring and narrowly definitional exercises would suggest.

Chapter 5 gives an account of the principal academic debates that have featured in the attempts to define the form. It also argues that recent notions about the blurring of fact and fiction actually tell us more about current cultural fears and anxieties than about traditions of practice. Our present obsession with borders and boundaries reflects in part an end-of-century fearfulness and uncertainty, in the face of which the (apparent) certainties of other times become attractive. The mixing of – if not blurring between – drama and documentary has a cultural history, the understanding of which necessitates some account of the antecedents of television forms (in journalism, theatre and film). The theoretical and practical influence of the pre-Second World War documentary film movement is examined in Chapter 5 to establish a foundation for the historical survey in Chapters 6 and 7.

Central to the argument throughout the book is the hybrid term of my sub-title: 'dramadoc/docudrama'. Different histories and traditions collide in that designation and I hope this coinage will prove useful in keeping the focus on two distinct traditions of usage. Chapters 6 and 7 give an account of the contrasting but complementary histories and practices of British and American television networks. It is in these institutions and their practices that 'dramadoc' and 'docudrama' first acquired significance. Examples offered throughout the book have been chosen to provide formal templates against which not only to measure pretty well any example of the genre but also to establish important lines of demarcation between the dramadoc and the docudrama. This is being done at an important historical moment: when the British tradition may become detectable only as a trace.

British and American traditions produced contrasting methodologies that are present in what I have classified as three phases of historical development, spread across more than fifty years of postwar television history. I define these phases and also give an account of the first two in Chapter 6. Within the twenty-five years of the two early phases can be found the reasons for the shifts in emphasis in the form between journalistic and entertainment priorities. Those crucial points of common practice led to the gradual merging of the British and American traditions in our own time – the third phase, which will be analysed in Chapter 7.

I shall make comparisons throughout the book between the more solemn British tradition of dramadoc and the parallel, but more entertainment-led, American tradition of docudrama. There are both positive and negative features to co-production, and I do not present an entirely pessimistic view of possible developments in the future. I shall pursue this topic in the final chapter via a theoretical account of the pleasures of the form. The 'ways of seeing' offered by dramadoc/docudrama have, I believe, been too little discussed and understood in the past; this has led to a routine downgrading of the form, especially in its 'made-for-TV movie' manifestation.

The case studies

I shall refer to a number of examples of practice, but there are eight films from the 1990s that are particularly important. *Fighting for Gemma* (1993) and *Hillsborough* (1996) are examples of campaigning films with a national focus. By contrast, *Hostages* (1992) and *Goodbye My Love* (1997) are films with 'international' subject matter. These British 'dramadocs' were made by Granada (part of ITV), a company that had operated continuously since commercial television began in Britain in 1955 and one of the foremost exponents of the form; the institutional history of this commercial television company will be a focus – particularly in Chapter 7. Modern American docudrama will be examined principally through discussion of the 'Long Island Lolita' trilogy (1992–93) in Chapter 8. The 'tabloid' tendency of current American practice will be broached (and not necessarily dismissed) here, and Jane Feuer's (1995) concept of the 'trauma drama' will be central to the debate. But there is also a counter-tendency to the tabloid docudrama, which is present in the co-productions promoted by Home Box Office (HBO). This aspect of modern practice will be considered in Chapter 7, when *Hostages* will again be used to examine the possibilities and dangers inherent in co-production. World Productions/HBO's 1997 *Hostile Waters* will also be used occasionally to illustrate the potential of co-production.

All these films are crucial markers of the dramadoc/docudrama's current status in a volatile world of television dominated by technological change. Not only does this threaten the very concept of 'documentary', it also has implications for dramatic realism – the staple form of television drama for most of the medium's history. Brief summaries of these films from the 1990s will indicate the range of content in current practice (but a glance at the television schedules of almost any month is likely to produce a not dissimilar range).

Hostages covers the period when Western citizens were being taken by Arab organisations in the Middle East in order to pressurise

Western governments. An Arab captor in the film defines hostage-taking as 'the poor man's weapon' – using individuals as hostages for the Middle Eastern policies of their respective governments. They were widely perceived in their own homelands as martyrs in the clash of opposing ideologies and world views. The Granada/HBO film is structured around American, Irish and British captives and their campaigning loved ones at home.

Fighting for Gemma tells of the brief life and tragic death from leukaemia of Gemma D'Arcy, a young child who lived near a nuclear generating plant in Cumbria, England, where her father was a worker. The plant – once called Windscale, now Sellafield – is owned by the company known in 1993 as British Nuclear Fuels Ltd. (BNFL). The story of her struggle against a cancer that many believed to be the result of her father's exposure to radiation is juxtaposed with that of a legal team also struggling – to establish a claim in law for Gemma's family and for other families similarly afflicted. Their equally formidable adversary was a huge corporation with vast resources and power. These individual narratives are set against a history of the development of nuclear power and an account of the laws of physics involved in it, which the legal team have to master to fight their case.

Hillsborough is the story of a disaster in 1989 in which over ninety football supporters were crushed to death in a crowd waiting to watch an FA Cup semi-final soccer match. The programme, made seven years after the event, investigates the failure of British institutions to deal responsibly not only with the event itself but also with its aftermath. As in the previous example, the television programme linked the private tragedy of apparently needless death with on-going public campaigns for justice. A rising popular distrust of public institutions was evident in both dramadocs; this factor offers a clear link with the American tradition of docudrama and particularly with what the American television industry calls the 'trauma drama' (see Chapters 7 and 8).

Goodbye My Love too fits the pattern of programmes exploring millenarian social anxieties. It is about euthanasia, or, as its main protagonist Derek Humphry resonantly calls it, 'physician-assisted death'. Played out against the twin trajectories of Humphry's establishment in the 1980s of the organisation Hemlock and the occasions in his own life when he has practised what he preaches, this film rehearses arguments for and against voluntary death – arguments that are becoming heard more insistently in Western societies with ageing populations.

The so-called 'Long Island Lolita', Amy Fisher, claimed to have had an affair in 1992 with a garage mechanic from New York, Joe Buttafuoco. She tried to kill his wife, Mary Jo, and the story generated tons of newsprint and occupied hours of media time in the USA. All three main US television networks made docudramas from the story: the National Broadcasting Company (NBC) made *Amy Fisher: My Story* in 1992, the American Broadcasting Company (ABC) produced *Beyond Control: The Amy Fisher Story* in 1992 and Columbia Broadcasting Systems (CBS) made *Casualties of Love: The Long Island Lolita Story* in 1993. All were broadcast in Britain in 1995: *Amy Fisher: My Story* – re-titled *Lethal Lolita* on BBC1 by the British Broadcasting Corporation (BBC), *Casualties of Love* on Independent Television (ITV) and *The Amy Fisher Story* on Channel 4, thus achieving a clean sweep of British networks too.

Hostile Waters is about a collision between two submarines – one American and one Russian – off the eastern seaboard of the USA in 1986, just before the Reagan–Gorbachev summit at Reykjavik, which was so crucial to the 'velvet revolutions' of the late 1980s. The sixteen missiles carried by the Russian ship *K219* were locked on to targets from Florida to New York, and 'fail-safe' mechanisms were set to trigger their launch in the aftermath of the collision. An Eastern seaboard nuclear disaster (not to speak of the inevitable re-writing of subsequent political history) was narrowly avoided because of the heroic actions of two ordinary sailors from the 'evil empire'. A co-production, this film linked old and new methodologies in particularly thought-provoking ways.

Making the news, not reflecting it – *Hostages* 1992

Of all these examples of 1990s practice, however, it was *Hostages* that provoked real controversy. As a first step, I want to establish the form's occasional, but manifest, impact on the public world by focusing on the day in 1992 when *Hostages* encountered opposition from its own subjects – the Beirut hostages themselves. On Wednesday 21 September 1992 *Hostages* was about to be transmitted. The film was made in Granada's studios in the centre of Manchester and on location in Britain and Israel. Over a period of two years the film was developed within the context of Granada's well-established current affairs department, which had produced the news magazine programme *World in Action* since 1963.

The programme was to be screened in Britain during prime time that very evening, and US transmission would follow in February 1993 (in the prestigious 'Showcase' slot of the cable television company Home Box Office). Although it had been diligently researched by Granada personnel, it could not be called a documentary programme; and although it was acted by well-known professionals, it was not just a television drama either. The dramadoc form had been used to tell this particular story because, at the inception of the project, it was believed that there was 'no other way to tell it'.

This classic formula is one that was invented by Leslie Woodhead, one of the major figures in the development of the drama-documentary in Britain.[5] It highlights the journalistic imperative which causes a Granada dramadoc to be made. This was always journalism of the 'last resort', whereby public interest considerations demanded that a story enter the public domain by this means or not at all. Because there were no cameras present when the historical events represented in the film took place, the extra dimension of dramatic presentation (and, necessarily, speculation) was used to enable the story to be told. The ultimate aspiration of the category of programme that forms the subject of this book is to make a difference in the historical and political world beyond the television screen by going to places that are originally denied to the camera.

However, this high-minded aspiration was put into another context on the morning of the day of transmission. Four of the Beirut hostages depicted in the film – John McCarthy, Brian Keenan, Terry Waite and Terry Anderson – published a letter in the *Guardian* newspaper. It read, in part:

> We are greatly concerned that Granada Television is promoting the film *Hostages* (to be shown this week) as the 'true story' of those depicted in it. From the information released from Granada's publicity department it is clear that the film contains scenes involving us that are pure fiction. Granada is grossly misleading the public by giving them the impression that they will see what actually happened.

The letter was the culmination of a campaign to have the film withdrawn by Granada and it ensured a level of controversy for the actual transmission that raged on for some time. With the real hostages claiming 'pure fiction' and an 'untrue' story, Granada's 'documentary' claim was thrown into doubt and the issue was energetically taken up by the press.[6]

Whose story, the hostages were asking, was it? How could the facts of a real-world situation be adequately rendered in someone else's drama when they could only really be known, agonisingly, to those who had actually endured it? Later in the letter they made it abundantly clear that they would have no objection to a documentary treatment of their captivity; it was the drama to which they objected so vehemently. So far from reconstructing a situation to which cameras had not been privy, the film makers were in their view 'grossly misleading the public'. And yet, the hostages had not actually seen the film in question and were therefore pre-judging the very issues they raised.

On the morning of the letter's appearance in print the film was complete and arrangements for its transmission on both sides of the Atlantic had been finalised. The business of advertising British transmission through trails was well advanced and the press preview had taken place. Ordinarily at this point the programme makers would be awaiting press and audience reaction and preparing to assess the project's success or failure. However, because the situation to which *Hostages* referred and which it had hoped to influence – the Beirut hostage crisis – had altered so fundamentally, *Hostages* inadvertently exposed the vulnerability of this form of drama to history itself.

The groups holding the hostages (always described in the Western media as 'terrorist', 'fundamentalist', 'extremist', or combinations of these terms) began to release their Western hostages shortly after work on the film got under way. The American journalist Terry Anderson, the last of all to be held, was released in December 1991. Happily for the real hostages, but ironically for the film makers, the individual crises dramatised in *Hostages* were over in news terms by Wednesday 21 September. Most of the former hostages were by then working on reflective, personal versions of their years in captivity. Thus, the real-world news events had ceased and had become instead the source for competing mediations (in books, articles, interviews). In this context some of the real hostages were not in favour of any dramatisation of their story that was not owned or endorsed by themselves, and especially one so close to the event.

Campaigning films and programmes habitually claim to provide new information when they appear; it is one way of attracting audiences to subjects they may already feel they know about. The use of fiction to support factual evidence is admission that any historical reality is only ever partly available to the photographic and electronic media (and, indeed, to any human agency). But this claim was thrown back at Granada and HBO by the hostages' counter-claim that not only did the film have nothing new to say but it was also 'misleading' and, in fact, simply added a new dimension to their torment. What was the prospective viewing public to make of all this? How, if at all, would it affect their views of history, current affairs and television representation? Indeed, would they even want to watch a 'factual fiction' (absurd paradox) at all after such an appeal from the real-life subjects of the events depicted? The complicated and controversial personal and public issues raised by such cases as this, and the interpretative difficulties raised by the dramadoc/docudrama, will be explored in this book.

Dramadoc/docudrama – preparation and production

Research

The first points to make about the preparation of such programmes as *Hostages* and *Goodbye My Love* concern the level of research, a key marker of difference between the dramadoc/docudrama and other kinds of television drama. The information-gathering methods used to provide material for *Hostages* were not just similar to those which would have been used for a documentary, they were identical. The programme was prepared like any other piece of television journalism, making use of the same information agencies. Kathy Chater notes that there are 'two forms of factual research' in current affairs programmes (1992: 16–17). In the first the researcher simply collects the generally accepted facts of a case. In the second, which she calls 'the exposé method', the aim is to find 'facts that have either not been considered or which have been rejected by the general consensus.' This broadly covers the research input into *Hostages*. Granada has its own collection of newspaper cuttings as well is a visual archive made up of film and video tapes. Computer technology now backs up these 'hard copy' archives in a library that is available only to Granada personnel. In addition, 'field work' interviews were done with returned hostages (such as Frank Reed) and families and friends working to get them out (such as Jill Morrell).[1]

Although Chapter 2 will deal in detail with the lawyers' role in the programme-making process, it is worth mentioning now that the producers constantly referred the research work for *Hostages*, and the script it generated, to Granada's lawyers to ensure that it was legally defensible. The US co-producers, although not involved directly in research, also had lawyers check the script and programme against American law. Everyone was anxious to get the facts of the film right for professional, ethical, legal and financial reasons; it is worth recording that these facts were never disputed in court. The material consulted was mainly, but not exclusively, already in the public domain; it constituted a base for the programme's dramatic activity. Research was ongoing and new angles of approach were sought constantly. Pre-production research and development provides the main link between documentary proper and dramadoc/docudrama. But it was not a case of facts followed by programme, because a fluid and evolving historical situation demanded continuous input from the research team during the shooting and even beyond – into the post-production period.

In addition to its researchers working with facilities not unlike those of a major daily's newsroom and using working methods not unlike those of newspaper journalists, the film also employed a writer to turn the factual material into dialogue that actors would exchange in scenes organised into a continuous narrative text. Like any work of the imagination, this text was composed with aesthetic considerations never far from its writer's consciousness. The 'shooting script' – a more or less final version – went through several drafts. The method by which the production team then worked on the text was broadly that of any fiction film: they laboured to make it 'work' as film drama. Actors rehearsed with a director then performed for the camera during a precisely organised production schedule. The process involved casting, negotiating with actors' agents, finding a director and a crew, organising the schedules to ensure the actors' presence at read-throughs, rehearsals, location work and studio sessions. Finally, realisation in performance before the camera depended on skills from outside the world of factual journalism – skills of credible performance in a simulated environment recorded on film by technical means.

So *Hostages* could not be called a 'documentary' in the usual sense of that word, even though it was prepared like one. The very fact that actors had rehearsed a specially written script was enough to deny it that categorisation. But nor was the programme strictly a 'drama' in the sense of a freely imagined work of fiction, made 'originally' in the mind of its writer; Bernard MacLaverty had been obliged to adhere too closely to the factual material collected during the pre-production stage for that to be the case. Furthermore, during shooting, the film's documentary base intruded into the very processes of rehearsal and performance. In truth, the two producers intervened so often on the set – to correct or to insist on particular matters of fact – that they had been dubbed, only semi-jokingly, the 'fact fascists' by the cast and crew. The 'fact fascists' at this point in the proceedings were the on-set mouthpieces of Granada's off-set researchers and legal team. For the 'artists' – the director and the actors – any suggestion of improvisation outside the legally vetted script was out of the question.[2]

Treating facts

Hostages began – as do television programmes of all kinds – as someone's idea. When an idea is accepted as having potential it is developed into a formal 'pitch' or 'proposal' made to a producer. Given enough initial interest, a 'treatment' of the subject develops it further. 'Treatment' is the industry term for a document that outlines not only the subject matter of a proposed television programme but also the way in which it will be approached. *Hostages* producer Sita Williams says, 'the treatment isn't a straitjacket, it's only to give whoever needs to know a kind of feeling for the story.' From a treatment it should be possible to determine the genre within which the programme could be categorised, the precise form it will take, the audience to whom it might appeal and even the kind of scheduling slot that it will eventually require. Williams remarked that the already researched facts, evident in the treatment itself, were what gave *Hostages* 'its journalistic basis', effectively marking out its intended territory for the planners of the television schedules.

A successful treatment may itself have to go through many drafts, but once accepted it becomes the basis for subsequent budgetary and logistical planning. In dramadoc/docudrama it eventually shapes a writer's work in fundamental ways. In the USA the process is very similar. Todd Gitlin describes it as the 'filtration step[s]' by which the industry controls ideas (1994: 21). In the open competition that characterises American television the process reduces the thousands of ideas pitched each year to the three main networks 'by a factor of five, ten, or thirty' at each stage – until only a few shows get on the air. This initial filtration ends when the programme enters the shooting stage.

The dramatic element undoubtedly makes for many of the complications. Just as the concept of the 'unrehearsed' is fundamental to documentary, so the 'rehearsed' is integral to drama. In the classic narrative film the spectator is sucked into the frame through the cathartic power of identification with a fictional 'other'. By contrast, the spectator in documentary is positioned as a 'person-to-be-addressed' and held at a distance as a dispassionate observer. The clash between these competing 'ways of seeing' can be read as a sub-text to the hostages' letter quoted in the Introduction.

In the USA it is increasingly common for some problems to be resolved by paying actual participants in historical events to be 'consultants' on docudrama projects. Alan Rosenthal notes that 'most of the [US] networks and major producers of docudramas not only employ scouts to search for the hot stories, but also spend vast amounts of money in purchasing the story rights' (1995: 26). This can lead to strange consequences, which I will examine further in Chapter 8 when I consider the case of the 'Long Island Lolita', Amy Fisher. HBO wittily satirised the tabloid excesses of this kind of film making in 1992 with *The Positively True Adventures of the Alleged Texas Cheerleader-murdering Mom*. The jokey self-referential nature of this docudrama is evident in one scene that depicts the eponymous 'Mom' objecting vociferously to the idea of the actress Holly Hunter playing her in the film. It is of course Hunter whom we are watching in the scene.[3]

The British dramadoc tradition is very different because it is closer to the project of the journalist and documentarist. Jeremy Tunstall notes that 'British documentary film-makers see themselves as heirs to two great traditions – one in public service broadcasting, the other in 1930s documentary film-making' (1993: 33). Historically, Granada has highlighted its journalism, working always with stories already in the public domain. In refusing to enter into auctions of the 'Long Island Lolita' kind it has always invoked the rights of the investigative journalist. But the gathering momentum of feeling about who owns a real-life story and the increasing convergence of the broadcasting institutions promise to complicate this straightforward moral stance in the twenty-first century.

While the stages of proposal, adoption, production and transmission have remained broadly unchanged, the 1990 Broadcasting Act legislation in Britain has caused a growth of the independent production sector and co-production. Many of the Granada dramadocumentary team are now operating as independents and working with co-producers like Home Box Office.[4] The much-expanded sector has caused competition which has had two effects: it is now harder to place single drama in the schedules, and factual drama needs more than ever to plug into a controversial issue. Needing the publicity boost of the campaign on the one hand, but finding schedule space difficult to come by on the other, the dramadoc form has become more and more like the American docudrama.

The growing synergy between American and British television has, as I remarked in the Introduction, led me to use the term 'dramadoc/docudrama' in this book. It has the merit of enacting typographically the meeting of distinctively British and American traditions signalled by the separate words 'dramadoc' and 'docudrama'. The form remains different from conventional television drama in its research dimension and in the attention given in its preparation to regulation and to the law (again, see Chapter 2). In the research and project-development stage there is more going on behind the scenes, more sensitivity to possible repercussions, than in any other television drama genre.

The process of production

The process of production can now be summarised as follows:

Pre-production   'Pitch' or concept → research → treatment → further research → draft scripts/ongoing research → final script → (continuous legal vetting) → cast and crew assembled.

Production   Read-through → rehearsal → shooting in studio and
  on location → ongoing research, re-drafting, legal checks.
Post-production   Editing → dubbing → research updating/
  continued legal checks → scheduling → (press preview) →
  transmission.
Reception   Post-transmission discussion → follow-up programmes.

The final category is a reminder that the process does not terminate
at transmission; the moment of reception is equally important, as
are any repercussions arising from this moment. Only at the time of
its meeting with its audience is any programme finally complete.
Here the dramadoc/docudrama sometimes collides in unexpected
ways with the world from which it emerged (I shall discuss this in
more detail when I return to *Hostages* in Chapter 7).

In recent years media studies have shifted into a more reflexive
interest in the audience for television than can be derived from
audience research that simply quantifies ratings or seeks explana-
tions of 'uses and gratifications' of television watching.[5] Especially
if it is controversial, the form becomes really interesting at this point
because one can observe the historical process itself feeding back
into reception. The history to which the dramadoc/docudrama
points can work in and through the programme, creating turbulence in the real world. This was clearly the case on 21 September
1992. The acute awareness of the boundaries between fact and
fiction during the pre-production and production periods was
mirrored closely at the point of reception. Here we find a more
active questioning of what was seen than in any other genre in any
other medium, whether print or audio-visual.

The costs of preparing and making these programmes are
generally less than those of drama but more than those of
documentary. *Hostages*, for example, cost over £1 million to make in
1991–92. This is cheap by film standards, but it is a considerable
commitment of resources for a television company, even with co-
production. I will return to this matter in Chapter 7, but it is worth
noting here that British and American network executives tend to
see the dramadoc/docudrama as a cheap means of marketing single
television dramas, and the serious subject (such as *Hostages* and
Hostile Waters) can attract big stars for reduced fees.[6]

Making the drama

In the remainder of this chapter I shall focus on the occasion of the dramatic performance itself. First of all, I shall go into the film studio to look in detail at the pro-filmic moment (in other words, the real-time dramatic action that takes place in front of the camera). From time to time in this book I shall use the language and vocabulary of film and media studies theory, as I have here. This is not intended to baffle, but there are times when the precision of such theory is useful in making a distinction. 'Pro-filmic event' is an especially useful term because what happens in front of the camera can still be regarded as markedly different in documentary and in drama. Dai Vaughan asks: 'What exactly is the pro-filmic? Fiction does not need to ask, since its only interest in the pro-filmic is to eradicate it'. The documentary, on the other hand, relies on a 'total assimilation of the pro-filmic' in order to make its meanings (1986: 174–5).[7]

Much has been written on the documentary aspect of the mixed form (and this too will be considered further in Chapters 3–5), but an initial focus on the drama of present-day practice will illustrate that, fundamentally, there is no real difference at the point of performance between the generality of film and television drama and the dramadoc/docudrama. This is because the disciplines of performance are pretty much the same for both. The documentary element in the modern form is now mostly to be found in captions. It also exists 'off set' of course: in pre-production research activity, in publicity and, increasingly, in 'legalling' (see Chapter 2).

In the television or film studio the principal audience is a 'surrogate' one. The instruments of the camera and the microphone stand in place of the eventual watchers and listeners. Their business is to record for the eyes and ears of a deferred 'real audience'. Performance-before-camera is the pro-filmic event of the dramadoc/docudrama. Here the camera and the microphone have an agency that is different from, but similar to, that deferred audience. My observation of television rehearsal/camera-performance is filtered through the prism of the theatre, because that institution is still a primary site of acted performance (and of training for that performance).

Drama is the most problematical element of the mixed form because its basic qualities seem so different from the more evidential qualities of the documentary – this was the basis of the hostages' objections as set out in their letter. I shall therefore make comparisons between the television studio and the theatre space, between the activities that take place within each, and between the relative juxtapositions in the two media of performer, technical crews and audience. My purpose is to illuminate the shift to film values that is part of contemporary television practice. This view of practice will, I hope, be helpful when more abstract concepts of 'documentary' and 'drama', and when institutional factors, are discussed later on.

31 October 1995 – Filming *Goodbye My Love*

Granada's Quay Street, Manchester, complex has affinities with both film sound stages and 'black box' theatre studios. This latter became very popular in commercial and educational theatre during the 1960s. Quay Street's 'Studio 12' most resembles a giant Cottesloe Theatre (the 'experimental' space at the National Theatre's South Bank site in London). It is, in other words, a large, high-ceilinged, light-tight box with flexible units of seating available for a studio audience if required. 31 October was the fifth day of a sixteen-day studio schedule. The screenplay being filmed had the working title *Final Act*.

Much television drama is now shot on film, and this has been the case since portable film cameras offered television programme makers an alternative in the mid-1960s. Many workers on both sides of the camera either have made films already or aspire to do so. The crew I observed had mostly shuttled between the two media throughout their careers. 'Screen drama', like all drama, has its semi-accepted hierarchies, and the feature film is still the apex of achievement for many screen-drama workers (as mainstream theatre continues to be for many theatre workers).

Work on *Final Act* began with eight days of location shooting in the USA (13–21 October 1995), followed by a read-through/ rehearsal of Peter Berry's script in Manchester (24–5 October). Finally, intensive filming took place in the Granada studios and on location in the Manchester area (from 26 October to 13 November). Shooting was followed by the post-production processes of editing and dubbing (early 1996). At the time I attended shooting the producer Sita Williams' best guess was that the film would be transmitted in a two-hour slot on the ITV network 'somewhere around April 1996'. Having first been offered a poorish summer slot, it was promised a more prestigious Christmas schedule slot on Sunday 29 December 1996. Eventually it was transmitted in the late evening feature-film slot on Saturday 4 January 1997. This was hardly prestigious scheduling, given that it was in the aftermath of the New Year sales, a notoriously cheap period for advertising and one of low expectation in terms of audience. One of the programme's many problems was that *Hillsborough* was fast-tracked by the ITV network (partly for its news value, partly because it was written by a 'hot' writer – Jimmy McGovern) and screened at the end of 1996.

The project underwent two changes of title. Its original working-title, *Final Act*, was felt to sound rather pessimistic and was uncomfortably close to the title of a book by the main protagonist Derek Humphry: *Final Exit: The Practicalities of Self-deliverance and Assisted Suicide for the Dying.*[8] The film was re-titled *Act of Love* in early 1996. However, a 1981 NBC 'made-for-TV movie' had already used that title. This might not have mattered, except that the NBC film had been very successful and Granada had hopes of selling its film on to Public Broadcasting System (PBS) in America. Ron Howard, who made his name playing the character Richie Cunningham in the hit television series *Happy Days* (and who has subsequently become a noted film director), starred in the NBC film. Although it was adapted from a novel rather than from actual events, it also addressed the subject of euthanasia seriously, achieved a 21.7% rating and a 35% audience share when first transmitted and acquired a high reputation. It has been repeated frequently on US television since its first transmission (see Gitlin, 1994: 172). Granada duly changed the title of its film to *Goodbye My Love*.

Studio realities

For six days of the shooting of *Goodbye My Love*, Studio 12 contained ten sets of rooms built according to the production designer's research in the historical locations where some of the events depicted had originally taken place. Details of the interiors of two houses had been noted and photographed during the eight-day trip to the USA. Location shooting in the USA provided exterior views of the houses now replicated in Studio 12 as well as contextual 'neighbourhood' shots. Heavy with naturalistic detail and for all the world like West End/Broadway theatre sets, the structures were erected on Sunday 29 October during a break in filming – a process not dissimilar to a theatre 'get in'. The rooms included ceilings, but were open on one side. For one of the 'houses', the whole of the downstairs floor-plan had been reconstructed. The upward proportions of Studio 12 and the usual requirements of television studio lighting were irrelevant to the needs of a filmed drama-documentary that aimed at the faithful reproduction of an anterior reality. The studio's provision of seating for a studio audience was similarly irrelevant.

Each change of scene during the day involved the crew re-locating camera, lighting and sound equipment in new set-ups, all organised with a view to economy. As is usual in such cases, the schedule was not in story-order but in filming-order to reduce unnecessary hiatuses in a process that is characterised by a hyper-awareness of costs. Within each scene camera set-ups required the re-arrangement of the equipment to cope with the exigencies of the new camera angle, and the technical crew were busily occupied for anything up to a quarter of an hour between takes. During this time the actors returned to their dressing rooms. The scene on location was not dissimilar, except that dressing rooms were coaches and caravans, camera set-ups could be miles apart, and the whole process was to some extent dependent on weather conditions.

Filming on 31 October began at 8.00 am and was scheduled to finish at 7.00 pm but continued into an hour or so of overtime. During this long day the team filmed half-a-dozen A4 pages of 'dialogue' (some scenes were in fact wordless). Ten scenes were shot from a number of angles, the main establishing shots at times needing three or four takes. Reaction shots were sometimes accepted as satisfactory after a single take. Any rehearsal was mainly for camera position, movement and focus. Again, location work was broadly similar, the only logistical difference being in the transporting of equipment and personnel from one location set-up to another (but all within the Manchester area).

The camera on this particular day was mounted throughout on track and hydraulic trolley to facilitate movement backwards and forwards, up and down. On the previous day there had been a good deal of hand-held operation – more often a feature of location filming. For some shots two microphones were used, but more usually a boom microphone picked up the speakers' lines. Actors, after being given or finding a position on set, had to move to their marks in multiple takes. Lighting, rigged and re-rigged for each set-up, made much use of diffused, 'bounced' light from large gold and silver reflectors. 'Key lighting' was the dominant convention, with a suitable naturalistic acknowledgement of 'real' light sources within the room set-ups.[9]

The technical work contrasted interestingly with the no less precise but broader requirements of stage lighting and sound. Since the sets were such realistic room simulations, lighting followed two main priorities: to light actors for the camera and to maintain the naturalistic illusion of real-room light as required by the script. Some of the sound and lighting equipment being used had originally been developed for news programmes that relied mainly on on-scene lighting boosted by lightweight equipment (digital sound recording, radio mikes, clip-fixing mini-spots). This equipment is now standard for television drama too; thus the major priorities of a network television service – news and entertainment – are enacted at the level of technology.[10]

Technology was, of course, ever-present in a way it is not for most theatrical rehearsal. The majority of those present were camera/lighting crew concerned with the image; they were tending the camera and what it was focusing on. The sound crew was smaller but was equally intent on creating through the medium of its technology a sense of the reality of that room. The only other person besides myself from 'outside' the film crew was a photographer who was present throughout the day, taking publicity shots (for use pre-transmission and in press reviews). We all moved around the studio for the different scenes in some sense like (and unlike) an audience at a promenade theatre.

At any one time the actors had anything up to twenty people watching their work; but no one watched in the manner of any theatrical audience, even a promenade one. Most people were there to give attention to some particular aspect of the proceedings. They were 'servicing the image', as it were. Many of the watchers (including the producer) gathered during takes around a small black-and-white monitor, even though the real actors were six feet away. What the camera was seeing was more important than any quasi-theatrical view of the action obtained by watching the set.

For anyone whose training is in the theatre, accommodations to the camera are the most striking feature of the rehearsal/filming process. At the level of actors' performances these were constantly being made. The requirements of the camera were paramount. This is not to say that the feeling of being 'right in the situation' did not concern the actors and the director, Richard Signy, it was more that there was an unspoken consensus about the greater importance of getting things 'right for the camera'. The necessities of framing and focus marked the parameters of the action, just as the concepts of sightlines and lit space mark the parameters of stage action, but they were non-negotiable givens rather than adjuncts to the process of performance.

On takes that were likely to be supplementing the main action (for example reaction shots and reverse-action shots) minor changes in the positioning and orientation of the actors (the film set equivalent of 'cheating' a stage position) were speedily accepted and even volunteered. The focus on eyes and faces in these dialogue scenes was most apparent, perhaps, in the camera crew's frequent measuring of distances between actors' eyelines to ensure precision of focus. Television drama, even when filmed, is still pre-eminently a drama of faces and eyes and of small (room) spaces, the smaller screen allowing proportionately less to the drama of space than cinema. The fixed audience perspective of the theatre, meanwhile, is less flexible in terms of focus.

The routine before a take illustrated the more technology-driven concerns of the screen drama. Where a theatrical rehearsal would tend to settle after a break with perhaps a call for quiet from a stage manager and instructions from the director ('Let's pick it up from...'), in the film studio preparation for re-entering the drama has a distinctive and different rhythm of words and action. These accommodate carefully to the camera and microphone. The assistant director (AD) calls, 'Turn over' to the camera operator once there is quiet, and the sound recordist then announces, 'Sound on.' Even then clapper-board information is marked for the crew (and, later, the editor) before there can be any performing activity.

At the end of the unit of action the AD calls 'Cut!' on the director's instruction. The lens of the camera is then checked for specks of dust before the take is included in material to be seen later in 'rushes'. The director has the last word on whether a particular scene requires another take or whether it is time to move on to the next, but (as was evident in this case) takes the decision after frequent consultation with the producer. All this has the ritualistic quality of the finely honed work routine – but, again, the concentration of effort is on technological 'eyes' and 'ears', busy about their task of recording faithfully for the audience's human eyes and ears.

Just as a theatrical deputy stage manager (DSM) runs the rehearsal or show logistically, the first AD runs the studio, with the second AD assisting 'back stage' in the studio (like a theatrical assistant stage manager). The third AD is mostly responsible for moving the cast between the studio and the dressing room. The parallel is not total, for in theatre the DSM will normally record stage movement on the prompt copy in rehearsal and call cues in performance, and an assistant stage manager will normally look after props in both situations and/or operate sound (or other) effects in performance. In the film studio the task of marking up a copy of the script is undertaken by continuity personnel, the other tasks by 'Action Props' and by 'Set Dressers'. The heavily-annotated continuity script, with pens of various colours clipped to it, resembles the theatrical prompt copy. Continuity, props and make-up also makes much use of Polaroid cameras; prop desks scattered around the studio bears evidence of the importance of this activity.

The practical exigencies of delivering a television product exacerbate the habitual state of working-against-time that characterises all drama. Originating from departments that are more usually concerned with factual programming, dramadoc is not always accorded the resources television drama departments (let alone major studio feature films) will tend to take for granted. In an ideal world, Sita Williams felt, *Goodbye My Love* would have had three more days of filming. Forced as the film was through budgetary considerations into a race against the schedule, occasional urgent conferences between Williams and Signy were often to do with the cuts and elisions in the script that would be needed if the production team were to stay on the right side of its tight timetable.

The agencies of organisation and technical presentation have a far greater prominence in television at the fragmented moment of performance. In the theatre these matters would come under the aegis of two theatrical sub-groups – stage management and lighting/sound personnel. The former group facilitates the rehearsal and 'runs the show' in performance. The latter group will be involved in design and logistics pre-performance, with occasional input at rehearsal, and will be involved in technical operation in performance (though this is sometimes the province of stage management, especially in small-scale touring). The only time that a show is given over to the stage managers, lighting and sound designers and technicians is during technical rehearsal. In 'mainstream' productions actors are excused this rehearsal, as junior stage managers 'walk' their parts to mark technical cues and actors are kept fresh for other technical/dress rehearsal(s). Once cues have been fixed and tested, the expectation at subsequent technical rehearsal, whether 'cue to cue' or 'continuous action', is that actors will hold back from performance levels, reserving their full commitment for the presence of an audience.

On the set of *Goodbye My Love* the pace and rate of the action were determined almost entirely by the wants and needs of sight and sound, camera and tape recorder. All this caused a different rhythm to the event of shooting – and a different kind of focusing for performers – from the rhythm at a theatrical rehearsal. It was like working on individual pieces of a large jigsaw where the printed script is the picture on the box. The business-like (though co-operative and friendly) atmosphere was similar to that in a theatrical rehearsal but was noticeably more low-key. The presence throughout of technical personnel (where in the theatre they would only be present at the technical rehearsal) was undoubtedly a contributory factor.

In contrast to the theatre director's somewhat mythical power of textual interpretation and the film director's equally mythical power of inspired seeing, the television drama director is more concerned with co-ordination. Richard Signy's efforts were focused on the attempt to realise the script as written for the camera and the microphone within the time constraints, where excision and elision were to be used as last resorts. For example, at 4.15 pm a rapid conference between Signy and his two assistant directors concluded that the day's filming would need to run into overtime to stay on course with the remaining part of the schedule. The priority was to record as much of the script as possible given the time, in as acceptable an amount as possible, so that sufficient 'raw material' existed for the editor(s), director and producer to work on in post-production. Whereas the technical matters are more in the nature of 'actor-support' in the theatre, the balance shifts noticeably in the film/television studio. The concept of author/authority is in any case a problematic one, but it is easy to see why producers have a higher profile in the logistically demanding world of television drama. They have the privileged overview – metaphorically and literally.[11]

Acting in miniature

In many ways there was a reversal of the 'normal' processes of rehearsal for a theatrical performance; and nor is any template of performance in the theatre useful. This is in part because the theatrical process that sees an occasion when audience and actors meet – the performance – is denied to the television (and film) actor. Any receiving is always in suspension in the television studio; it is deferred in a more profound sense than is the case in theatre. The individually crafted pieces of the jigsaw of recorded performance are actually assembled in the post-production phase. Here, actors may be present for the dubbing of sound, but the significant shapers of the audience experience are editors, directors and producers.

The overall effect is to miniaturise dramatic moments, driving actors inwards rather than outwards. The actors take what in themselves are tiny sections of dialogue, then expose these moments (and themselves-in-role) to the camera over and over again. In this sense acted performance can be contrasted with the very different pro-filmic event of the documentary film, which occurs in real time and records the behaviours of people caught up totally (or supposedly totally) in an unfolding actuality.

Theatrical rehearsal, especially early on in the process of realisation, may concentrate heavily on moments in a drama in just this way, but directors will generally have more opportunity to help actors establish themselves-in-role in continuous temporal action, thereby developing the 'through line', which in character terms is the *sine qua non* of the Stanislavski-based Western acting tradition. At least, this is true of all naturalistic performance and it is necessary to compare like with like. *Goodbye My Love* was a determinedly naturalistic film script (most are), in which dialogue is present as an accompaniment to, as much as a provoker of, action. Its characteristic modes are ellipsis and indirection; it rarely communicates directly or didactically. Sita Williams called it 'the most filmic and therefore least verbal' of the scripts for which she has been responsible as a dramadoc producer.

It was evident too that this kind of script had no need for 'fact fascists' on set. Although interventions at the level of fact were entirely absent from the set, this film actually caused more difficulty to Granada's lawyer, Patrick Swaffer, than most (see Chapter 2 for further detail). In becoming 'more filmic and less verbal' the modern dramadoc/docudrama is steadily pulling out of the more discursive documentary functions that governed earlier manifestations (see Chapters 5 and 6). *Goodbye My Love*, like most of my 1990s case study examples, was anchored to documentary primarily through its captions and credits.

Theatrical rehearsal may 'chop up' the chronology of a naturalistic drama for specific developmental purposes, but rarely to the extent of a film's shooting order. In performance of naturalistic theatre part of an actor's split consciousness will be managing a chronology that is usually supported by the play. On their return to an off-stage, whether designated as 'dressing room' or whatever, actors may even (according to levels of conscientiousness) seek to retain their character through exercises of various kinds. But their task in filming is different given the sheer length of the 'perfor- mance' in real time (although some film actors, Marlon Brando for example, have become fabled for their efforts to stay 'in role' over long periods). The lack of performance continuity in film reinforces miniaturisation by magnifying the moment and by privileging it against the sequence.

The read-through period, brief though it be, is one of the few occasions in television drama when the actors can engage in the kind of free-ranging, intuitive and associative activity that consti- tutes 'building a character'; time before the camera for this purpose is extremely limited. The read-through of *Goodbye My Love* was spent mainly in discussion between the principals about the major motivating characteristics of their 'characters' (which is often the case, according to Williams). Scare-quotes are a necessary reminder that drama-documentary does not have characters in any conven- tional dramatic sense. It attempts to portray real-world individuals who are accessible in a way that fictional characters are not (a factor that often raises the temperature of debate about this genre and to which we will return).

Some of the words that the writer Peter Berry gave the actors to speak were on the public record, others not. Minor figures can be made into 'composites', but if this happens with major protagonists the film becomes generically different (see Chapter 3). To take just one example from *Goodbye My Love*, the main protagonist was Derek Humphry (played by the actor Robert Lindsay). The real-world Humphry has written books on euthanasia, has direct and contro- versial experience of involvement in the 'voluntary' deaths of people (including that of his first wife) and is a proponent of changes in the law through the organisation that he co-founded. Thus, the read-through discussion could not be entirely speculative and imaginative within the parameters of a given 'text'; the subject, in a sense, is focused in and through this particular real-world individual. Even at this point the activity of the rehearsal room reverberated with the outside world in a qualitatively different way from other kinds of play. And because television is also a journalistic medium (and drama-documentary is in part driven by journalism) the reverberation has different consequences from those of the stage documentary play.

In the acting the keying of performance was towards interiorised realism rather than exteriorised naturalism. The effect of a good amplifier in a hi-fi system is what comes to mind; the aim was to turn the gain or volume of (theatrical) performance down without losing (televisual) power. The action during these studio scenes took place within a room to which the camera, as it were, allowed the audience privileged access; this sustaining illusion would be irrevocably shattered by any of the projection involved in theatrical performance. The trope of 'privileged access' is what connects all television genres and it certainly forms an umbilical connection between the drama and the documentary of the dramadoc.

'Scene 85' of Berry's shooting script provides an example (and the sheer number of scenes is itself evidence of the process of miniaturisation). Humphry's second wife Ann (Gwen Humble) and her mother Ruth (Judy Parfitt) spend some of Ruth's last living moments looking through a family photograph album. Ruth has decided to die with her husband Arthur (E. G. Marshall). Both will depend on the active assistance of Ann and Derek. There has been rational discussion of this decision and Ruth appears to be both decided and determined. But as a full, visceral realisation that she has decided to end her life strikes home for the first time, Ruth has a panic attack. The 'stage direction' in the sparse filmic script reads: 'Ruth's sudden intake of breath. And she panics – the thought of it – she doesn't want to die. She suddenly stands up. Looks around, lost.' Then she says: 'Is that all I've done ... ? I can't ... I can't ... I can't absorb all this ...'

There was little in the way of building through rehearsal to sustain the actor in portraying this all too credible moment in a one-page scene. Played in the theatre, its success for actor and audience would undoubtedly reside in a high emotional key triggering a directness of response from an empathising spectator within the elasticity of theatrical time. In theatre naturalism we participate in moments such as these rather than passively 'watching' something.

The word 'spectator' seems more appropriate. In television realism our fly-on-the-wall access offers a different kind of scrutiny – the distanced stare of surveillance, the activity of the viewer/*voyeur*.

In the theatre success with an audience habitually depends on Stanislavskian controls that have been developed during acting training and mobilised through rehearsal to ensure the actor's dominance over, and channelling of, the energy inherent in the theatrical moment – a moment that is as much vocal as it is physical. If it is done badly, the audience drifts, becomes atomised, ceases to be an 'audience'; if it is done well, enough spectators can be relied upon to be 'in' the moment with the actor to weld an audience into a self-reflexive, collective unit, jointly absorbed in that moment and carried by the energy of performance from moment to moment.

On the film set, for the camera, in a moment to be seen by a fragmented audience months later, the split second of Ruth's surprise (the look rather than the words) was the emotional trigger and the focus was inevitably on eyes and face – distant entities in most theatres. The requirement was therefore not exactly underplaying, but more precisely a low emotional (which does not mean 'no-emotional') key in the moment of recording – as near to 'performance' as television drama gets. The moment must be strong enough to withstand our viewer-gaze; any 'falsity' is cruelly exposed.

Judy Parfitt first 'marked the moment' fairly prosaically in a couple of rehearsals for camera. Experienced as she is, the insecurity that is part of the element that any actor breathes led her to tell the crew that this was what she was doing (just in case, perhaps, anyone watching thought it was all she could manage). For the actual takes, she concentrated on the physicality (not the vocality) of the character's situation – the sudden fear propelling an arthritic old women into a standing position. She was gasping rather than projecting the words for the close-up ear of the listening microphone rather than for a far-off listening audience.

The force (and ultimately the success) of the film lay in such underplayed dramatic moments, not in any discursive statements about the moral rights and wrongs of 'assisted death'. Underplaying the enigmatic Derek Humphry himself was the key element of

Lindsay's characterisation too. The debate about euthanasia, which first drew the producers to research and write their original treatment, was focused by open questions about motivation resulting from the opacity of the behaviours on view. The real historical Humphry has an almost messianic belief that the law should be reformed in respect of an individual's stated wish to end his or her own life, and his aim is to bring this change about. The dramatic question remains: why?

This question has two parts in *Goodbye My Love*. First, how do you read Humphry's pursuit of his aim in personal terms? (What makes him in particular do this?) Second, what moral overview should be taken? (Is he right, whatever the personal complications?) Our involvement in this character-based enigma before, during and after the film may be complex and ambiguous enough to cause fluctuations in views on both questions, and herein lies the potential appeal to drama. Is Humphry's conduct to be read as bravely single-minded, or as callously ruthless? And how does an audience map its own judgement on the matter on to its understanding of the issue of active choice in death? To answer the former question, an audience reads a dramatic situation; to answer the latter, it must take account of the documentary elements in the film.

Robert Lindsay is an actor who is particularly well suited to television – a medium that, as developed in Western cultures, is pre-eminently one that scrutinises individuals. *Goodbye My Love*, like other Lindsay television films, made much use of his timely talent. In the script the camera is frequently instructed to dwell on Humphry/Lindsay's face as his character treads a path from sympathy to ambiguity, from advocacy to obsession. Many scenes in the script are wordless dwellings on his face as it simultaneously reveals and conceals motivation. In this dramadoc the enigma of the real at the level of the individual (what we are faced with when we look at anyone we meet or know and try to fathom their thoughts and motivations) met the apparent force of the fact.

Such an ethical problem can only be portrayed non-verbally in terms of screen realism, given the fragmentation of language as a trustworthy referent (and the resultant distrust of words in representation). Lindsay's distinctive range of concentrated but ambiguously-hurt facial expressions and his apparently unstudied but evidently troubled body language have given a powerful emotional charge to British television dramas such as *GBH* (1993) and *Jake's Progress* (1995). In these two scripts by Alan Bleasdale, where Lindsay's characters stood on moral questions and where one might place them on a highly subjective (but indispensable) moral spectrum was rendered profoundly ambiguous in on-screen performance.

At the British press preview of *Hostile Waters* (19 June 1997) Rutger Hauer, who played the Soviet submarine's captain, Britanov, talked of similar features in the script of the World Productions/ HBO film. *Hostile Waters* had attracted him, he said, both because of 'the size of its Chernobyl-like subject' and because it was 'a good adventure too'. The acting challenge in portraying Britanov lay precisely in the lack of words and the emphasis on actions and expressions in the script. Hauer observed: 'The script is structured as a series of commands – there's no room for overt characterisation... Character is not in how they talk, but in what they do.' The synergy with film drama could hardly be more evident.

Television drama, 'audience-less' at the moment of its performance for the recording agents, is remade for transmission in post-production through editing and dubbing, just as film drama is. In the deferred moment of reception, with an audience that is both closer to and further from the performance, it is remade yet again. The moment of reception for television drama is different in certain regards from that for film. This has, I believe, important consequences – and not just for performers. We must seek to understand the dynamics of these moments, the better to deal with them as audiences. In theatre the moment would need to be outwardly displayed – in semiotic terms, 'ostended', or held up for view.[12] Before the camera something more interior, more private, is required. Television is a private medium in more senses than one; with the sets literally real except for a missing wall, the pro-filmic moment in *Goodbye My Love* was set in 'fourth-wall realism' as opposed to naturalism.

Credibility/belief/understanding

Euthanasia has become a headline issue in Britain and the USA because both countries contain large ageing populations. As a means of focusing the moral issues surrounding a subject that is likely to become more important in the next century *Goodbye My Love* offered much for an audience to talk about the day after transmission. The atomised audiences of television drama must also defer their reactions to some extent – until there is an opportunity for the 'TV talk' that comes after particularly interesting and widely seen programmes. The drama-documentary form increased this possibility by referencing the debate to the real life and work of Derek Humphry.

During the shooting, however, the methodology of drama took over from that of documentary almost completely. The 'factual basis of the story', in David Edgar's classic formulation, '[gave] the action of the play its credibility' (1988: 52). It was the task of the drama to persuade an audience to take a view on the issues (defined through research) by believing in the performance. The 'fact fascists' had no role to play in this film, and Sita Williams' main concern during the shooting was to ensure that some balance in the arguments (for and against euthanasia) survived the process of visual realisation. Her view was that, however careful you are to ensure what she calls a 'debating balance' in the script, you can never know until you begin to see the images whether the film will sustain the ideal of a for-and-against forum. The success of the enterprise, for one viewer at least, was evident in Desmond Christy's review for the *Guardian* (6 January 1997); *Goodbye My Love*, he wrote, 'was worth any number of discussion programmes about mercy killing.'

Granada executive Ian McBride takes the view that 'drama-documentary's power has to do with whether the audience are attracted to the subject' in the first instance. Thereafter, he believes, a subject's potential in the abstract must be sustained by the particular of the drama.[13] Williams, too, believed that in this case a documentary (rational) account of the issues of euthanasia could be encountered by an audience in dramatic (emotional) terms. In this sense *Goodbye My Love* is a classic of the re-formed genre: it exists in a clear line of development from the kinds of programmes that will be analysed in Chapters 6 and 7. But in its emphasis on personality it resembles most the US 'made-for-TV movie' genre, which Todd Gitlin has described as 'little personal stories that executives think a mass audience will take as revelations of the contemporary' (1994: 163–4).

In common with other writers, I have argued elsewhere against this inexorable individualising of issues which is an almost inevitable concomitant of naturalism's descendant, television realism.[14] The industry itself, however, has no sympathy with this view. Williams, for example, defines dramatic coherence itself as 'a story told through character', saying: 'If you're doing drama-documentary you're inevitably locked into naturalism. I don't see how else you can do it. I don't see what you would gain by stylising it in any way, really.'

From the legal angle, however, a different view begins to emerge. The more filmic and dramatic a programme is, the more difficulty it has become to 'legal'. In the legal process the documentary part of the dramadoc/docudrama must be accessible if a lawyer is to be able to defend it. An increased emphasis on the drama of the unsaid is re-inflecting the distinctive contribution of lawyers to the making of modern dramadoc/docudrama, and it is to this aspect of the preparation of these programmes that I will now turn.

2

Dramadoc/docudrama – the law and regulation

'Legalling'

My argument in this chapter will be that the law has become ever more important to the dramadoc/docudrama, partly because of the ambiguity of dramatic realism as practised in film. Responsibility for the documentary element has increasingly devolved on to legal teams partly as a result of changes in the television institution and partly because of the shifts in form that were noted in Chapter 1 (and will be considered again). This further examination of the conditions of 'actually existing' practice will inform the study of codes and conventions that follows in Chapter 3.

The legal and regulatory frameworks that have grown up around dramadoc/docudrama are more significant than for any other category of television programme, which is strange given that dramadoc/docudrama is an occasional rather than a regular part of scheduling. 'Legalling' is the term that has come to designate the process of legal checking of programmes before and during their making. Although the ultimate responsibility rests with the owners or governors, programme makers have to accept that they are the ones who may be asked, in court, to justify their decisions and to demonstrate that the factual basis for their programme is legally sound. Legalling provides a kind of anticipatory defence for the media institution – one that is designed to avoid the courts and the costs of a successful suit. Some claim that this can act as a brake on creativity, amounting to censorship, and can lead to a 'writing by committee'. The constraints that are allegedly placed on the imagination of writer, actors and director can be discerned in the making of *Hostages*, where the 'fact fascists' were merely the on-set representatives of a legal team under whose surveillance the whole enterprise proceeded.

Drama that is 'based on fact' is something of a legal minefield precisely because it relies so much on information both in and at the edges of the public domain. Even where events are a matter of record, the extent of the understanding of those records can be an Achilles heel. Facts can easily be contested by those who claim to know more or to know other facts or who assert that certain facts have been misunderstood. The investigative thrust of research can lead the drama into difficulty. It is easy too for similarities to exist in work in different media based on the same facts and for accusations of research plagiarism to arise. Mixed forms are more in danger of breaching copyright laws than freely imagined fictional forms.

In 1996 several writers accused Granada of using their work without acknowledgement in the factual drama series *In Suspicious Circumstances*. This popular programme presents crime costume dramas in which historical cases are re-enacted and is in many ways the direct descendant of the illustrated newspapers of the nineteenth century and of the 'True Crime' type of periodical of today. Although the series has the obvious advantage over drama-doc of telling stories from the past, so that protagonists are beyond suing the producers, its reliance on research means that overlaps with the work of other researchers have occurred.

One such writer, Andrew Rose, felt things had gone beyond overlap; he believed that his book *Scandal at the Savoy* had been plagiarised for an episode of *In Suspicious Circumstances* ('*Crime passionnel*'). While Granada openly acknowledged that the book was known to their researchers, their defence was that the episode and the book happened to be based on the same material, which was in the public domain. Ian McBride said in the *Observer*: 'I don't think some writers appreciate how much research we do from a wide variety of sources, such as the Public Record Office, Crown Prosecution Service and newspapers' (27 October 1996).

The level and quality of the research in dramadoc/docudrama are not only what set it apart from other television drama, they are what enable lawyers to defend producers and television companies against such charges of plagiarism. When the case against Granada came to court, of twenty-one claims made for infringement of copyright, four were upheld and the others dismissed. Being challenged on authenticity of research is, in terms of response, perhaps rather like being in a traffic accident – you should never admit liability but you have to be aware that blame could eventually be apportioned according to the law of the land.

The territory of the dramadoc/docudrama, however, is living individuals and the organisations they work for. The principal worry here is that persons who have become unwilling dramatic protagonists will claim they have been 'defamed' by the programme (in other words, had their reputation damaged in the eyes of the world). If they think they can show that the programme's view is inaccurate or unfair according to the facts they may seek damages by becoming the 'plaintiff' in a court case. Similarly, if an institution thinks it has been defamed it can have recourse to the law. Institutions and their representatives can command large resources and are often very jealous of their public image.

Geoffrey Robertson and Andrew Nicol, in their standard British work on the subject, note that media law is 'lucrative... high in profile... and in a state of exponential growth' (1992: xvi). Costs are increased in a controversial programme category like dramadoc/docudrama, and in co-production further costs are incurred because legalling must also be done by lawyers from the co-producing nation or nations. Although the two legal systems in Britain and America have many common points of reference, there are key differences. In any event, the legalling process is a necessary and unavoidable one, which takes account of both the legal responsibilities of broadcasters and the requirements of the law. I shall first summarise the latter.

Defamation

Defamation in legal terms is the publication or broadcast of false information that causes damage to the plaintiff's reputation. It is understood as either libel (the written form of defamation – hence 'publication') or slander (the spoken form – or 'broadcast' in its most general sense). In terms of these definitions, a television programme can be regarded as both publication and broadcast. Although dramadoc/docudrama is especially vulnerable to charges of defamation, court cases are relatively rare. This is partly because of the expense and uncertainty associated with litigation, partly because the research element can be mobilised to justify what has been published and/or broadcast to the satisfaction of the law, and partly because the law on both sides of the Atlantic is still amenable to the notion that 'fair comment' on a public subject, made in an informed manner, is justified in the wider public interest.

Fundamentally, media lawyers assess risk by applying 'a working test of "potential actionability"' to the material contained in programmes they legal (Robertson and Nicol, 1992: xvii). They must be satisfied that the possibilities are low to non-existent before they can perform their most significant pre-transmission task – the signing of the insurance certificate that protects the television company and its employees from legal action by third parties. 'We cannot start shooting,' Sita Williams told me, 'until Goodman Derrick [Granada's London-based legal representatives] underwrite the script.' Having sought reassurance that the programme defames neither persons nor organisation, the lawyers' opinion persuades insurers to give 'E & O' (errors and omissions) cover to the programme maker. In the event of action this insurance will pay for a defence (and any costs incurred should the case go against the defendants).

But the kind of public argument about dramadoc that we saw in the case of *Hostages* is much more frequent, so a good deal of legal comment on the form occurs at the margins of the law. The notion of dramadoc/docudrama as a 'media event' is useful here, as it points up the fact that debate in a society continues around and beyond a transmission, especially if it is controversial. There are similarities with the 'moral panic' of sociology (or the flurry of discussion that can occur around some contentious social problem or event). The agenda for wider public debate is at least partly set by the media, and in particular cases politicians and even governments join the fray. This occurred, for example, in the case of the 1980 Associated Television (ATV) dramadoc *Death of a Princess*, which famously occasioned a Middle Eastern nation, Saudia Arabia, to break off diplomatic relations with Britain (see Chapter 7 for further details). It is not unusual for the opening exchanges in the public argument to be evident in pre-publicity and at press previews. When controversy is generated by the contesting of the programme's view of the facts, the news media tend to become very active, as *Hostages* demonstrated.[1]

At such times the air can become thick with the threat of legal action. Solicitors, especially those retained by wealthy individuals, are particularly fond of the 'letter before action' as a ploy to try to prevent publication or transmission. The letter characteristically warns an organisation or individual that action may be taken against them. The request for withdrawal and/or emendation of the offending material is then made either overtly or tacitly. The print media are willing enough on such occasions to follow up on the implication of such manoeuvres: that there may be some kind of inaccuracy in a planned programme. Casting doubt on factual provenance, as the Beirut hostages' letter does, can be a problem at the point of reception.

With drama-documentary, the Granada executive Ian McBride remarks, 'there's always somebody who doesn't want it made.' Both *Hostages* and *Fighting for Gemma* were opposed, the former by the hostages themselves, the latter by a powerful commercial organisation, BNFL. In neither case did opposition result in legal action, but lawyers' letters are nonetheless routine elements in the making of a dramadoc/docudrama. John McCarthy's literary agent Mark Lucas was particularly active in this regard before the transmission of *Hostages* and, although he was unable to prevent the broadcast, he may have helped to reduce the audience for the programme (see, again, Chapter 7).

The lawyer's work

During the production process legalling involves regular, even daily, consultation between producers and lawyers. At Granada complete scripts are sent, and alterations to scripts faxed, to Goodman Derrick. As scripts are honed and refined, so the assembly of docu-

mentary material authenticating the script also proceeds and
lawyers cross-check the factual basis for particular lines and whole
speeches with the producers and/or researchers. Of course, all television drama is checked for potential legal problems, and to some
extent dramadoc inherits the potential for controversy possessed by
the factual, documentary side of its provenance. But it is a form that
needs even more careful vetting because of the sensitive nature of
the material that often dramatises the lives of living people and
active contemporary institutions. In practice, this means that lawyers must see scripts at all stages of their production – from treatment to post-production – for them to be able to advise and
comment.

The producer's marginal comments in working scripts of *Fighting
for Gemma* demonstrate the close interface between the creative and
legal teams. Although aesthetic questions are sometimes raised, the
bulk of marginal comments refer to legal matters and the programme makers' fear of running foul of a large institution like
BNFL. On Sita Williams' 'Principal Working Script' of *Fighting for
Gemma* such marginal comments as 'Q RP', 'Send to RP' and 'RP'
are by far the most frequent ('RP' is the lawyer Robin Perrot of
Goodman Derrick). Next in frequency is the comment 'Check',
which refers to the research base within the Granada organisation
itself. In practice, this usually means files that are compiled and held
by producers themselves. The present costs of making television
programmes tend to preclude the option of the writer-researcher, so
the responsibility for the factual base lies very much with the
producer, aided by the lawyer.

There are many places in the script of *Fighting for Gemma* where
'input' was very direct and a speech or section of dialogue was cut
or amended as a result of legalling. In general, this produces a
circumspection that is the antithesis of plain speaking. There is a
good example on page 48 of Williams' script, where Susan D'Arcy's
line: 'Sellafield caused her [Susan's daughter Gemma] to have
leukaemia' was changed as a result of Robin Perrot's view that such
a statement might be taken as defamation by BNFL. It became a
more circumspect but less passionate interrogative: 'Are you saying
Sellafield didn't cause her leukaemia?' Lawyers find such a phrase

altogether easier to defend. On page 75, a line of Susan's was again altered for similar reasons: 'That place caused Gemma to have leukaemia!', became 'Gemma's got leukaemia.'

The effect of the linguistic shift is inevitably to diminish the real mother's 'fight' somewhat. The contrast with the language the real Susan D'Arcy tended to use during her traumatic suffering could not be more stark. When she was interviewed by the *Today* newspaper's reporter Penny Wark (10 November 1993) she described how she refused to allow her husband, a contract-worker at Sellafield, to blame himself for their daughter's illness: 'I said, "That's not true. It's Sellafield done it to you without you knowing.".' The article's headline is even stronger, paraphrasing Susan D'Arcy in a way that would certainly have caused problems in a dramadoc: 'I want them to admit they [Sellafield] killed my girl.' In law, 'Susan D'Arcy' (the character in a filmed drama) does not have the same rights of free speech as Susan D'Arcy (the real-world individual).

Because the lawyers work a good deal with the media, their sensitivity to legal requirements is tempered by their recognition of the values and aspirations of the programme makers. They become quasi-media professionals as a result of collaboration. In Alasdair Palmer's words, a lawyer 'has this very difficult job – not wanting to destroy the film, but wanting to protect us legally.'[2] Robin Perrot and Patrick Swaffer of Goodman Derrick have often been involved with Granada dramadocs (Perrot legalled *Hostages* and *Fighting for Gemma*, Swaffer *Goodbye My Love*), and Oliver R. Goodenough of New York's Kay, Collyer and Boose and Harvard Law School has legalled extensively for HBO (including *Hostages* in the USA). As lawyers particularly experienced in entertainment law in general, and dramadoc/docudrama in particular, their work is a little-understood but vital part of the process. The success of the collaboration can be measured in one sense by the infrequency of court action.[3]

Regulatory bodies and frameworks

Programme makers are constrained not only by the law but also by the various regulatory frameworks that exist in Britain and the USA. In recent years these have developed rapidly, especially in

relation to factual broadcasting. So, for example, the members of
the Granada team interviewed for this book were bound by the *ITC
Programme Code* and the ITV Network Centre's *Statement of Best
Practice*. They had also to be wary of offending the Broadcasting
Standards Council (BSC) and the Broadcasting Complaints Commis-
sion (BCC). In 1996 these two organisations became one.

The BBC is of course bound by its Charter and has broadly similar
internal publications to those of ITV (its *Producers' Guidelines*, for
example). Patrick Swaffer observes that broadcasters in general tend
to find this panoply of regulation 'onerous and burdensome', but
makers of documentary and documentary derivatives find it especially so, particularly when they look in the direction of theatre and
film, and even journalism. They feel people are, relatively, freer from
restriction in these industries.

The *ITC Programme Code* is a representative example of the
assumptions, language and declared intentions of such regulatory
instruments. Its Section 3 deals with the question of impartiality
and gives the Independent Television Commission (ITC)'s response
to the 1990 Broadcasting Act's strictures on the preservation of
'due impartiality ... as respects matters of political or industrial controversy or relating to current public policy.' 'Due' is here defined as
'adequate or appropriate to the nature of the subject and the type of
programme'. Paragraph 3.7 of this section deals specifically with
drama and drama-documentary. It recommends that 'plays based
on current or very recent events be carefully labelled' and asserts
that dramadoc (it does not use the term docudrama) 'is bound by
the same standards of fairness and impartiality as those that apply
to factual programmes in general'. In a crucial sentence it also
recommends: 'The evidence on which a dramatic reconstruction is
based should be tested with the same rigour required of a factual
programme.' The *Statement of Best Practice: Factual Drama on Television*, published by the Independent Television Network Centre in
1994, underscores these regulatory requirements. Its 'Guidelines
for drama-documentary' contains almost identical statements (see
Corner and Harvey, 1996: 253–4). The *BBC Producers' Guidelines
1993*, meanwhile, talk similarly of the 'obligation to be accurate'
(see Kilborn and Izod, 1997: 153).

Additionally to the requirements in other kinds of factual programming, the *ITC Programme Code* document recognises that: 'Impartiality may need to be reinforced by providing an opportunity for opposing viewpoints to be expressed.' The dramadoc, which is bound in part by the constraints of what are called 'fictional elements', becomes something of a special case, and the regulations specifically recommend 'a studio discussion following the drama itself, or a separate programme providing a right of reply within a reasonable period' to ensure impartiality. An example of the dramadoc-followed-by-discussion format was BBC2's *The Late Show* of 21 September 1992, when one item was a follow-up discussion of *Hostages* (I shall refer to this again in Chapter 7, as an 'extra-textual event').

The *ITC Programme Code* acknowledges cultural anxiety about the form by providing this self-reflexive scheduling. Acknowledging that 'the boundaries between what is fact and what is fiction may become blurred', it attempts to legislate by stating: 'a clear distinction should be drawn between plays based on fact and dramatised documentaries which seek to reconstruct actual events'. Its answer, in many ways the 'custom and practice' answer of the Granada dramadoc tradition itself, is that anything which attempts reconstruction should be 'clearly labelled as such, so that the fictional elements are not misleadingly presented as fact'.

Because dramadocs often address issues of public policy, there are always likely to be vested interests contesting the view taken by the programme. The form's claim to be a vital part of the democratic process in Britain and America rests partly on this factor. Todd Gitlin quotes Barbara Hering, an NBC lawyer: 'If justified by the facts, [docudrama] performs a public service, but if the facts are not as portrayed, the possible undermining of the public's faith in their institutions would be not only unfair but a real disservice to our audience' (1994: 173). This distinction is crucial, and the public's faith in the main source of its day-to-day information – the television – is at issue here.

In the USA there is a central regulatory agency, the Federal Communications Commission (FCC), which was developed from the earlier Federal Radio Commission in 1934. This body is currently extending its control of modern media to include the new tech-nologies of cable television and the Internet. Historically, it has been concerned primarily with such matters as the allocation of frequency bands for transmission and the limitation of monopoly in broadcasting. It has had some influence over the content of com-mercials and programmes, but is often seen by media commentators as a somewhat craven servant of the commercial interests that have always dominated American broadcasting. First Amendment guar-antees of free speech have ensured a rather looser monitoring of US docudrama (see Chapter 6). At times, monitoring can come down to State, rather than Federal, legal precedent.

Before a docudrama can be transmitted by an American network, the script must pass through three layers of scrutiny: by the net-works' own legal, 'errors and omissions', and 'broadcast standards and practices' departments. All networks have guidelines, just as the BBC and ITV do. Guidelines offered by the NBC (see Rosenthal, 1995: 248–50) do not refer specifically to docudrama but to 'fact-based movies and mini-series'. This is a much broader swathe of fact/fiction drama, which is to be expected in view of the less sub-stantial cultural commitment to the investigative dramadoc tradi-tion in the USA.

If the reasons for this looser definition are historical and cultural, the demands made are very similar to those in the *ITC Programme Code*. NBC requires the producer to provide 'substantial backup, including multiple sources', and to 'send one copy of the annotated script to the NBC Program Standards Department and a second copy to the NBC Law Department.' The *NBC Annotation Guide* offers detailed instructions on this aspect of the script preparation. Finally, NBC draws the attention of producers to various independent research agencies whose assistance they recommend; specifically, they mention Fact or Fiction, an organisation formed expressly to deal with the fact-based movie and the mini-series. Granada, of course, still has its own research department to assist its producers.

'Release forms', which are used extensively in documentary proper, are recommended for use in docudramas too. A release form, signed by the real protagonists in a true story, will ensure that they cannot take action after they have been portrayed in a drama.

As Robertson and Nicol put it, 'Consent to publication is a complete defence' (1992: 94). Rhona Baker reproduces a dummy release for would-be producers to copy (1995: 258–9) and Alan Rosenthal gives advice on waivers (1995: 212). Granada dramadocs have yet to go down this road; they are still governed by the rights of the investigative journalist to comment on matters in the public domain. This resistance to allowing a power of veto to protagonists has advantages, and not just financial ones. The British tradition has, perhaps, more room for manoeuvre. Oliver Goodenough remarked in his 1996 conference paper that in the USA 'the legal end [wa]s more advanced', but described British dramadoc as 'creatively stronger'.

In and out of court

Goodenough observes that 'the [US] courts have worked out a First Amendment analysis that permits [docudrama] to be made with relative safety from legal challenge'. He stresses, however, that 'staying in this area of safety… depends on the producer acting responsibly'. The case which helped to establish this situation legally was that of Davis *versus* Costa-Gavras (1987), in which the latter film director's depiction of historical events in his 1982 *Missing* was challenged. His opponent in court represented a US State Department unhappy with the way American involvement in the Chilean Army coup of 1973 had been portrayed in the film. Goodenough quotes the final view of Judge Milton Pollack:

> Self-evidently a docudrama partakes of author's license – it is a creative interpretation of reality – and if alterations of fact in scenes portrayed are not made with serious doubts of truth of essence of the telescoped composites, such scenes do not ground a charge of actual malice. (Goodenough, 1989: 29)[4]

What should be especially interesting to the student of the media here is the judge's apparent invocation (and misquotation) of the celebrated definition of documentary given by John Grierson in the 1930s (the 'creative treatment of actuality' – see also Chapter 4). As is often the case, Grierson's 'treatment' is rendered as 'interpretation', and his 'actuality' becomes 'reality'. Such semantic shifts bear out a widely held critical view that documentary's aesthetic power of 'creative interpretation' has been at least as important as its claim to represent the actual/real. The slippage between 'real' and 'true' has a long history. It would be a mistake to expect the law to have anything other than a pragmatic view on this; as Goodenough said in his conference paper, 'the law is a working-through at a societal level of ethics and morality'. The status of documentary as a mode of communication is routinely collapsed into its status as a mode of social exploration (a tendency I shall examine further in Chapter 4). But problems multiply as soon as drama is introduced into the equation. It is no wonder that cultures that have developed a 'documentary perception' struggle with forms that merge aesthetic and informational functions.

At the legal level, however, producers on both sides of the Atlantic are channelled towards a notion of 'due impartiality' by both legal and regulatory frameworks. The balance in both legal systems is in favour of the 'responsible producer', and it is this which ensures that programmes continue to be made. What can happen if the process goes wrong, however, was illustrated all too clearly in the case of a 1989 BBC television play *Here is the News*, written by G. F. Newman, in which a character called David Dunhill was so closely modelled on a real journalist – Duncan Campbell – that he was able to sue the BBC (and win) in 1990.

Deploying his own investigative skills to devastating effect, Campbell demonstrated just how much detail of his own life had gone into Newman's Dunhill, proving that a change of name is not a sufficient tactic to avoid the charge of defamation. Goodenough says on this point: 'Merely changing names, events, locations or physical features will not in itself prevent recovery by someone who claims to be recognizably portrayed.' He cites a 1983 case in America that was similar but racier: an actual 'Miss Wyoming' 'was able to win the issue of identity against *Penthouse* magazine when it ran a story about a fictional Miss Wyoming of a different name, who twirled batons and levitated men through oral sex' (Goodenough, 1989: 5).

In the UK particularly there is a further, unfortunate dimension: the lawsuit has become the privilege of the rich and litigious.

Robertson and Nicol remark: 'Libel actions launched by wealthy and determined individuals can be enormously expensive to combat' (1992: 43). The notion that you have to be rich to get justice is not a happy one for the British legal profession: 'Massive libel awards to unprepossessing plaintiffs contrast too starkly with the inability of the average citizen to obtain a right of reply or to be protected against media intrusion into private joys and griefs.' (Robertson and Nicol, 1992: xviii).

Although Granada's programme makers have become inured to the occasional 'furore' and to the solicitor's 'letter before action', they did face legal action on the 1990 film *Why Lockerbie?* (called *The Tragedy of Flight 103: The Inside Story* in the USA). This had just concluded when I interviewed Alasdair Palmer in 1994. According to him, the problem with *Why Lockerbie?* was that it was 'critical of a large American company which hadn't yet gone bankrupt'. On this occasion Palmer had to go beyond the normal legalling procedures and provide lawyers with 'a script in which each line had a number which referred to a document attached to it'. The case was eventually settled out of court.[5]

Nor is reference to the regulatory body for independent television an unheard of event. The ITC censured Carlton for its film *Beyond Reason* (a 1996 film based on a sensational 1991 murder case in which an army officer's wife was murdered by his lover). By contrast, in 1997 it upheld as valid the treatment of the subject of child abuse in a Meridian Television dramadoc, *No Child of Mine*, against a series of complaints. The censure followed complaints by the murdered woman's parents. Doubts about the facts in the second example were dispelled by the programme's use of confidential files made available by a real-life victim. Oliver Goodenough believes that more developed American precedents on the matter of privacy will soon become part of British law too and that the days of reliance on regulatory checks and balances are as good as over.[6]

The BBC's problems with fact/fiction mixes in recent years have made the organisation more cautious. In addition to *Here is the News*, two other films caused controversy: the Charles Wood teleplay *Tumbledown* and Alan Bleasdale's *The Monocled Mutineer*. *Tumbledown* told the story of Robert Lawrence, a Guards officer who was badly wounded in the 1982 Falklands War. Necessarily, it depicted in a way that might he seen as controversial not only a number of Lawrence's actual colleagues but also the institution of the British army itself, and it was due for transmission on the eve of a general election. Alterations were made to the film and its transmission was delayed until 1987. Ian Curteis' *The Falklands Play*, meanwhile, caused almost as much of a problem even though it was not transmitted at all. I have argued elsewhere that this particular controversy over representations of the Falklands War betrayed a society deeply troubled by, and unable to resolve, antithetical views – unable any longer to smooth them into the kind of consensus that was evident in, say, 1950s films representing the Second World War.[7]

In 1988 *The Monocled Mutineer* was shown as a four-part dramatisation based on a book by William Allison and John Fairley. It told the story of a First World War deserter from the British army, Percy Topliss. The film was heavily attacked for allegedly taking liberties with the truth. The *Daily Mail* was prominent in claiming errors and several newspapers ran editorials on the subject. In the context of a decade in which the government in power was prone to regarding the BBC as a left-inclining, hostile institution it was perhaps not altogether surprising that the BBC lost its appetite for factually based drama for a while after these problems. The institutional aim of Charter renewal left the BBC vulnerable at this point in its history – the last thing it needed was controversies over fact-based drama.

The end-result of a combination of regulation, increased legal activity and general cultural suspicion of the form has been a defensive-mindedness on the part of broadcasters. They are after all likely to be under simultaneous attack (in the worst scenario) from several quarters: persons or institutions depicted in a dramadoc (and unhappy with their depiction); the legal representatives of such persons or institutions; regulatory bodies; their own employers; and a wary public. Granada's Ian McBride takes the view: 'Because you know this kind of thing will happen, the demands on you are so much higher. We do quite a lot of work in pre-production in trying to construct what kind of attacks are likely to be launched against us.'

Nevertheless, there is a tendency towards strategies that avoid risk, which is to some extent reinforced by the training and institutional practices of lawyers themselves. Robertson and Nicol make the point that lawyers are 'inevitably more repressive' than the law itself:

> 'because they will generally prefer to err on the safe side, where they cannot be proved wrong. The lawyers' advice provides a broad penumbra of restraint, confining the investigative journalist not merely to the letter of the law but to an outer rim bounded by the mere possibility of legal action. (1992: xvi–xvii)

Libel actions are customarily fought on a combined defence of 'justification' in terms of available facts and 'fair comment' following from this, and Patrick Swaffer notes that 'a jury finds this difficult'. With courts finding it more difficult to attribute meaning than any student of literary theory, it is no wonder he admits that 'lawyers are cautious about meaning'.

International co-production makes the process of legalling still more difficult and the likelihood of cautious solutions more probable, because of inherent differences not just between two legal systems but also between two cultures of broadcasting. In Britain and the USA the test of potential actionability takes slightly different forms. For Americans, as I have noted, the First Amendment to the Constitution grants a right of free speech to citizens. Britain currently lacks a constitutional guarantee of this right. In the USA the principle has also been established, through precedent, that 'recovery [for public individuals] is only possible if it can be shown that the publisher of the false libel acted with actual malice'; for private individuals, 'a showing of negligence in the publication of the defamatory falsehood' is required (see Goodenough, 1989: 5). In Alasdair Palmer's words, 'the burden of proof is not on you as the film maker [as it is in the UK], it's on the plaintiff to prove that you're wrong'.

There is no doubt that US broadcasters have benefited from First Amendment-protected precedental cases such as the *New York Times versus* Sullivan case of 1964 (in which the US Supreme Court ruled that a newspaper had a right to make allegations against a public figure provided these could be proved to be 'honestly and diligently made'). As Robertson and Nicol remark, this judgement paved the way for such historic exposés as Watergate and Irangate; in the UK this kind of investigative journalism tends to attract a debilitating barrage of writs (1992: 103). As a result, caution is the watchword in Britain. Although Robertson and Nicol define journalism as 'not just a profession [but] the exercise by occupation of the right to free expression available to any citizen', they acknowledge that histori-cally, Britain has hedged around this right with 'special rules' devel-oped by Parliament and the courts. In the absence of any legislation on freedom of information a largely precedent-led tradition of free speech has grown up (1992: xv–xvi).

Significantly, in offering advice to would-be programme makers, Patrick Swaffer notes three principal legal 'worries' for any British lawyer dealing with dramadoc:

1 Defamation Is anybody identified in the programme whose reputa-tion is likely to be reduced as a result of the programme?
2 Confidentiality Is any material used in the programme that is confi-dential or was obtained in confidence?
3 Regulatory framework [Swaffer lists some examples of this].

So Swaffer's training causes him to take the position of the defen-dant having to prove a case against a plaintiff.

In contrast, Goodenough lists four areas of potential difficulty in relation to media depictions of [real people]':

• Libel and slander
• Privacy
• Publicity
• Trade name   (Goodenough, 1989: 5)

The shift from defendant to complainant, and the more commercial awareness inherent in 'Trade name', clearly marks out a difference in the American legal view (as does the apparent absence of worry about regulation). But the absence of a strict liability, which in the UK puts the burden of proof on the defendant, is the most notably different feature.

Differences in State and Federal legislation do make for some potential confusion in the USA. With 'privacy and publicity', for example, 'each of the 50 states has its own laws' (Goodenough, 1989: 5). It is true, also, that the American system is prone to entre-preneurial activity as a result of the 'contingency fee system' (a kind of 'no result – no payment' arrangement which actually encou-rages litigation). The real difference in the two systems, however, remains in the positioning of the burden of proof: in the British system it is necessary to prove that everything that is claimed is true; in the American the plaintiff must demonstrate malice and negligence. Goodenough summarised in his 1996 conference paper: 'In the UK, the question is, is it the truth? In the USA, the question is, did they do their homework?'

Regulating, legislating or censoring?

If the basic structures of criminal law, civil law and legally man-dated regulatory bodies are broadly shared by both British and American broadcasting, UK media agencies have been hedged around historically by the kind of informal, gentlemanly (and I use the word deliberately) lobbying and state-sponsored benign repres-sion that have resulted from a self-protecting culture of caution in public matters. But the USA is not necessarily any better. The pre-eminence of the commercial interest has made things simul-taneously freer in terms of the legal framework and more restricted in terms of the kinds of programme it is possible to make. Because advertisers want above all programmes that will draw popular audiences, US television has a tendency to take fewer risks with the formats of programmes – and its docudrama tradition is not as 'fact-rich', to use Goodenough's phrase, as the comparable British dramadoc tradition.

In recent years, however, the two cultures and their media institutions have been moving closer together under global market pressures. Robertson and Nicol comment: 'The recent history of moral and political censorship in Britain has been characterised by a move from criminal law to statutory regulation' (1992: 594). As the amount of regulation has increased, so the degree of freedom in Britain has reduced; and as the commercial competition in the USA has become hotter, so the capacity to be innovative and daring (and to be free in that sense) has equally reduced. The co-production dramadoc/docudrama provides a site for the analysis of these cultural pressure-points.

Unlike the USA, Britain still has two fundamentally different forms of terrestrial television broadcasting – the public service BBC and commercial television – which are at present more or less equally balanced in terms of their access to audiences:. The BBC was formally constituted as an organisation in the 1920s, as were the first US broadcasting networks. But whereas the latter have always been commercial (the USA only acquiring a public service network in the 1960s), the BBC has presided over seventy-five years of continuity in the public service tradition.

Following the British General Strike of 1926 the government of the day ensured that the constitution of the fledgling broadcasting organisation guaranteed the right of military take-over. Section 19 of the BBC Charter gives a Home Secretary this power and Section 13(4) gives her or him an additional right of veto on any pro-gramme or item within a programme (see Robertson and Nicol, 1992: 26). Although Section 19 has never been used in anger (so far), the threat that it holds has sometimes caused the BBC to dither and procrastinate on matters of public policy. When commercial television came to the UK in the 1950s, the Independent Broad-casting Authority (IBA) was similarly positioned in relation to government judgements about sensitive issues, and Section 10 of the 1990 Broadcasting Act transferred the government's power to intervene to the newly constituted ITC. The USA, partly because of its sheer size, has always given local stations greater autonomy, and the regulatory function of the FCC is more akin to that of the new, post-Broadcasting Act, 'lighter-touch' ITC than to previous models of broadcasting regulation.

A good example of the British way is the so-called D-notice, through which British governments are able to restrain the broad-casting of subject matter deemed to be against the national interest. Its purpose was defined as well as upheld by the government itself. The tendency of such convenient secrecy is at odds with the concept of civil education for responsible citizenship that is so much the defining tradition both of British broadcasting and of British education, and so a fundamentally ideological argument is played out at the level of the individual programme whenever dramadoc becomes controversial. The break-up of the post-war consensus in Britain has led to challenges to the network that once guaranteed acquiescence in a gentlemanly square dance between legislators and broadcasters.

The paradoxical difference between a non-commercial organisation that is easily subject to government pressure and a commercial but more independent one was shown most remarkably in the 1980s. During those years the deteriorating situation in Northern Ireland caused the Thatcher government progressively to remove the various voices of the Irish Republican Army (IRA) from television screens. In the case of *At the Edge of the Union*, a 1985 BBC documentary in the *Real Lives* series, the BBC bowed to pressure and removed the programme from its schedules. In 1988 the Thames Television documentary series *This Week* investigated the killing in Gibraltar by the Special Air Service (SAS) of three IRA members earlier that year. The programme, *Death on the Rock*, went out after the IBA and the television company resisted the government's attempt to have it removed from the schedule. The consequence of this resistance was that the Conservative government was forced to legislate, in 1988, to deny the IRA 'the oxygen of publicity'. Robertson and Nicol's words about the move from criminal law to statutory regulation are neatly illustrated by this example.

The Broadcasting Act of 1990 shifted the ground further and altered the outlines of commercial television's regulatory framework. Thames lost its franchise in 1993 in a follow-up to the new legislation; many commentators saw this as a direct result of its resistance to covert censorship on *Death on the Rock*. These changes in broadcasting were set in train by a government incensed by what it increasingly regarded as meddling by the media. The combative attitude of the Thatcher Government, with its belief verging on paranoia that the British media was a hot-bed of left-wing agitation, focused the debate in the UK on the regulation of the media. Robertson and Nicol (1992) take the view that the model of Article 10 of the European Convention on Human Rights may lead Britain eventually towards the kind of guarantees enjoyed by American journalism, but this must be dependent on the overall position of the UK within the European Union.

All this affects British drama-documentary inasmuch as it is documentary; the rigour expected of a purely factual programme is the base from which the programme must be made. The main laws that must be acknowledged by the makers of dramadoc/docudrama are, therefore, the criminal laws of contempt of court, official secrecy, sedition and obscenity, and the civil laws of libel and breaches of copyright and of confidence. These are reinforced by the various regulatory bodies on both sides of the Atlantic, behind whose rhetoric lurk the twin concepts of 'due impartiality' and 'good taste'. These rough rules of thumb can seem as if they are intended mainly to dissuade programme makers and broadcasters from taking risks, but they can also be seen as a permitted freedom-within-boundaries rather than a free-for-all.

For Granada, the requirements of the *ITC Programme Code* govern all practical decisions, anchoring the drama-documentary to rules of 'due impartiality' inherited directly from the news and current affairs programme. Film, of course, is similarly subject to the law and to censorship, but Ian McBride, for one, believes there is effectively no comparison between the two media:

> The requirement of due impartiality is actually a duty; no feature film maker has that responsibility. Cinema is not regulated like that because it's not seen as carrying a public information role. It's not current affairs, it's essentially seen in an entertainment role, in which the audience elects to go along and watch.

His view as a programme maker is that 'the reasons for the television regulations are actually sound given the more random way television is watched.'

Of all the laws likely to impede the making of a dramadoc/docudrama, libel laws are now foremost in the minds of media lawyers, especially as the form focuses more and more on the 'personal story'. British dramadoc producers like Alasdair Palmer look at the US system with something approaching envy: 'I have to think the American system is best because they actually do believe in the freedom of the press – it's constitutionally protected.' He feels that the

US system is more enabling in matters of genuine public interest. On the other hand, he is also in favour of the kind of *sub-judice* procedure that obtains in the UK and that prevents the pre-judging of trials, or 'trial by media'. The events surrounding the O. J. Simpson trial of 1995 would seem to bear out this view; an in-built disadvantage of the First Amendment, perhaps, is that it virtually guarantees the trial-by-television that the UK Contempt of Court Act of 1981 prevents.

Robertson and Nicol, however, sound a note of caution: although 'the British media enjoy relative freedom from censorship by comparison with most Third World countries', the situation in America, Canada, France, Scandinavia and Australia is much better from the point of view of freedom of expression. These countries use Article 19 of the Universal Declaration of Human Rights of 1975 as their definition of that freedom. The Declaration reads, in part: 'Everyone has the right to freedom of opinion and expression; this right includes the freedom to hold opinions without interference and to seek, receive and impart information and ideas through any media and regardless of frontiers' (1992: 35). According to international studies quoted by the same authors, the UK was 'sixteenth in the league table of countries that most enjoy freedom to publish'; and this was before the changes in Eastern Europe in 1989 occasioned further slippage. There can be no doubt that the rhetoric of democracy in the UK is beginning to look decidedly windy and that the controversial drama-documentary is at a point at which the culture is very clearly at odds with itself. Brian Winston suggests that 'for non-commercial, state-funded broadcasting not inevitably to mean state control requires, as a first essential, that freedom of expression be constitutionally guaranteed' (Hood, 1994: 39).[8]

Legal advice

In spite of all the difficulties, broadcasters can and do get programmes on matters of public interest on to television screens in Britain and America – a part result of the complex but not ineffective history of tradition, case law and precedent. A decreasing consensus on the degree of openness in public information has generated an increasing public distrust of information agencies. As a result, the running check that is legalling has acquired more and more importance since dramadoc first became controversial in the 1960s. The legal contribution to the process is now so direct that it can easily be read as a kind of censorship, and many writers now fight shy of working in a field that is overdetermined by legal and regulatory constraints; no wonder Rob Ritchie (writer of Granada's *Who Bombed Birmingham?*) warns: 'It is a hard and exacting task to write dramadoc.'[9]

It is against this background that we must view the making of drama-documentaries in the British tradition, which is to say programmes that attempt to provide public information on issues of collective importance by means of dramatisations that are firmly backed by research and documentation. It is, however, unsettling to note the sober advice offered by the two media lawyers most closely associated with the programmes discussed in this book.

Oliver Goodenough lists the following 'Suggested Procedures':

- Select a Topic and Characters of Legitimate Public Interest.
- Get Releases.
- Do Voluminous Research.
- Have a Factual Basis for Every Aspect of the Script.
- Stay as Close to Literal Truth as Possible.
- Respect Chronology.
- Do Not Use Composites for Major Characters.
- Depict Dead People [death wipes out rights of libel, slander and privacy].
- Take Particular Care With Certain Topics [gloss: especially 'sex and nudity'].
- Have a Legal Review of the Script and Film.
- Use Disclaimers.

(1989: 29)

Patrick Swaffer lists four 'Golden Rules' for dramadoc. These are briefer, but not dissimilar:

1 Firstly, fairness and accuracy.
2 Detailed and good-quality research must underpin your description of any events.
3 Work with the evidence you have got, rather than [the evidence] you

wished you had; don't listen to rumour and gossip.
4 Best of all make a programme about historic events where the participants are dead and therefore can't sue.

The example (given earlier) of *In Suspicious Circumstances* demonstrates that dead protagonists of course only protect programme
makers from the most directly obvious litigants.

While Oliver Goodenough, like many Americans, admires the
'fact-rich and fact-rooted' British tradition, the increasing tendency
in dramadoc/docudrama is to focus on specific stories – often of
private individuals projected by some experience or other into the
public domain – and to steer clear of politically dangerous topics. US
networks, like tabloid newspapers, actively seek and often pay for
personal stories of unusual (and frequently salacious) experience.
Co-production and shared culture have ensured that this tendency
is gaining ground in the UK.

Patrick Swaffer notes that in dramadoc there 'is always the risk
that, in the most extreme cases, the dramatisation of the story will
overwhelm or remove the documentary element of the programme'.
This is a tendency that he sees as increasing: 'More recently, this
problem has become more acute with the development of
drama/documentaries [*sic*] dealing with personal life stories.' The
specific programme he had in mind, and which he cites later in his
paper, is *Goodbye My Love*, which was examined in Chapter 1. As
I remarked then, the filmic emphasis on personal detail, buttressed
by naturalistic acting techniques, shifts the ground on which the
dramadoc stands somewhat dangerously. Even with a subject of
proven public interest, such as euthanasia, there is now a real possibility that the documentary element may be implicit rather than
explicit and that legal cases will increase. As Swaffer remarks,

> more acute problems come with drama/documentaries of personal
> stories where events have often taken place both in public and in private
> and there may be entirely conflicting viewpoints on individuals' motives
> and, indeed, the actual events.

His view appears here to bear out Julian Petley's conclusion that the
debate about dramadoc/docudrama 'has become far less politicized
in the 1990s' (1996: 24).

'Again and again,' Swaffer says, 'you review with the [creative] team the meaning of the film.' The lawyer must therefore be 'part of a team to assist you with identifying and reducing, or removing, risks'. As a result, the lawyer will have 'a good deal of input into the meaning of the programme'. This is seen as a mixed blessing. Programme makers, as we have seen with Palmer and Williams, will often praise the sensitivity of their lawyers on this issue, but the creative shoe undoubtedly pinches at times. At a public debate in 1997 the Channel 4 executive David Aukin called the control exerted by lawyers 'a terrible compromise' – to general acclaim from an audience principally composed of film makers and writers. Charles McDougall, director of Granada's 1996 *Hillsborough*, offered this stoical view: '[lawyers] are there right through to post-production and you have to put up with them.'[10]

I have characterised the new-style programmes more as American docudrama than British dramadoc, and I hope to justify this claim in later chapters. They are more fraught with danger than ever before because they aim to be more filmic and less logocentric. Kilborn and Izod note that they claim to offer 'a different level of understanding' (of the documentary) and 'a qualitatively different level of viewer involvement' (as far as the drama is concerned); but perhaps the latter begins to obtrude on the former (1997: 143).

It may be tempting for programme makers to see lawyers as people who pick away at lines of dialogue, whereas artists work beyond words, trying to capture a visual and aural *Zeitgeist*. It is perhaps better to see modern media lawyers having a cultural as well as a legal role. In these times of uncertainty about, and increasing challenge to, facts and information they have become a kind of arbiter of meaning-in-the-text for the industry and within the culture. As well as trying to fix meaning, they have come to represent a figure past whom it is necessary to smuggle other meanings. The job of 'meaning-making', theorised almost out of existence in the modern academy, has devolved on to the lawyer. Patrick Swaffer observed to me caustically that theoretical finessing of the concept of meaning would not get far in a court of law.

In order to give a context to examining the terms most commonly used in academic writing to define and describe the dramadoc/

docudrama, I want to move on in the next chapter to a review of the codes and conventions of dramadoc/docudrama. Together with the research dimension of pre-production, it is these production devices which most usefully mark out dramadoc/docudrama from the general flow of television schedules.[11]

3

Codes and conventions

Dramadoc/docudrama

The 'Siamese twin' term dramadoc/docudrama not only highlights the differences between British and American practice over the second half of the twentieth century but also reflects the fact that the separate terms have now become almost interchangeable in English-speaking cultures. Where American culture dominates, usage favours 'docudrama', and this term is used often in British writing on the form; 'dramadoc', however, is rarely used in American writing.[1] Whichever term is used, the principal codes and conventions of the form are now common to both traditions. In general, it is codes and conventions to which people in a media-literate environment respond and which they recognise prior to categorisation. I hope the reader will cross-check what I say about this against their own experience of dramadoc/docudrama and that this chapter will provide a basis for the more theoretical discussions that will follow in Chapters 4 and 5.

Dramadoc/docudrama has almost always set out to do one or more of the following:

(a) to re-tell events from national or international histories, either reviewing or celebrating these events;
(b) to re-present the careers of significant national or international figures, for similar purposes as (a);
(c) to portray issues of concern to national or international communities in order to provoke discussion about them.

Increasingly in recent times it has also aimed

(d) to focus on 'ordinary citizens' who have been thrust into the news because of some special experience.

And finally, almost as a by-product of all this, it has
(e) provoked questions about its form.
The last feature is an indicator of a 'coming of age' for dramadoc/
docudrama in particular and for the media in general.

Questions about 'referentiality' and 'representation' (see Corner
1996: 42–3) probe the extent of the documentary coding in a
programme. The moral (and legal) justification for having actors
depict real-life events is often debated, especially when a dramadoc/
docudrama is controversial (as in the case of *Hostages*). Controversy
about dramadoc/docudrama is like the issue of portraying violence
in the media: everybody has a view (even if they have not seen a
particular programme). Some commentators will always hold that
the inherent representational dangers of dramadoc/docudrama
(especially of misleading a gullible public) far outweigh any informational advantages claimed. Drama coding increases debate about
what John Corner calls the 'manipulation' issue.

The dramadoc/docudrama, then, contains material that is
usually already familiar to its audience (or, if not familiar, accepted
by it as already widely known). Trails before programmes, print
media advertising and captions/voiceovers in transmission highlight this familiarity for promotional purposes. Closeness in time to
contemporary historical events helps, because the audience's memory of events that are still recent will not need much refreshing
prior to their representation. *Hostages* followed up a major news
story with which people throughout the Western world would have
been (relatively) familiar in 1992–93. The structure of the current
affairs story (kidnap, incarceration, torture, 'ransom', possible
escape/ release) was arguably already in the minds of the audience
when the programme was first transmitted. The original treatment
written by Alasdair Palmer counted on just this factor. Its first sentence reads: 'This is the story of how five men reacted to being kidnapped, chained to the floor, beaten, and held under the constant
threat of death.'

Failing the presence in the story of well-known names and
events, the dramadoc/docudrama links specific events to a more
general set of historical events. A historical 'macro-story' is thus
hooked on to a lesser-known 'micro-story' (especially in pre-

transmission publicity). *Fighting for Gemma* thus took its place in the history of television programmes investigating the long-term effects of the nuclear fuel industry on the environment and on public health. The real life and real death of little Gemma D'Arcy acted as a metonymic device through which the dangers of nuclear power could be debated publicly. Even though it was located within a narrowly British frame of reference, this debate is part of the culture of all nuclear fuel-using nations.

Hostile Waters presented its account of the saving of the world from nuclear holocaust by framing its story of a heroic submarine crew (a story allegedly suppressed in the West and still denied by the US military) with two well-known narratives from recent history. The first (and older) one was a 'Cold War' narrative – of submarines shadowing each other in the depths of the Atlantic, endlessly practising the moves of a nuclear end-game. The second concerned the more recent story of the *rapprochement* between East and West in the 1980s, which led eventually to the collapse of the Communist bloc. This story featured Reagan – the movie-President – and Gorbachev, the 'modern' Soviet leader trying to move his nation beyond the Brezhnev time-warp.

Captions

The first key convention of the form is direct reference to such real-life events, usually by means of *captions*. Nowadays programmes are generally topped and tailed by them, and as often as not they use white lettering on a black screen or the device of the news agency teleprinter clattering out the latest news. There is a verbal equi-valent: the sepulchral *voiceover* telling an audience that 'The Events You Are About To Witness Are True' (such voices habitually capi-talise words); but this device is seen as rather old-fashioned, and mixtures of still and rolling captions are usually preferred (see below for other functions of the voiceover). *Hostages* and *Fighting for Gemma* provide good examples of the use of captions.

The *opening caption* used in the pre-credits sequence of *Hostages* is typical of a contextualising device connecting the film to its real-life referent. The very first film frame seen by the viewer contains white

.lettering centred on a black background. Music in a classical style builds and we see/read:

> Between 1984 and 1992 more than fifty
> Western citizens were held hostage in Beirut.
> This film dramatises incidents which illustrate
> what happened to some of them.

Thus the first, contextualising, caption gives us time, place, indications about character (a focus on 'Western citizens') and the beginning of a disclaimer (dramatisation that 'illustrates'). The visual and aural values are emphatically 'high concept' (see Edgerton 1991).

After about five seconds the caption starts to roll and the black background lightens to reveal the dawn scene of a bay with a town (Beirut) left of frame and in the middle distance. The frame is carefully composed and the scene is both imposing and peaceful, an impression reinforced by the string-dominated music. The rolling captions extend both the disclaimer and the description of the 'illustration' proposed by the programme:

> Dialogue has been created based upon publicly
> available material, interviews with former hostages,
> their friends and relatives, diplomats and
> politicians from the United States, Europe and
> the Middle East.
> No endorsement has been sought or received
> from anyone depicted.
> To compress six years into two hours, chronology
> has been changed and some events have been
> amalgamated. The names of minor characters
> have also been altered.

Opening caption material often incorporates this kind of disclaimer, acknowledging (as per television regulations) the partial nature of versions of events offered in dramatisation. Such lengthy statements would be unthinkable in 'documentary' and unnecessary in 'drama'. The disclaimer in *Hostages* was especially important in view of the published objections of the real hostages. Such captioning is regarded with almost talismanic reverence by the Granada team and is part of the tradition pioneered by *World in Action* in the 1970s (see Chapter 7). It has several purposes: it places the film historically; it sets the scene dramatically; it argues a representational case; it protects against legal action (see also, '*disclaimer*', below).

Some of these features are mirrored in *closing captions*. For example, historical time-scales that looked backwards into the past at the beginning of the programme look forwards at the conclusion. Dramadoc/docudrama is a form that is 'opened up' to historical time, its 'story time' complicated by other contexts and further contingencies. The closing captions of *Fighting for Gemma* demonstrate this forward-pointing convention at the moment of closure. The final caption (white on black and again framed as a static statement in the middle of the screen) begins:

> Gemma D'Arcy died in September 1990,
> aged six.
>
> In October 1993, after an eight-month
> trial, a High Court judge decided that
> no link had been proved between a
> father's exposure to radiation and his
> child's cancer of the blood.

This caption fades, giving way to a second:

> British Nuclear Fuels, and its operations at
> Sellafield, were therefore not responsible,
> on the balance of probabilities, for the
> death of Elizabeth Reay's baby daughter or
> for Vivien Hope's illness.

Again a fade out brings in the third end-caption:

> Twelve days later, the government's Health
> and Safety Executive published a study
> indicating a possible link. The study showed
> the risk of illness to children in Seascale
> whose fathers worked at the plant before
> 1965 to be 14 times the national average.

And finally, we see/read:

> Martyn Day began re-assessing evidence
> of environmental exposure to radiation
> from the plant, for possible use in further
> cases against BNFL – including that of
> Gemma D'Arcy.

The whole sequence takes forty seconds, and is presented solemnly – in total silence with all captions still rather than rolled. The effect is rather like reading an inscription (on a gravestone, perhaps – an appropriate model given the child-death which the programme treats).

Just before the final caption fades to give place to the (rolling) cast list and credits, Gemma's 'theme tune' (Otis Redding's song 'My Girl') breaks the silence, fading in on sound at about the time an average viewer might read as far as Gemma's name, the last words on the final caption. This too is 'high-concept' presentation and the essentially discursive nature of dramadoc/docudrama is well illustrated here. The story of *Fighting for Gemma* is a complex one, and the final captions acknowledge this. However, their projection of the story's complexity into its next historical phase is editorially angled to reduce the impact of BNFL's case for the defence (that their complicity in the death of children like Gemma is not proven). While steering to the right side of the legal matter of defaming BNFL, *Fighting for Gemma* nevertheless implies a view of moral responsibility. In that sense it continues the fight for Gemma that was undertaken historically by her parents and legal representative (Martyn Day of the final caption sequence, who led the legal team 'fighting for Gemma').

American docudramas follow a similar line, but the tone of captions on 'low-concept' programmes can be varied more and take on less solemn tones. In NBC's *Amy Fisher: My Story* (entitled *Lethal Lolita* in the UK), white italic writing on a black background is used to inform us:

> This is Amy Fisher's story – her version
> of the truth. She says she had a partner
> in crime, the man she claims was

her lover, Joey Buttafuoco.

He has consistently denied any sexual
involvement with her and any knowledge
of the criminal activities you will see portrayed in this film.

All this is read out by a female voice just for good measure. When
the caption clears the voice goes on to read out a second, one-line
caption:

Only they know what really happened.

A similar format is used for the end-captions. Low-concept arch-
ness is in stark contrast to the high-concept, voiceless prose of the
other two examples.

Captions, then, set the scene, put the audience in touch with 'out-
of-story' events and characters and, increasingly, deny legal responsibility. The *disclaimer* is a particular kind of opening or closing
caption. Once, a standard rubric, such as 'No reference intended to
persons living or dead' or 'Based on a True Story', was sufficient, but
now many films carry increasingly reality- (and law-) sensitive
disclaimers. In litigious times it is worth looking at the credits on
reality-based feature films too. Tim Robbins' 1995 *Dead Man
Walking*, for example, ran this disclaimer caption before its credits:

This film is inspired by the events in the life of
Sister Helen Prejean, C.S.J., which she describes in
her book *Dead man walking*. As a dramatization,
composite and fictional characters and incidents
have been used. Therefore no inference should be
drawn from the events and characters presented
here about any of the real persons connected
with the life of Sister Helen Prejean, C.S.J.

The hand of the studio lawyer is evident in this meticulous stating
of the obvious; there is all the difference in the (legal) world between
Sister Helen Prejean, C.S.J., the real-world individual and author of
a book about her own life called *Dead Man Walking* and 'Sister Helen
Prejean', a character played by Susan Sarandon in a film called *Dead
Man Walking*.

In addition to having opening and closing functions in films captions are sometimes used to locate the time and place at the beginning of a fresh sequence in the narrative. *Hostile Waters* makes much use of such *linking captions*. The narrative shuttles – often quite abruptly – between the Russian *K219*, the US submarine *Aurora* and the headquarters of both the Soviet and US navies. The linking captions supply a narrative function, helping to cut rapidly from scene to scene. A teleprinter style for such captions increases the urgency of the dramatic situation and provides the equivalent of on-screen stage directions. Dramatic tension is enhanced thereby, and the sense of the cut-off world of submarine crews is vividly evoked. This kind of device, however, derives more from the codes of documentary than from those of drama.

Voiceovers

The *voiceover* is another convention that dramadoc/docudrama shares with documentary more than drama. Either it takes the form shown in the Amy Fisher example above, in which a voice reads out a visible caption, or it is direct-address narration by an actor from the drama, a news anchor commentator, or even a real person involved in the pro-filmic events depicted. As the aural equivalent of the visual caption, the device has been used in the past to convey facts and information (see Chapter 6), but today it tends to function as part of the dramatic *mise-en-scène*. In *Hostages* the voices of news reporters are used in the opening sequence, for example, to contextualise the conflict in Beirut (see next section).

The term *diagesis* is useful here. Developed by film theory, it refers to the method of narration employed in a film and is used to mark the degree to which necessary information is conveyed to an audience from within the world of the film story. In the realist film information mostly comes 'diagetically'. The audience receives it from the words of characters, from the *mise-en-scène* (or 'what is seen in the frame' of the individual shot) or from what the camera picks out for its attention (in terms of depth of focus, angle of vision, etc.). In dramadoc/docudrama both the caption and the 'authoritative' voiceover are 'non-diagetic' – they come from outside the story world. Their function is threefold: to start us off with the necessary prior knowledge of the non-story world; to help the story take temporal and locational leaps as the narrative unfolds; and to project us back into the real (non-story) world at the end of the film. Dramadoc/docudrama has a higher level of information to convey (as has documentary) and there is little choice but to mediate it non-diagetically from time to time.

Documentary material

Use in the film of actual *documentary material* is an important and distinctive convention by which both information and authentication are achieved. Drawn from the same archives as those which supply news, current affairs and documentary programmes, such material authenticates a programme at the documentary level and connects it visibly to its documentary claims. At a dramatic level in contemporary dramadoc/docudrama it rarely disrupts the narrative flow as it provides vital contextualisation. Like captions, documentary material frequently sets the scene in time and place for the unfolding drama.

After the opening captions in *Hostages* the film cuts to a montage of contemporary newsreel footage with voiceover commentaries. They establish clearly the nature of the conflict in Lebanon. The peace of the tranquil dawn-over-the-ocean opening shot is shattered in a very specific way by the documentary footage. Rocket launchers, for example, fire right to left of frame (in film terms, towards the peaceful seaside town of the opening frames). The first voice we hear says: 'Lebanon is not the scene of one war but many...' in the tones of a front-line television reporter. News footage/commentary is then intercut with the credits for the film, the voices of Western newsreaders fading in and out with the visual material. The scene is thereby set in two ways: we see literal scene-setting in the form of landscapes and places and we hear metaphorical (and historical) scene-setting in the form of facts and information about the Lebanese conflict. The joint visual/discursive mode is distinctive in the balance that is effected between the pictures seen and the words heard; the codes are principally documentary.

The *Hostages* newsreel footage and its accompanying voiceover, however, are tricky: they partly function as a non-diagetic caption, but they are 'semi-diagetic' – both in and out of the story world. So, although the footage is there to inform us directly about the historical situation in the Lebanon between 1984 and 1992 and to 'set the scene' (as a caption might), it is also used seamlessly within the dramatic action in order to progress the drama naturalistically. The technique that achieves this result is a montaging of the documentary with the drama. The first drama scenes in the opening section of *Hostages* are intercut with the documentary news material in a rhythmical balance that, additionally, includes actor-credit information.

Credit sequences in today's television drama are always multi-layered and designed to maximise the viewer's interest. In *Hostages* we see first Jay O. Sanders (as Terry Anderson), then Josef Sommer (Tom Sutherland) being snatched from the streets of Beirut by Hezbollah kidnap squads. These dramatised scenes are confirmed by (simulated) news voiceovers that identify the victims. In the first scene proper we see John McCarthy (played by Colin Firth) making just such a news report about Brian Keenan being taken hostage. In three neat dramatic steps we are presented with the four main players in the drama, the historical sequence of their abduction and the general context of the war in Lebanon.

That we are in the realm of drama on these occasions is obvious from the deliberate contrast in quality of the film stocks and shooting styles. The documentary footage reads as news – it has all the rough-and-ready hallmarks of being shot in natural light and under pressure (simple set-ups, lens flarings, occasional lack of focus, camera shake, arbitrary framing). Whereas its quality as image is affected by being copied from archive sources, the drama footage is quite the opposite. Here we have multiple camera set-ups and self-conscious framings as well as the smooth transitions of continuity editing. There are establishing shots of bombed-out streets; there is clear point-of-view identification of kidnappers and kidnapped through close-ups and eyeline matches. Dramatic depth is achieved in sequences such as that in which Anderson is metonymically mal-treated (his glasses are knocked to the ground and shattered).

Sutherland's point-of-view of the back of the limousine that will carry him into captivity has clarity of framing and focusing, but camera wobble conveys the naturalism of Sutherland's struggle against his captors while simultaneously alluding to the documentary values of the earlier newsreel footage.

In the dramadoc/docudrama these are supporting rather than opposing camera rhetorics, but drama is prioritised; in the last example the camera shake of documentary is simulated. That which is forced on the news camera operator in the field (and which we saw in the montage of Beirut) is affected for dramatic purposes. Like the experienced speaker who uses the debating trick of putting facts and figures alongside an entertaining anecdote, the dramadoc/docudrama uses the continuous experience of viewing to fold two quite different techniques into one. The codes and conventions are mixed as a result of the development of the form, so that within such a sequence as this they can scarcely be separated.

In the first scene proper of *Hostages* the programme-makers connect the simulated event with the news and quasi-news material we have just been watching. The drama thus draws additional credibility from the documentary that has 'set the scene'. A (fictional) news crew is shown in an establishing shot (Firth/McCarthy at centre of the frame). Firth/McCarthy gives us information about Keenan (whom we have yet to see) while the camera closes in on him. The camera finishes up in medium close-up on Firth/McCarthy's face. Around him the 'news crew' become part of the *mise-en-scène* establishing him as journalist-in-the-field.

Jill Morrell comments on this scene:

> It was weird seeing other people play us, but it all fell into perspective in the opening few minutes when John had been curiously transformed from producer to reporter. We all burst out laughing; it was simply incorrect. (McCarthy and Morrell, 1994: 616)

It is certainly possible to read the scene as 'McCarthy the television reporter' doing a piece to camera. In a way he *is* – in the television dramadoc for which we are his audience. The producer Sita Williams pointed out, however, that the camera set-up foregrounds the Worldwide Television News (WTN) sound-recordist's microphone and that there is no camera in sight – personnel wander about in a way that would not be possible for any piece to camera. Acknowledging that it was possible to misread the scene as depicting a television crew, she refuted the idea that this had been deliberate and also rejected the accusation that McCarthy's work in Beirut did not include reporting. McCarthy describes his work as acting bureau chief for WTN as: 'co-ordinat[ing] the activities of the camera crews and liais[ing] with London on the details of their coverage and the best means of shipping the cassettes', but Williams was adamant that occasional reporting could and did occur. McCarthy himself corroborates this, writing in *Some Other Rainbow* about conducting interviews, accompanying the crews as they went about their work and filing a report on Keenan's kidnapping (McCarthy and Morrell, 1994: 31–8).

This section of *Hostages* usefully illustrates the kind of slippage that is always likely to occur when documentary becomes dramadoc/docudrama. Disputes tend to take place at the (dramatic) edges of the (documentary) truth claims. This is why the form is hedged with disclaimers from makers and denials from participants, all of which can create doubt in viewers. The elisions declared in the captions to *Hostages*, although manifestly necessary for the two-hour drama, will always tend to work against the claims of authenticity. For the viewer the very suspension of disbelief necessary to accept the drama reinforces disbelief at any subsequent consideration of the documentary.

In the form in which it is currently presented in the English-speaking world documentary is increasingly used rhetorically and diagetically. For example, archive news footage is used several times in *Hostages* and its primary function continues to be the authentication we saw in the opening sequence. But additional dramatic points are usually made in today's practice. In *Fighting for Gemma* the nuclear past is held up for our attention in Scene 54 of the script, in which Martyn Day's legal team view some 1950s newsreel footage about Windscale, the nuclear plant that became Sellafield. Yorkshire Television's 1983 documentary *Windscale – The Nuclear Laundry*, which first exposed the problems associated with Sellafield's reprocessing plant, is also used in the film. This has several functions:

documentarily, it helps the audience understand the 'backstory' of nuclear power; dramatically, it enables the audience to share the legal team's learning curve on the issue.

The mix of archive/library material and acted reconstruction in the early part of *Hostages* amounts to a *simulation of documentary material*, so closely do the two intercut. Increasingly, this is used to develop character in the narrative, producing dialogue between figures in the drama who sometimes exist at different levels of representation. For example, President Reagan appears so often in *Hostages* that his documentary image becomes a character (a highly suitable role, perhaps, for the Hollywood President). First seen calling the Arabs 'barbarians' in the pre-credits sequence, he 'participates' directly in a scene depicting Terry Anderson's Christmas 1988 video message. The recorded message is a faithful 'note for note' copy of Anderson's actual video, so this part of the sequence is demonstrably a simulation. But whereas the scenes of the making of the video in Beirut, its transmission on US television and its reception in the home of his campaigning sister Peggy Say (Kathy Bates) are wholly acted, they are intercut with Reagan's documentary reaction at a White House press conference. With the actor Charlton Heston also in shot, Reagan gives his response to Anderson's video: 'I don't think that was Terry speaking. I think that was...I think he had a script – that was given to him. When I was given a script, I always read the lines!' The sycophantic laughter that follows this shaft of wit, in which Heston joins enthusiastically, underscores the film's theme of official muddle-headedness and collusion in keeping the hostages imprisoned for so long. A president-actor performing to camera does not get you out of a Beirut jail.

What I am calling 'simulated documentary material' – both faked footage and the device of editing together documentary and acted footage to create dialogue – is not unusual. In *Fighting for Gemma* the cutting together of footage from a Granada *Update* regional magazine programme and David Threlfall's performance as Martyn Day enables a 'virtual documentary' of Day's original dialogue with representatives of BNFL to take place. This device brings the dramadoc close to American docudrama practice. In the 1988 *Shootdown* (about the downing of Korean Airlines flight KAL 007 by

Russian planes in 1983) Angela Lansbury (playing the mother of a victim) similarly 'participated' in an edition of the syndicated American talk show *Donahue*. The same technique was used whereby an actor's simulation replaces a real individual's side of a conversation, which is edited-out.

This is something of a 'high-concept' technique, however. The 'Long Island Lolita' trilogy, by contrast, is packed with stereotypical simulated press conferences and journalistic ambushes of the protagonists. Broadcast and print journalists did indeed pursue the real protagonists in 1992, eagerly signing them up as soon as they could. In the docudramas they are portrayed as a kind of 'Rent-a-Media-Mob'; they jostle each other, thrusting microphones and cameras forward, but the babble of questions always quietens quickly so that the story can be advanced when the audience hears a key question. 'Low-concept' docudrama offers the conventions of news reportage purely as a narrative aid, confident that its audience is sufficiently used to the codes and conventions of news reporting itself to be able to transpose them enough to 'read' the drama.

Conventions aim increasingly to knit together the documentary and the drama rhetorically, from within the parameters of film realism. News hounding of Amy Fisher *et al.* is recreated to preserve the visual values of the made-for-TV movie. High-concept programmes are more likely to incorporate poor-quality but 'dramatic' original news footage and devices to signal their presence. A 'channel-zapping' visual/aural blip in *Hostages*, for example, helps the regular switches between archive and re-creation. When we surf the channels with our remote controls we not only interrupt individual programmes, we discover – indeed make – connections between different television genres. The snow-and-static of the connective frame 'sutures' the polished frames of the drama to a documentary footage authenticated partly by its poor quality (a camera operator under fire will be unlikely to study the finer points of framing and focus).[2] Reagan's comment on Anderson's performance is thus simultaneously within the drama (and is itself 'dramatic') and without the drama (as a documentary image). Anderson's sister Peggy Say comments in the drama as she watches her brother: '[the State Department] will say he was forced to read that.' A visual blip later

Reagan does just that documentarily, and the dramadoc/docudrama narrative sequence is complete.

The channel zapping convention is a direct acknowledgement of the continuum of mediations available in the world of television. All mediations, from news to cartoons, are necessarily conventionalised, and the device is 'knowing' in the sense that it expects the audience to be media-literate enough to be able to see both with and through it. The device also betrays an anxiety: interrupting the dramatic diagesis is to be avoided at all costs, therefore documentary must function actively within the drama – or not at all.

Drama conventions

Most of the other conventions of dramadoc/docudrama lie in the realm of *realist drama*. As I tried to show in Chapter 1, modern practice in television drama involves multiple camera set-ups on realistic sets or actual locations, 'key lighting', sound recorded for maximum clarity of narrative flow, continuity editing (minimising the interruptions to the narrative flow) and non-diegetic music dubbed in during post-production to influence mood. For performers the avoidance of direct address to camera is linked to believable behaviours that are reproducible to order and filmed out of sequence with the narrative. Documentary makes its presence felt in the research contribution to the *mise-en-scène*, in the unwritten rules of casting (where a broad resemblance to the real-world original is an advantage) and in the favouring of a 'low-key' acting style.

The modern thrust towards simulation and re-enactment, where actors cast for resemblance perform in patiently recreated interiors, has one anomaly: the simulation of exterior scenes is often much more of an approximation. Alasdair Palmer did obtain some footage of Beirut for *Hostages*, but most of the location filming was, rather paradoxically, done in Israel.[3] In *Goodbye My Love*, although there was location work in the USA, it was mainly to film the exteriors of houses and to provide car journey footage. By contrast, for a late scene set in the airport in Oregon (Scene 183) Manchester Airport was substituted without any problems. There is a routineness in the exchanges of real and fake at this level that is rarely mentioned (because it is accepted by most audiences as a matter of course).

However, exceptions do occur. The town councillors of St Bees, a seaside resort in Cumbria, objected both to Granada and to their local MP, William Whitelaw, about a scene in *Fighting for Gemma*. They alleged that the scene in question showed tests for radiation levels being made on a beach that was recognisable as theirs. As a result, suspicions about its radioactivity would harm tourism. Such claims are perfectly understandable at a simple level of representation. The drama's establishment of place used the beach metonymically – it stood for 'beaches tested for radiation' – but the councillors read the scene documentarily against the intentions of the film makers. In fact, in reception terms the recognition of somewhere one knows in a film drama is always more likely to cause alienation from the drama, puncturing the suspension of disbelief, than to cause concern about what might be being said about that particular place. This intrusion of the (unintended) documentary into the drama is irritating for the programme maker, but comes with the representational territory.

In the matter of *casting*, the convention for well-known public stories is to go for the 'look-alike' performer, then to use the considerable skills of costume and make-up departments to enhance the resemblance. Actors are chosen who resemble their real historical counterparts sufficiently for an audience to accept the simulated identity with no significant interruption to the suspension of disbelief necessary to enjoy realist drama. In *Hostages* there is such 'sufficient resemblance' between, say, the actor Jay O. Sanders and Terry Anderson and between Colin Firth and John McCarthy. In less well-known stories, such as *Fighting for Gemma*, this convention is not quite so urgent, but there is always some awareness that, in publicity at least, there may be advantages in being able to put the performer and the real person side by side without too much dissimilarity being evident. If anything, and inevitably, performers are usually slightly more glamorous than their real-life originals.

The conventions (referred to in the *Hostages* caption above) of *telescoping events* and creating *composite and fictional characters* deserve mention, since they point up the structural nature of drama's meeting with documentary in the dramadoc/docudrama.

'Compositing', or folding a number of real-world individuals into one dramatic unit, is done principally for dynamic purposes. If necessary, a totally fictional character can be invented. Whichever route is chosen, the scripting action is taken to progress the story at the necessary rate within the requirements of the slot in the schedule for which the programme is intended. Without these devices the story could become clogged with detail that might well be of interest documentarily but is regarded as extraneous dramatically and much feared by makers of dramadoc/docudrama. Just as I claimed (in Chapter 1) the people in Studio 12 were 'serving the camera', so documentary detail can only be justified while it continues to 'serve the narrative'. The most obvious compositing in *Hostages* is in the presentation of the hostage protagonists' dramatic antagonists – their Arab captors and the politicians/diplomats. The latter are the real villains of the piece, and the film's composites are actually stereotypes. In structural terms they have such limited functions to play – because they are at the margins of the experience being depicted – that they can only be stereotypes. By contrast, the Arab guards, although recognisably stereotyped, are treated with some sympathy.[4]

Moments of *inherent dramatic tension* and/or *dramatic irony* within actual situations are actively sought and highlighted in treatments. In Alasdair Palmer's original treatment of the hostages' story, for example, the relationship between Keenan and McCarthy is a dramatic key:

> If McCarthy saved Keenan from self-destructive rage, Keenan put steel into McCarthy's soul, and helped him to the strength he needed not to be scythed into submission by the guards and the dirt and degradation of his situation.

The moment when McCarthy and Keenan eventually meet is a dramatic climax in Part 1:

> Without explanation, they are suddenly hurled, both naked and blindfolded, into the same pitch dark room. They say nothing for some time. Then McCarthy gradually slips down his blindfold, sees the stinking hirsute Keenan and says: 'Fuck me, it's Tom [*sic*] Gunn!' He then has to explain to Keenan who Tom Gunn is.[5]

Although the convention in the credit sequence to *Hostages* told us directly who was representing whom, we are denied a sight of Ciaran Hinds as Keenan until this 'Treasure Island' moment. In the drama's emotional trajectory of hope and despair the dramatic impact of the relationship between the central characters must be maximised. The separation of the two at the end of Part 1 provides a televisual equivalent of a theatrical 'curtain line' as Keenan tries to convince himself: 'He'll be back. They'll not kill him. Just a few questions. He'll be back in a minute.' Structurally, the conventions of the modern dramadoc/docudrama are arranged around the dramatic, not the documentary, dynamic. Similarly, Sita Williams' concern was for the dramatic irony of McCarthy reporting on the already captive Keenan (in the disputed early scene mentioned above) rather than nit-picking about what McCarthy's actual job was in Beirut.

Editing out

The fear of losing an audience's attention determines to some extent what factual material stays in and what is edited out, since such material is sometimes excessive in relation to the dynamic of the drama. *Editing out* is thus a vital feature of the organisation of dramadoc/docudrama, and it is unavoidable when plots are driven naturalistically. It is no wonder that Leslie Woodhead takes the view that 'the most effective programmes satisfy almost Aristotelian rules of dramatic construction'. In his experience, 'the Aristotelian shape is an instinctive human impulse for narrative order rather than a planned strategy'. Sita Williams put it this way: 'One thing you have to do with dramadoc is not simplify but rationalise and structure in a more definite pattern than actually happens in reality.' To rationalise and shape in dramatic terms means to edit out in documentary terms.

One of the reasons for the failure of *Hostages* was the large number of characters. The cramming in of hostages, their helpers, their captors and their governmental representatives crowded the narrative. Keenan's sisters, Jill Morrell and Anderson's sister Peggy Say are all underdeveloped within the drama. Sita Williams now admits that the women were 'undersold', yet feels that 'being properly ruthless' would have improved the film as drama:

we should probably have dropped them altogether... In dramadoc you filter out the number of characters so that the ideas and the issues are open through a limited number of characters whom the audience get to know and relate to.

But because the functions of the characters in the film duplicated their real-life roles (helpers to the heroes/hostages in the battle with the diplomats) the women could not be edited out completely.

Even so, it is difficult in this genre to resist the sheer randomness inherent in the detail of real events: in *Fighting for Gemma* there is a lawyer called Martyn Day and a scientist called Philip Day. These two protagonists are not related. No dramatist, however dedicated to realism, would write such a coincidence into their play for fear that the audience would ask the irrelevant question, 'Are they related?' In 1990, a Yorkshire TV dramadoc *Shoot to Kill* treated the events of the John Stalker inquiry into the Royal Ulster Constabulary's alleged policy of that name. Its writer Michael Eaton noted that all the main participants were called 'John' and that this 'problem' for the writer could only happen in a form of drama compelled to some extent to stick to known facts.[6]

The dramatic narrative of the contemporary dramadoc/docudrama may be primarily one of character and relationships, but the documentary narrative is of events in the public domain in which certain personalities feature irreducibly. Perhaps the salient point about the mixed form is that it is more likely to present a relationship between individuals and institutions than mainstream television drama, even if they are now being mediated via 'dialogueing' between documentary image and drama. It depicts citizens against their governments in *Hostages*, 'little people' against giant corporations in *Fighting for Gemma* and individual reformers against medical, legal and ethical institutions in *Goodbye My Love*; these films are both more public and less private in their content.

The extra-textual

As sport on television features pre- and post-match analysis and discussion, so the dramadoc/docudrama is often preceded and followed by interview and discussion programmes. Sometimes they are intended to ensure balance and are part of the codes of practice that were examined in Chapter 2. They are *extra-textual* events in themselves; Jane Feuer calls them 'nonstory materials' (1995: 35). The turbulence that results from screening a version of an anterior reality cannot be accommodated without further television talk (for this is what such programmes inevitably contain). This is another convention of the form. In a similar way documentary theatre performances often trail in their wake foyer displays of documentary material and extensive programme notes (sometimes containing facsimile documents).[7] The extra-textual includes continuity announcements, talk-show appearances, discussion programmes, even newspaper campaigns (both for and against). They are as much a feature of the modern dramadoc/docudrama as the captions of their opening and closing sequences.

As part of pre-publicity in the USA Tom Sutherland met his impersonator Josef Sommer on ABC's *Good Morning America* (16 February 1993) in front of an audience of nearly five million people. In contrast to this publicity-driven exercise, BBC2's arts magazine programme *The Late Show* offered a polarised debate (between those in favour of the form and those against) on the night of the British transmission of *Hostages*. The level of the debate was signalled by its framing question (asked by presenter Sarah Dunant) – 'Is *Hostages* exploration of fact or exploitation through fiction?' – and by a news clip of Brian Keenan expressing the view that Granada's film was not helping the hostages to find 'a new bond of trust with the world'.

Alasdair Palmer was then called upon to defend the film against three 'opposers' (four, if you count Dunant herself) and two familiar charges: that *Hostages* was underdeveloped dramatically; and that its authority as fact was fatally undermined by the limitations of its form and the absence of approval of the hostages themselves. This is the 'bad documentary/bad drama' line I mentioned in the Introduction; *Hostages* stood condemned as bad on both counts. The issues rehearsed included: individual privacy versus public interest, 'copyright' on personal experience, impartiality in broadcasters, and public trust in the inherent 'decency' of broadcasters.[8]

Another kind of extra-textual vehicle frequently found is the advertising of support systems for victims and those similarly traumatised. Following the screening of Granada's 1996 *Hillsborough* a continuity announcement talked through some on-screen 'helpline' numbers: 'If you are distressed by this programme a helpline is now open [Hillsborough helpline]...or if you have been affected by the loss of a child and would like to talk to someone [child death helpline].' On regional television the next morning, discussion programmes further examined the continuing trauma of the 1989 football stadium disaster and the notion of police culpability raised both in the campaign of the Hillsborough parents' group and in the film itself.

Just as the negative reaction when *Hostages* became a media event caused a 'turn-off' amongst the audience, so the support mechanisms around *Hillsborough* carried the film forward on a tide of sympathy that culminated in a television award in 1997. More populist – and much more sympathetic – newspaper coverage reported on the making of the film in the months leading up to transmission and in the days following. The *Daily Mirror* ran a series of articles that supported the campaign of the Hillsborough victims' relatives, and reporters doorstepped the police officer who had been in charge on the fateful day (and who had by now taken early retirement on grounds of health). The extra-textual phenomenon can therefore be supportive of, and not antagonistic towards, the dramadoc/docudrama.

Definitions

In the dramadoc/docudrama, documentary's promise of privileged access to information is added to drama's promise of understanding through 'second-order' experience. The camera accesses two different kinds of reality – a record of external events (which still constitutes the basis of the documentary's appeal) and a simulated reality of acted events. The promise of the camera (its documentary offer to show events to an audience distant in place and time as though that audience were present) is extended, but only as a defining paradox. The camera's promise cannot be fully delivered in actuality since there are places either where it cannot go or where it has missed its chance of going. In the dramadoc/docudrama those things which the camera has missed (because its ubiquity is a convenient fiction rather than an actual fact) or which it can't get at (because 'the actual participants are dead or dutifully dumb', in Ian McBride's words) can still be shown – but only up to a point and at a price. Audiences who accept the extension of the camera's documentary showing do so increasingly within the context of dramatic suspension of disbelief. There is also, perhaps, a general cultural need to believe the camera's universal access to be more than just mythically true. All this guarantees the codes and conventions of dramadoc/docudrama as we watch. Following the moment of reception, the form's bid for belief is as often *dis*abled by these factors as it is *en*abled. It is dramadoc/docudrama's cultural role to be believed and then disbelieved, so to speak.

The establishment of broad conventions permits provisional definition to take place at this point. It is often the case in the arts that definition lags behind practice. But the difficulties peculiar to the docudrama/dramadoc have often been focused on the question of definition – as if clear categorisation would somehow solve everything. The purpose of such definition has too often been to hold back a tide of journalistic unease about the form.[9] Attempting for the moment to ignore unease about the ethics of the form (but acknowledging that this will need to be discussed), my definitions of the four key terms are as follows:

1 *Drama-documentary* uses the sequence of events from a real historical occurrence or situation and the identities of the protagonists to underpin a film script intended to provoke debate about the significance of the events/occurrence. The resultant film usually follows a cinematic narrative structure and employs the standard naturalist/realist performance techniques of screen drama. If documentary material is directly presented at all, it is used in a way calculated to minimise disruption to the realist narrative.

2 *Documentary drama* uses an invented sequence of events and

fictional protagonists to illustrate the salient features of real historical occurrences or situations. The film script may or may not conform to a classic narrative structure; if it does not, documentary elements may be presented non-naturalistically and may actively disrupt the narrative. But 'documentary' in this form is just as likely to refer to style as to content (and to be about the 'look' and 'sound' of documentary proper), in which case the structures of film naturalism once more obtain.

3 *Faction* uses a real-world template of events and characters to create the basic structure of a fiction. Factions rely on their audiences to connect with the 'out-of-story' factual template in reception and do little within the film to effect this connection. Film naturalism is, almost inevitably, the staple dramatic means of representation.

4 *Dramadoc* and *docudrama* are contemporary shortened terms that describe television programmes that mainly follow the drama-documentary methodology. The two words are now used virtually interchangeably (thereby partly denying thirty years of practice – see Chapters 6 and 7).

I want to use these definitions experimentally in an analysis of the form that is simultaneously specific (to instances of practice) and general (in terms, especially, of the history of fact–fiction mixed forms of broadcasting within institutions). In the rest of the book I shall try to explain how I have arrived at these definitions, and my reader will, I hope, understand through this process both how the dramadoc/docudrama has evolved and how important it is to an understanding of the complex representations that are available to the medium of television.

I shall now trace some conceptual origins to this controversial televisual form whose difficulties arise from its challenge to the limits of representation. Where, ultimately, has it come from? The answer to that question is very simple: it comes from a belief that truth can be established from evidence. Central to this belief is the almost mythic status of the camera as a provider of this commodity. The camera's power as witness is central to the representational code of the dramadoc/docudrama.

The camera's gaze

It is still not unusual to find people for whom 'seeing is believing' and for whom 'the camera cannot lie'. And this is in spite of greater sophistication of the media in the developed world and in spite of the efforts of media theorists to demonstrate the constructed nature of all representation. A belief in the evidential seems more than likely to survive and to continue to provide a basis for both the document and the documentary. In the advanced nations there are few people alive today who have not spent much of their lives subjected to the camera's gaze. Even before being initiated into the realm of language, we are initiated into the realm of the 'being seen' by eager parents wishing to document first smiles, first steps, etc. through the agency of the camera lens. Indeed, it has now become customary to document the very moment of birth with the camera. On hand to record the primal moment are the Polaroid and the video, midwives to the realm of representation into which anyone born after about 1975 is metaphorically thrust even as they take their first lungful of air outside the womb. Major industries in photography and video have grown up as the ability to record moments has been democratised through the social extension attendant upon ever cheaper equipment and processing.

The camera must surely be accounted one of the key inventions of the industrial age. Like the internal combustion engine, the telephone and the home computer, the camera has been part of the twentieth century's transformation of time. Ways of being and seeing that are now accepted as the norm are actually part of a world created after the first Industrial Revolution. This world, by general consent, is one that is more individualised and less collective than the previous one. The broad drift of civilised life since about 1850 can be summarised in Judith Williamson's succinct description of photography as 'a process developed historically alongside the modern bourgeois family' (1986: 125). Like so many of the great inventions since the mid-nineteenth century, the photographic and electronic camera as developed by Western civilisations have been inexorably privatising instruments.

Faith in the camera is grounded on two basic, and linked, premises that patrol the boundaries between private and public experience. The first is that the camera will 'hold back time' (both private and public). This is the leap of faith made by all of us as we use our cameras to record those moments in our lives which we wish to fix into memory – to record for deferred contemplation. In photography they become, to use a paradoxical phrase, 'still moments'; they have no movement and are 'still' in one sense, yet in fixing a moment they stand as emblems of that moment. Snatched from the flux of time by science, they are 'still in' the former moment as we look at them at other times. Roland Barthes has referred to this camera-supported process as 'our mythic denial of an apprehension of death' (1993: 32). He claims that the camera's activities 'puncture' our perception of the flow of time in unexpected ways. Within the unstudied detail to which it is always alert, he argues, lies the camera's power to fold time inwards (towards the past) and outwards (to the future). The camera is the indispensable precondition for what has become known as 'the postmodern' – that unfixing of linear, chronological time that has characterised the end-of-century mind-set of Western civilisation.[10]

As true for public as well as private moments, the 20/20 vision of hindsight will sometimes imbue a picture, especially a moving picture, with a significance unimaginable to the actual recorder of the moment. Consider, for example, the 'moment' of John F. Kennedy's death in 1963 as recorded by Abraham Zapruder, or the 'moment' when the Challenger space shuttle exploded in 1986. On both occasions cameras recorded the split second when a public event became 'history' – something important to represent at other times in order to try and make meanings beyond the specific, the time-bound and the individual.

Bill Nichols has noted:

> The indexical bond of photochemical and electronic images to that which they represent, when framed by optical lenses that approximate the properties of the human eye, provides endless fascination and a seemingly irrefutable guarantee of authenticity. (1991: 149–50)

Access to moving images via the movie- and video camera increases the paradox of the moment snatched from time even more, grounding memory not in lived reality but in re-produced photographic and electronic images that are 'not still' but in motion as often as the images are shown. In the realm of public affairs news footage takes on the role both of national historical family albums and of evidence.

Evidential status both reveals and conceals meaning. John F. Kennedy certainly dies again whenever the Zapruder footage of his assassination is re-viewed, but do we understand this death any better? The 'absent–present' tantalises again and again with its promise of telling us what really happened on 22 November 1963 in Dallas, Texas. It is surely no accident that Oliver Stone could make a whole film (the 1993 *JFK*) solely about interpretation of the evidence available from that day.

This is the other major premise upon which the supremacy of the camera is built: that it will give us access to external events that would otherwise be lost except through the very different agency of report. The Zapruder footage is viewed again and again partly because it is always apparently more than an eye-witness report. As such, it ought to tell us more than a simple witness can, because witnesses can only ever describe discursively what has passed before their eyes in the moment of its occurrence. A permanent image on a film from a camera at the scene ought to be able to say more – to solve the ongoing mystery of whether Kennedy was killed by more than one assassin, for example. This no-longer-innocent home movie has been scrutinised again and again; it has been the subject of renewed examination by new frame-by-frame technology. Yet, sphinx-like, it refuses attempts to empty it of meaning. The more it is studied, the more it becomes evident that it is not, nor has it ever been, a transparent record of the event it purports to depict.

In the moment of Kennedy's death the twentieth century discovered that the camera lied; or rather that it was inclined to riddle in a paradoxical and inscrutable way. This was a moment fully as significant to a technological age, and subsequently as much mythologised, as Oedipus's ancient discovery that to take filial relationships on trust and circumstantial evidence was potentially tragic. The emphasis has now shifted to the possibilities of construction and invention inherent in new post-production technologies, which increasingly threaten the camera's potential as an objective recorder of pro-filmic events. Naïve faith in direct access to events through the camera may have been challenged through theoretical

debate since the Second World War and may now be under threat
from new digital technology (Scitex, for example), but Western cultures continue to keep the faith because deferred promises of objective proof are historically grounded in ongoing technical advance.

Examples of this tendency to keep the faith despite intellectual
scepticism are easily found and often assume that technical advance
will make mediations somehow 'more real' than they were before.
The record of an event, whether private or public, is always more
authentic if it offers immediacy. But ultimately this immediacy –
this authenticity – is felt by an audience rather than being inherent
in a technical process. It is easy to assert authenticity but more
difficult to prove it philosophically. As long ago as 1972 Nicholas
Garnham was pointing out: 'the appearance of progress within [the
documentary] aesthetic has been largely technical, the search for
the Holy Grail of a totally transparent technique' (1972: 111). The
search is ongoing and in more recent times has come up with the
now-ubiquitous Steadicam (a camera that allows its operator to
move around during shooting without jerkiness resulting in the
subsequent film image). The search for transparency has more
recently given us the 'mock-documentary', which turns transparency within the work itself in order to reveal its constructed
nature. In Ross McElwee's *Sherman's March* (1986) or Michael
Moore's *Roger and Me* (1989) the self-aware directors 'declare' their
agency in constructing their self-reflexive films, making technique
transparent in a more provocative and amusing sense. Moore and
McElwee act as *faux naïf* reporters in their work, opening up the
objective stance of the traditional documentary record by inflecting
their reports with their personalities – anxious and neurotic in
McElwee's case, ebullient and insouciant in Moore's. On British television (in Channel 4's *Brass Eye* – 1997) Chris Morris apes the conventions of the documentary magazine programme both to satirise
them and to subvert 'official' views.

Accepting convention

Dramadoc/docudrama's particular set of representational codes
and conventions appeals to belief just like any other kind of convention in representation, and the appeal to belief is anchored in a

distinctively twentieth-century faith in images – especially moving ones. We accept what we see according to our previous knowledge and experience. To the degree that we have been persuaded by the documentary and convinced by the drama in previous manifestations of the form, our knowledge and experience encourage us to think that we will enjoy further exposure to such representations.

Conventions of any kind are, as Richard Sparkes has said, 'the condition on which the bargain of the suspension of disbelief is struck with the audience' (1992: 147). There is pleasure to be found in any set of conventions that are well understood and widely shared (but not yet ridiculed or despised). If, however, the conventions become out of date or difficult to give credence to, or if they have been trumped in some way by new forms, significant change must occur otherwise a form will disappear. Conventions are always subject to a kind of 'Emperor's New Clothes' test, through which the majority of people will decline to question what they see most of the time. Indeed, the acceptance of mediated forms in general depends on this. But the fable of the emperor's new clothes is also salutary because it is important in another way to question what has been naturalised by convention. This is, of course, the very point of the fable: the unsophisticated child is so much more usefully critical than the sophisticated but sycophantic adult who cravenly kowtows to the emperor's vainglorious fantasy of importance.

The rise of television to prominence in the 1950s makes those years its primal decade – the time of emergence for generic conventions of all kinds. It was only gradually that these conventions began to be questioned, both inside and outside the television industry, and to be changed. In the formative historical period of television, as John Corner has written,

> A primary factor in the formation of generic styles was the search for the distinctively 'televisual', which perhaps worked from cinematic, theatrical, radio, newspaper or music-hall precedents, but which then reshaped the material in ways which used the medium to the best possible advantage. (1991: 13)

The generic conventions of drama-documentary and of documentary drama are quintessentially televisual.[11]

It is easy to see why the dramadoc/docudrama is likely to continue to have a place in broadcasting. In this form the camera's ability to go anywhere and see anything is both borrowed from documentary on behalf of the drama and extended by the drama on behalf of documentary. They go together to increase the camera's truth claim by denying its actual deficiency (it was not there in fact, but we can pretend it was in fiction). Our gaze as audience is disembodied; we are in the 'there-but-not-there' realm of the record at the same time as we inhabit the 'I-am-there' identificatory realm of the drama. In both cases the hidden corporeal presence behind the camera lens in real time is composed of a several-bodied film crew, but in television time (i.e. when we watch) there is only ever 'us alone' as we wrestle with the demands of evidence and belief. People sometimes want to ratify emotionally what they may already have understood intellectually. The camera's promise of complete seeing can only ever achieve completion if our emotions are stirred dramatically as well as our understanding increased intellectually.

The codes and conventions used in dramadoc/docudrama have been principally dependent on the changing nature of television drama. The direct influence of documentary has been less marked. Although there have been times when broadcasting institutions have tried to make programmes of this type a more permanent feature, they are usually made either by documentary or drama departments or by units of production formed especially to investigate something when there is no other way to tell it. The claim of 'no other way to tell it' is, pre-eminently, what makes dramadoc/docudrama such a controversial and disputed form. The ways in which the intellectual and affective debates that have circulated around the dramadoc/docudrama have been configured and reconfigured will be explored in Chapters 4 and 5. The least remarked thing that any controversy in the arts does is to measure the degree of our willingness to accept conventions. The provenance of those conventions which I have been discussing in this chapter can be clarified by examining some of the 'keywords' I have already been leaning on heavily so far.

Keywords

Wordsearch

The compound term of my sub-title – 'dramadoc/docudrama' – will now be subjected to a 'wordsearch' intended both to define present usage further and to reveal what has been lost over time. When the great cultural theorist Raymond Williams published his book *Keywords* in 1976, he described it as 'an inquiry into a *vocabulary*' (Williams' emphasis) (1976: 15). This vocabulary was the one by means of which the English-speaking societies tried to make sense of their world through their common culture. Williams took language fundamentally as a thing of use – shaped by the people who speak it, in the context of the living cultures within which it is embedded. He traced slippages in usage through which important nuances are produced in commonly used words. Keywords, he argued, acquired cultural resonance partly because the very commonness of their usage could lead to unquestioning acceptance that their meaning could be taken for granted. His book opens up the process by which meanings have been, are being and will go on being contested and changed. Cultures condense around such words, marking out as they do points of interest (and anxiety) within a society. They offer insights into how a culture works.

Williams' methodology of inquiry will be used in this chapter to scrutinise further the provisional definitions derived from present practice and offered in Chapter 3. The keywords in writing and discussion about dramadoc/docudrama are revealing of more than just a television culture. The sheer proliferation of words and phases that have been coined to categorise the forms of television that mix drama and documentary is in itself remarkable. The phrases, compound nouns and noun-coinages in question are drawn mainly from four root words – 'documentary', 'drama', 'fact' and 'fiction'.

I shall group them under three combinative categories:

1 Combinations that use *documentary* and *drama* and that begin with 'drama', or a corruption/derivative of that word:

- *dramatised documentary*
- *dramatic documentary*
- *drama documentary* (also *drama-documentary* and *drama/documentary*)
- *dramadoc* (and *drama-doc*)

The phrase *dramatic reconstruction* can conveniently be included in this list, 'reconstruction' identifying a documentary claim.

2 Combinations that lead with *documentary* or a variant of it, or that modify it with a prefix of some kind:

- *semi-documentary*
- *documentary-style*
- *documentary drama* (also *documentary-drama* and *documentary/drama*)
- *docudrama* (also *docu-drama*)
- *docutainment* (also *infotainment*)

The last coinage leads to the heart of a cultural dilemma that is focused as much on the information/entertainment binary as on the fact/fiction one, but I am arguing that 'info' here supplies a documentary function.

3 Noun-coinages and phrases based on *fact* and either using or implying the word *fiction*:

- *faction*
- *fact-based drama*
- *fact-fiction drama* (*fact/fiction drama*)
- *based on fact* (as in 'made-for-TV movie based on fact')

The common rubric *based on a true story* can also be incorporated into this category.

By far the commonest confusion in usage has been between categories 1 and 2. The British writer and producer Paul Kerr tried to resolve the problem by suggesting 'DD' (1990: 76). Using the initial letters of the two most popular coinages – 'documentary drama' and 'drama documentary' – he hoped to avoid having to distinguish between them. Though his shorthand is tempting (given one's tendency to use 'dd' in notes), I prefer 'dramadoc/docudrama' for the reasons given in Chapter 3. Recent additions to this long-running name game are *headline docudrama* and *trauma drama* (Carveth, 1993, and Feuer, 1995; see also discussion of these terms in Chapters 5 and 8). The acknowledgement of present-day tabloid sensationalism and interest in psycho-social problems are well brought out by these recent American coinages, the latest examples of a 'wordsearch' that has been going on since television became culturally important.

It is possible to argue for either sickness or health in the genre from such a proliferation of terms. In my view it indicates in almost equal parts a fascination and an uncertainty amounting sometimes to anxiety that is part of a generalised cultural and social concern. The form and the debates on it highlight questions about the nature of the real and the limits of representations, about television itself and its access to reality. Television's very ubiquity lies at the heart of the problem. This most popular and accessible of media has always provoked worry in governments of all hues and in all nation states, the idea of regulation (to control access and range) being never very far away. As John Caughie remarked, 'it is an uncertainty as to what can and cannot be shown which creates nervous reactions within institutional control' (1981: 329). These 'nervous reactions' are, of course, exacerbated by a mass medium; the effects of all mediation may be a cause for concern, but minority mediations – *avant-garde* theatre, for example – are generally perceived as less threatening and therefore manage to stay relatively free of regulation. In many respects the histories of both international and individual national development in television have been about the ways in which populations would be permitted to talk about themselves and to one another and about how they would negotiate with those permissions. The common culture created by television has raised more difficulties than with the older mass media. The idea that the dramadoc/docudrama might need more regulation, in a medium that is becoming more and more regulated, is endemic.

'Pure' documentary films have been (and still are) routinely described as 'dramatic' if they are made coherent through either narrative structuring or the foregrounding of character, or both, but such a claim is not contentious in quite the same way as when the 'documentary' claim is made by mixed-form drama. It is mainly in television that the terms listed above have become the focus for real discussion, because television has developed mixed forms more systematically than either theatre or cinema. It did this for two main reasons – one philosophical, the other technological. First, television's dual mission to instruct and to entertain determined matters of content and form; second, its need to overcome the early inadequacies of electronic reproduction led programme makers to 'reconstruct' almost as a reflex. These two factors will be explored further in Chapter 6.

Of all the words and coinages listed, 'documentary drama', 'drama documentary', and the shortened forms 'docudrama' and 'dramadoc' are the most used. The presence or absence of hyphens and similar links enacts conceptual uncertainty, anxiety and confusion at the level of typography. The hyphen can be seen as a sort of typographical nervous tick. When present, the grammatical umbilical cord makes a compound noun of an adjective–noun combination – proposing, perhaps, the kind of balanced equality for which practitioners still argue but which critics so often find lacking. It is tempting to regard the phrases, however they appear typographically, as always weighted towards the second word. Thus, just as 'dramatic' in the phrase 'dramatic documentary' acts as an adjective modifying the noun 'documentary', so 'drama documentary' is a documentary treated dramatically. But 'drama-documentary' claims a balance in which, perhaps, both will be equally present.

Logically, 'documentary drama' is a drama treated 'documentarily', but definitional problems can be illustrated by substituting the word 'historical' for 'documentary'. 'Historical drama' tells us immediately that we are to expect a play based on known history – it is a statement primarily about the *origins* of the narrative material with which a writer/film maker has chosen to work. 'Documentary drama', however, is just as likely to tell us about the *style* in which a film is made as it is about its basis in 'documents', however defined (see Chapter 3 definitions).

Unfortunately, and confusingly, both terms are used as if there were no difference and they have become routinely interchangeable even within the same book. So, the excellent collection *All Our Yesterdays* can describe *Cathy Come Home* as a 'documentary-drama' on page 95, whereas a still from the film on page 199 calls it 'the Ken Loach/Tony Garnett drama documentary' (Barr, 1986). Shortening these phrases has not improved clarity. 'Dramadoc' and 'docudrama' (with or without hyphens) are now frequently used and appear to be corruptions of the original compound nouns 'drama documentary' and 'documentary drama'. But these words too are used interchangeably in Britain. So, for example, *Killing Me Softly* (1996) was reviewed by Lynne Truss in *The Times* as a 'docudrama' on 8 July, whereas Allison Pearson in the *Observer* six days later referred to it as a 'drama-documentary'.

This is not simply lazy usage: the salient point is that American practice and usage, having always favoured 'docudrama', has begun to affect British usage. It is principally in Britain that 'drama-documentary' and 'dramadoc' have currency, but 'docudrama' is more widely accepted. As with all shortened forms, these corruptions are highly convenient, especially in speech. They began to creep into use in the 1960s, by which time television had been around long enough both to be familiar and to be treated in some quarters with élitist contempt. 'Drama' is a difficult word to shorten, but 'documentary' (with four syllables if pronounced 'doc-u-men-try', and five if fully enunciated – 'doc-u-men-ta-ry') almost begs to be reduced to 'doc' or 'docu'.

The shift to shortened forms has almost always signalled a perception that the documentary impulse has been downgraded and is to be treated with levity and even suspicion. A dramadoc/docudrama was thus marked down as a deviation from some notionally 'pure' documentary norm – less serious and more likely to be frivolously entertaining at some level. The 'drama', in this view, was considered to contaminate the 'documentary', the implication being that a documentary would be a more serious and more honourable treatment of the events in the external world to which the film/programme alluded. Dramas that 'protect the innocent' by changing names and locations (what I am calling 'documentary dramas') are sometimes perceived as more honourable but are still tarred with the brush of a frivolity that, in exaggerating for dramatic purposes, distorts serious subjects.

Ongoing attempts to negotiate a path amongst these competing terms have resulted in a confusion that can only be untangled by a discussion of the history of both practice and usage. Raymond Williams said of his own keywords, 'the problems of [their] meanings seemed to me inextricably bound up with the problems [they were] being used to discuss' (1976: 15). In general, writing about dramadoc/docudrama tends to betray a similar tendency. Like Barbara Foley's definition of the documentary novel, the form is 'near the border' between factual and fictional discourses, 'but it does not propose an eradication of the border' (1986: 25). The practical and theoretical traversing of the border between fact and fiction is of the utmost importance culturally. The mixed form of television discussed in this book, although perhaps a minority interest in terms of viewing figures, has constantly mapped the shifting nature of this border.

As Andrew Goodwin and Paul Kerr put it, 'Television "drama-documentary" is not a programme category, it is a debate. And that debate has ranged so widely across programme forms that it is very difficult indeed to pin down' (1983: 1). Kerr found it difficult to go beyond this notion seven years later. It is 'not so much a distinct genre', he wrote, 'as a debate about genre distinctions' (1990: 76). The academic view is endorsed by practitioners; Leslie Woodhead told me:

> I find it most helpful to think of dramadoc as a 'Spectrum', with all the blurry edges that implies. I can appreciate the value to your students of having access to a more defined taxonomy, but as a practitioner of this odd trade, I'm only too conscious of adapting the form anew for every dramadoc I'm involved with.

Practitioners, then, are almost as coy about definition as academics.

Two things keep the 'debate' going and keep fuelling the effort to define as well as describe. The first is a continued demand for clear definition (if not taxonomy) on the part of students, non-academic commentators and ordinary viewers. This fire is continually stoked by print journalists, who, according to television practitioners, feel threatened by the investigative power of the form. Ian McBride remarked:

> For the newspapers, there's what I would describe as a needle factor in all this – you're either treading on their territory or you're stealing their clothes. That ignores the fact that most of the substantial investigative journalism in the last five years, maybe in the last decade, has been on television.

Documentary's declared links with pro-filmic reality still gives it a sharper evidential quality and claim than fiction, and the dramadoc/docudrama borrows this. Try as academic post-modernist theorists might, the evidential conviction is difficult to shift from the common culture.

Second, as John Hartley has remarked, the inherent institutional conservatism of television leaves it 'characterised by a will to limit its own excess, to settle its significations into established, taken-for-granted, common senses' (1992: 37). In other words, there is a common desire in broadcasters themselves for what Hartley calls 'clean' boundaries in television. 'Dirty' forms complicate this, and it suits an industry reliant on combinations of governmental and commercial good will to argue that it can regulate itself (1992: 37). The effort to be precise acknowledges a kind of responsibility towards content which is fundamental to the contract that broadcasters have with their audiences. In recent times this has occasioned a proliferation of 'guidelines on practice' and an increase in the pressures on legalling, as I argued in Chapter 2. But it is still a fact that, as Ian McBride points out, 'television is much more tightly regulated than newspapers'. For him, journalists tend to pick on the dramadoc/docudrama because it is vulnerable to regulation and it invades their territory: 'It's in their interests sometimes. It makes a good story to "flam up" the row about drama-documentary.'

The occasional nature of such rows creates further difficulty. Mixtures of drama and documentary do not constitute a genre in quite the same way as, for example, soaps or sitcoms or the police/hospital series, all of which are regular features of terrestrial network programming and are ever-present in the schedules. They are found at least once a week and are regularly updated stylistically to suit new demands. But the dramadoc/docudrama is usually a response to a very particular situation. Because it is an occasional feature of the schedules, arguments about it do not appear to progress but are revisited again and again.

In an effort to unpick the confusions I shall first break down the commonest phrases into their constituent parts in order to discuss their historical development. I shall work with easily accessible dictionary definitions (from the *Shorter Oxford English Dictionary* (*SOED*) 1993 reprint – the most recent at the time of writing). For terms that are not in the dictionary I shall cite less accessible (but still available) critical writing on the form. I also hope that a use of Williams' methodology (indeed, of *Keywords* itself where its inquiry coincides with mine) will clarify current usage.

Keyword 1 – 'Drama'

It is relatively easy, though far from uncontentious, to agree on what constitutes 'drama'. Whenever mixed forms have been defined or described there has always tended to be a concentration on the word 'documentary' in the compound noun and a taking-for-granted of 'drama'. It is the programme's moral and ethical right to the designation 'documentary' that tends to provoke debate. Whereas people are happy on the whole to assume common understanding of 'drama', they want to know the basis for any documentary claim. With 'drama', an expressive and aesthetical basis for understanding is usually sufficient.

The etymology of 'drama' takes us to a late Latin word derived from the Greek word *dran*, 'to do' (*SOED* 1, 1993: 743). This word for a kind of action entered English in the early sixteenth century via a French word, *drame*. In the Elizabethan and Jacobean period the institution of 'theatre' – and the practice of 'drama' therein –

staked out its cultural importance as a representation of actions, and this has become established and accepted. The earliest recorded meanings of drama refer to 'plays', or dialogue compositions in verse and prose, that have 'high emotional content'. Their 'composition and presentation' were often termed 'the Drama' (a usage dating from the early seventeenth century).

This explanation ignores the fact that 'the Drama', like any human activity, is always situated in history. Even drama as apparently universal in its depiction of human motives, feelings and emotions as the plays of William Shakespeare was an important ground for contemporary discussion of essentially social and political matters. Otherwise, Ben Jonson would not have been imprisoned as a result of his part in the writing of the contentious 1597 play *The Isle of Dogs* and Shakespeare himself would not have been summoned to Star Chamber to explain why his company had been so willing to perform a play of his about regicide (*Richard II*) to an audience of rebels the day before an attempted uprising against Elizabeth I (Essex's rebellion of 1601).

More recent, and metaphorical, use of the word has been to describe as 'drama' happenings of high emotional content in the real world. Notions of 'narrative', 'plot' and 'story', and also of 'character', have been successfully transposed in order to describe actual occurrences. Psychological identification with 'protagonists' (main characters), dislike of 'antagonists' (opposers of main characters), and even the presence of 'catharsis' (or emotional release within a structured narrative) have been imported into current affairs and news coverage.[1] The end-result is that everyday events are routinely described as 'dramatic' when they exhibit, or seem to exhibit, the contrived structural elements of the staged drama. Narrative completion, another structural notion deriving from the early eighteenth century (now often referred to as 'closure'), has also been important to the development of this usage. Conversely, resemblances to 'real life' are a frequent feature of the definitions of 'drama' in non-specialist dictionaries.

Hence, there is a mid-twentieth-century inflection that offers: 'dramatic quality; interest, excitement', indicating that the presence of 'drama' in any action, fictional or otherwise, will infallibly spice it up. This is the very stuff of both tabloid print and television journalism and is the factor that makes the television news simultaneously informative and entertaining and guarantees it to its audience as both understandable and watchable. It ensures high audience figures for broadcast news programming and, ultimately, the profitability of specialist organisations like CNN. It is responsible for the 'Reality TV' strand of recent years (programmes such as America's *Rescue 911*, and Britain's *Crimewatch*).

In summary: we currently have notions of 'drama' whose history in the English language goes back more than four hundred years. There are two quite distinct resonances to the word: 'Drama', which is the practice of representation, and 'drama', the quality inherent in actions of all kinds, including those in the real world. 'Drama' itself, then, comes down to us clothed in elements both factual and fictional, which are difficult to disentangle. But it is worth insisting that in grammatical terms the word is a noun, which names or designates. The adjectival form is 'dramatic', which applies the attributes of the noun beyond its simple naming function.

The noun is examined by Raymond Williams in *Keywords* (1976: 109–10). He makes the important point that examples in the drama word group 'belong to a traceable habit of mind in which life is seen, or is claimed to be seen, through art'. It is this 'habit of mind' and its documentary mirror image – the seeing of art in life – that has established the naturalist/realist dramatic form as dominant in the twentieth century and that has also established the documentary impulse as a kind of equal-but-opposite means of understanding the phenomenal world in relation to the expressive dramatic one. The secondary experiential dimension to art-works is folded back into our 'real', ongoing, primary experience of life. If experience of life can be construed within art-work paradigms in this way, a further level of sophistication arrives when those paradigms themselves begin to define primary experiences.

This is of great importance to television. John Corner refers to 'centrifugal' and 'centripetal' tendencies in the medium (1995: 5). Through the former, television has a 'powerful capacity...to draw towards itself and incorporate (in the process, transforming) broader aspects of the culture'; through the latter, 'television seem[s] to project its images, character types, catch-phrases and latest creations to the widest edges of the culture, permeating if not dominating the conduct of other cultural affairs'. In this way television's construction of 'drama' has extended beyond the fictional to draw in news, current affairs and documentary centrifugally. It pushes out re-formed concepts that include the dramadoc/docudrama, which was unheard of until the advent of broadcast television (except in a very different theatrical form – see below).

The new medium has added to a cultural tendency to shape life through art, which has a very long history indeed. This is partly what leads Alan Rosenthal to reassure the would-be screenplay writer that 'the elements of drama are universal and exist as much, if not more, in real life than in fiction' (1995: 53). And, as we have seen in Chapter 3, the programme maker Leslie Woodhead has come to believe that 'almost Aristotelian rules' govern the best kinds of practice in dramadoc/docudrama. Such assumptions are the result of both centrifugal and centripetal tendencies, the former drawing in that which seems to work often enough for 'universal' qualities to be claimed, the latter pushing out the notion that there really is no other way for any story to be told.

As Woodhead's comment on Aristotle demonstrates indirectly, Western civilisation has an acute awareness of precedent in drama that stretches far beyond the four centuries of usage in the English language. There exists both a solid body of practice in drama going back to the Greek playwright Aeschylus in the fifth century BC and an equally solid body of dramatic theory going back to his fellow Greek, Aristotle, in the third century BC. Since Aristotle wrote his *Poetics*, writers have regularly engaged in the formal and theoretical tasks of definition and speculation about drama in the abstract, basing their explorations on observed practice and their sense of an 'ideal' drama. Dramatists and theorists, from Sir Philip Sidney in the sixteenth century through Diderot in the eighteenth and Brecht and Artaud in the twentieth to the semioticians of academic theatre of the present day, have pondered and theorised upon drama's capacity to produce a perspective on human behaviour and history that other kinds of cultural production cannot match. There is, so to speak, a track record on 'drama' that can make it seem unproblematical. In our own inexorably realist times we have to pretend that most drama is real if we are to get anything from it. In such a climate it is no wonder that claiming 'closeness to fact' came to seem an advantage. But this very claim thrusts us up against the apparently equal-but-opposite term 'documentary'.

Keyword 2 – 'Documentary'

In a 1950s American television cop show, *Dragnet*, the main character used to proclaim over the introductory music and credits: 'The story you are about to see is true; the names have been changed to protect the innocent.' This became a popular catch-phrase and secured this series' claim as a documentary drama that took its stories from police files. Had *Hostages* changed the names, perhaps there would have been no immediate problem. But the difference with *Hostages*, and with the generality of dramadoc/docudrama as currently practised, is that the truth claim is always taken one stage further – towards real-world namings and the resultant truth claims of a 'documentary' presentation that is always more (and less) than drama.

'Documentary' is etymologically much more recent than 'drama' – its history goes back about a hundred and fifty years (*SOED* 1, 1993: 719). Although it may be a relatively less theorised concept historically, it has generated a high level of definitional activity within our own period as a result of its identification with the camera in particular. As a cultural community we are more anxious about 'documentary' than we are about 'drama', and this shows in our attempts to define it. The first recorded usages of the adjective 'documentary' in English are from the early nineteenth century and can be linked to a post-Enlightenment faith in positivist science and rationality.

The word developed from a noun, 'document', which had been in use from around 1400. A verb, 'to document', was in use by the middle of the seventeenth century. Latin was the language of origin of both these words, and the law, which was heavily dependent on Latin models of practice, was the active source of their use. Importantly, these words are connected with 'evidence' and the 'evidential'. The 'document' and the process of 'documenting' constituted a means of 'objectifying' evidence that could then be produced and accepted as proof positive in courts of law. Jeremy Bentham used the phrase 'documentary evidence' when writing on the law in 1827. Thomas Carlyle, a secular 'thinker' in very much a nine-teenth-century sense, also used the word in *Sartor Resartus* (1831) as an adjective denoting proof of a material, rather than concep-tual, kind. The notion of evidence grounded the modern study of history; Lord Macaulay referred to 'documentary evidence' in his *History of England* in 1855. All this undoubtedly contributed to the innate worthiness and seriousness that hover around the concept of the documentary (and which I will consider further in Chapter 8).

The use of 'documentary' as a noun came later and was, ironically, associated with the new arts/technologies of the early twentieth century – the camera-based media of still photography and film. Each of these had its own evidential claims as both witness and recorder of reality. These claims resided partly in the belief that those modes of representation were inherently superior to those of other, older media. Many dictionaries tend to offer examples of early usage of the noun from books on film. Coinages from the mid-twentieth century, such as 'documentarian' and 'documentarist', derive from the media in a wider sense (see *SOED* 1, 1993: 719).

In 1932 John Grierson's celebrated definition of documentary – 'the creative treatment of actuality' – marked an important moment in which the discursive priorities of the documentary came to include the affective as well as the evidential. Today, such theorists as Brian Winston are claiming (as I did in Chapter 1) that it is the point of reception that actually closes the documentary category; the proof of the pudding, so to speak, is in its acceptance by the spectator. 'The claim on "truth" necessary for the documen-tary', he says, 'exactly depends on spectators "constructed" by the genre to have that prior faith in it' (1995: 104). This 'construction' began in the 1920s and was a widespread phenomenon.[2]

There are now strong traditions of 'pure' documentary practice in film, radio and television from which to work in discussions about the form. These too are not without theoretical dispute and could hardly be said to be uncontentious. But no one would deny that the 'documentary' has a place in the minds of viewing audiences and media theoreticians alike, at least as an indexical indicator – the word points to a kind of film that claims (and, more importantly, is known by an audience to claim) to access the external world directly. Theoreticians may tell us that we cannot trust what we see – and this is a valuable message to receive insofar as it makes us ask questions and positions us as sophisticated and not naïve spectators – but, fundamentally, we start from a position of acceptance that the documentary, however reflexive, offers an engagement with unrehearsed reality rather than the simulated one of rehearsed drama.

Historically, the attraction of early documentary was its seeming unstructured, 'unconstructed' nature – in comparison with the drama's inherently structured and constructed nature. A wish to hold on to this notion of the unstructured led the practitioners of American 'direct cinema' of the 1960s to base their claim to authenticity on a 'found' quality – the structure being un-premeditated and discovered in the events as they unfolded. Although modern theoreticians may have deconstructed this idea very successfully, and although the equally 'artful' nature of the documentary is now well established, a widespread faith in the form remains. The Beirut hostages specifically noted (in their letter of 21 September 1992, quoted in the Introduction) that a documentary treatment of their experiences would have been acceptable.

In the schedules 'documentary' offers first and foremost a guar-antee to its audience that the pro-filmic remains closer to its surface than it does in drama. But its credibility has been undermined as its own codes and conventions have come under scrutiny, audiences have become more media-literate and programme makers have been placed under more and more pressure to deliver commercially viable products. The status of the documentary as 'fact' is less certain than it once was. The 1997 Channel 4 series *Brass Eye* is evidence of this. This spoof-documentary series relied on a common understanding of the codes and conventions of the documentary magazine programme (and on the fact that these can be copied).

Keyword 3 – 'Fact'

'Fact' has come a long way from its late-fifteenth-century meanings of 'an action' or 'a deed', deriving from the Latin *facere*, to do (*SOED* 1, 1993: 903). It first picked up the inflection of 'truth; reality' in the sixteenth century. The apparently inevitable antithesis with 'fiction' began to develop in this period also, as did its connection with 'document' and 'evidence' (see the following section). In the seventeenth century it began to mark the notion of the verifiable – 'a datum of experience' – which again was useful in the emergent legal institution. This resonance facilitated the shift in the rationalist eighteenth century to the legalistic 'basis for inference' and 'interpretation', which enabled courts of law to accept verbal and other evidence of occurrences in their deliberations. Much of this legalistic activity was of course designed to protect the individual in a newly industrialised society that was developing the concept of 'private property'.

These meanings fed the twentieth-century notion that there is an essential factual level to lived experience, which is:
• prior to interpretation;
• 'unbiased' and free of ideology; and
• to be respected and protected as originary and disinterested.

The quasi-religious level to which 'fact' has risen is best epitomised by the famous 1926 dictum of the *Manchester Guardian*'s editor C. P. Scott: 'Comment is free, facts are sacred.' In the twentieth century, derivatives such as 'facticity' and 'factuality' (*SOED* 1, 1993: 903–4) are indicators of the kind of tinkering that attempts greater exactitude and that would now have 'fact' floating free as an ideal term. And yet suspicions tend to remain, encouraged by the post-industrial alienation of populations accustomed to mistrust. Who is offering these facts to us? How can we be sure we have been given all the facts? Are other facts being suppressed, and if so, by what agency? Can we trust the facts given, or are there others, equally credible, that will come to light later? An all-too human desire to trust in something (facts will do) is often undermined by an equally human suspicion that something is missing (even if we are not sure what).

Docudrama/dramadoc's truth claim, based as it is on 'fact' and derived from the 'documentary', is frequently wrecked on the rocks of this scepticism. And the more the photographic and electronic media have claimed the fact, paradoxically, the more we have tended to grow in doubt. The suspicion that facts are never what they seem is now so endemic in Western and other media-literate societies that it amounts almost to a millenarian creed ('Don't believe everything you see on television!'). The former belief that 'seeing is believing' is now countered by the suspicion bordering on certainty that mediation can obscure as much as it reveals.

Keyword 4 – 'Fiction'

The Latin root of 'fiction' is *fingere*, to fashion; so fourteenth- and fifteenth-century anglicisation of Old French produced the verb 'to feign' (*SOED* 1, 1993: 941). Although 'feigned' implied an untruth of a kind, it was not quite as loaded an implication as that which 'pretending' or 'faking' might carry today. 'Feigning' was an imaginative, even idealised, notion and was not necessarily perceived as a lie. We have to acknowledge here how sophisticated the early modern period was in its reasoning. Its sophistication was unlike our own, of course, but in an age when language itself was excitingly volatile the skill of apprehension was valued more highly than that of comprehension. So in Elizabethan times poets like Sir Philip Sidney leapt to poetry's defence, claiming that in its 'feigning' it was able to produce higher, purer, more ideal versions of truth than less imaginative forms of writing.

His 1580 defence of his art, *The Apologie for Poetrie*, marked the emergence of the imaginative, the fictional, into a classificatory system. The written output of narratives derived from the imagination solidified in later centuries around the composition and production of stories and novels in particular. By the nineteenth century the prose 'novel' (see *SOED* 2, 1993: 1948–9) had become the dominant cultural form with a reach well beyond a middle-class readership. Insofar as television has inherited a popular story-telling function from the nineteenth-century novel its dramatic products have also become classifiable as 'fictions' and are routinely described by the adjective 'fictional' (a nineteenth-century coinage that was itself dependent on the emergent novel).

By the early twentieth century the category 'non-fiction' had made its appearance. Williams calls this a 'curious ... back-formation' that is 'at times made equivalent to "serious" reading' (1976: 134). It depends, he says, upon 'the conventional (and artificial) contrast between fiction and fact'. Nothing could better illustrate the cultural distinctions routinely made between words that have come to symbolise the serious and the frivolous, the sacred and the profane. This binary divide bedevils discussion of the dramadoc/ docudrama; indeed, it bedevils the very study of culture. The level of seriousness inherent in the fact, the document and the evidential informs the concept and category of 'non-fiction'. The 'documentary' film and television programme exists historically within this category and this reasoning.

The 'documentary', then, descends to us trailing clouds of seriousness. Through its supposed access to the phenomenal world it holds the promise of a special kind of control of the external world. It is the control that comes from knowledge and information; herein lies the instructional and educational thrust of the documentary impulse. 'Fiction' and 'drama', on the other hand, come to us separated from seriousness by a nineteenth-century cultural shift, which makes some wish to see them as peripheral activities associated with leisure and 'non-serious' aspects of life. They may be fun, but they are inherently lying.

The American comedian George Burns once remarked of acting that sincerity in the performer was all-important: 'If you can fake that you can do anything!' Like all good jokes, this lays bare the cultural suspicion that performance can never be trusted completely. Yet the emotional reach of the drama promises another kind of understanding that, although we know it is simulated, audiences seek as much as they seek the documentary's access to the evidential. The desires that fuel these seekings after some kind of final 'truth', and the pleasures they offer, will be considered further in Chapter 8.

But it is as well at this point to remind ourselves that 'drama' and 'documentary' do not automatically map on to 'fiction' and 'fact'.

As Andrew Goodwin has pointed out, the first two words refer first and foremost to 'practices [that]...overlap considerably', whereas the latter pair of words 'are not...mutually exclusive' (1986: 11). And Andrew Higson warns that the 'powerful differentiation... between "realism" and "escapism"...is not...reducible to a distinction between "fact" and "fiction"' (1986: 81). Whenever the debate over dramadoc/docudrama raises its head, it is often as a direct result of a determination to regard all these categories as separable when they are not separable in history or in theory or in practice. The wish to separate is perfectly understandable at one level: a 'fully-fashioned imaginative reality' originating in the mind of an author or authors *is* different from an anterior one, if only in the sense that the anterior reality is doubly accessible – through both the research material (when recoverable) and the resultant constructed work. The 'fully-fashioned' version, meanwhile, is a thing of autobiographical fragments, of half-remembered and mis-remembered moments, of fantasy and imagination.

David Hare has described vividly the conscious/sub-conscious genesis of his 1978 play *Plenty*. Set during and after the Second World War, this became a successful film in 1985. Hare recalls: 'I had originally been attracted by a statistic, which I now cannot place, that 75 per cent of the women flown behind the lines for the Special Operations Executive were subsequently divorced after the war' (1984: 15). Nothing could better exemplify the distance between documentary and drama in practice; nor could anything better exemplify the difference between a documentary play and a 'history play', Hare's preferred category.

Coinage keywords

Dictionaries have increasingly been forced to take note of the coinages forged from 'drama', 'documentary', 'fact' and 'fiction'. 'Docudrama', for example, is categorised in the *SOED* as 'M20' (middle of the twentieth century) and is explained as follows: '[f. DOCUMENTARY + DRAMA] = DRAMA-documentary' (*SOED* 1, 1993: 719). The word is accorded a separate entry on the same page, as is 'docutainment' ('L20...documentary film or programme designed as entertainment'). It is interesting to note how unproblematically the *SOED* reverses the words on either side of the equals sign. But compilers of dictionaries are as much recorders of usage as readers of critical theory. Not even this kind of minimal definition is offered for 'dramadoc'. The noun and its definition are simply appended to the other meanings of drama, and no date is given: '*Comb*: **drama-doc** *slang*, **drama-documentary** a film (esp. for television) dramatising or based on real events' (*SOED* 1, 1993: 719).

The dictionary, then, proposes equivalence between the two compound nouns and their corruptions – effectively, they are one and the same. The attempts of film and media theorists to draw distinctions between them are now probably doomed to failure as common usage favours the more popular (television) terms, which depend primarily upon differential American and British practice.

The crucial coinage from 'fact' and 'fiction' is of course 'faction', which is given a separate entry and is again dated 'M20': '[Blend of FACT and FICTION *n*.] Fiction based on real events or characters, documentary fiction; an example of this' (*SOED* 1, 1993: 904).

The term dates from about the late 1970s, and its provenance is in American television drama (see Chapters 6 and 7, where I compare and contrast American and British television practice). 'Faction' is a term I have never cared for, since it interferes with a word that has a much longer pedigree (meaning a self-defining and self-interested group of people). I would much prefer the term 'faketion', since the 'mocking up' of the real event has been such a common factor in practice.

Compound noun keywords

There are two really important compounds – 'documentary drama' and 'drama-documentary'. To follow usage, I include the hyphen in only the latter, though it is possible to find it in the former. 'Documentary drama' has a well established history, which is complicated by the fact that its early models are theatrical not televisual. It derives first from the oppositional European theatre of the period between the two world wars. Beginning as an adjective–noun combination, by the time it was used to describe some celebrated stage plays in the 1960s the separate words comprising the term had acquired an equal status.

Particularly in the work of Erwin Piscator in West Berlin in 1950–65 documentary drama came to mean dramatisations that utilised technological features (such as slide projections and loud-speakers) to relay facts to an audience and to signify a dramatic methodology that diverged from the dominant naturalism/social realism to include two-dimensional 'characters' who could represent abstractions (rather like the creations of medieval religious drama). The US Federal Theatre Project of the 1930s had perfected a journalistic 'Living Newspaper', which excitingly extended the reach of such non-naturalistic styles. But this connection with a European left wing proved the undoing of early American theatrical experiment. The war years and the McCarthy period virtually expunged that type of theatre.

This history is more clearly rendered in the term 'documentary theatre', which had a resurgence in the 1960s, when a great many serious issues were investigated in a Piscatorian theatrical style which was in a sense rediscovered after the Second World War. When they were published, the texts of these later Piscatorian productions were labelled 'documentary dramas'. One example, Rolf Hochhuth's 1963 play *The Representative*, was about the Holocaust. Its documentation was mainly achieved via lengthy published 'stage directions' (which were in effect footnotes), but other documentary dramas openly displayed their factual basis in the manner of Piscator's earlier productions in Weimar Germany. Such plays in Britain as Theatre Workshop's *Oh What a Lovely War* (1963) and Peter Brook and the Royal Shakespeare Company's compilation about the Vietnam war, *U.S.* (1965), were sometimes called 'theatre of fact' at the time, as were American plays like Father Daniel Berrigan's 1968 *The Trial of the Catonsville Nine* (about Vietnam 'draft dodgers') and Donald Freed's 1970 *Inquest* (about the Rosenberg trial).[3]

Specialist reference books on theatre and drama tend to follow either the theatrical or the television traditions but usually fail to make clear which. The *Batsford Dictionary of Drama*, for example, defines 'documentary drama' as 'a drama which deals with contemporary social problems, usually in a direct and naturalistic way'

(Hodgson, 1988: 100). But the plays show that you infer the naturalism only if you stick to some types of play and exclude others. This definition relies more on the *Cathy Come Home* type of television play than on *The Representative* (a play written in blank verse) or on *Oh What a Lovely War* and Arthur Kopit's 1968 *Indians* (which use non-naturalistic styles). By contrast, *A Handbook of Contemporary Drama* notes that there are 'certain similarities to the historical and political play, but [the documentary drama] relies more on modern techniques of mass media and reportage to present a version of recent history in a new light' (Anderson *et al.*, 1972: 125). The writer of the entry clearly has in mind the Piscatorian theatrical tradition.

I would describe documentary dramas as plays with a close relationship to their factual base – a twentieth-century extension of the historical drama or the *pièce à thèse*. The 'close relationship' can mean that the documentary material that has inspired the play in the first place can be exhibited directly in the performance and can 'show through' the fiction in a variety of ways – the 'extension' is inherent in the technological means of presentation. Normally, all this is done with a polemical purpose, the company and/or writer(s) wishing to argue a case forcefully, which generally opposes an established point of view.

In this sense theatrical productions in this tradition share the campaigning aim of some documentary film/television. Productions are put together rather in the way a prosecuting counsel might assemble a case from the facts available, and often it is governments or their institutions that 'stand accused'. This was one intention of the makers of *Hostages*, but it turned out not to be achievable in performance (see Chapter 7). 'Documents' as evidence of facts are either quoted or shown directly to the audience in the theatrical, Piscatorian tradition. In the television tradition they are embedded in a predominantly naturalistic playing style via voice-over, documentary footage and visuals.

It must be stressed, however, that the corruption of 'documentary drama' – 'docudrama' – has little or no connection with a theatrical tradition that endures to this day as a weapon of opposition in the Third World.[4] Whereas television professionals in the UK routinely use the terms 'drama-documentary' and 'dramadoc', Americans have always tended to use 'docudrama' to describe their plays-based-on-events. This is probably why the compilers of the *SOED* have declined to engage in the kind of cultural exploration in which we are now involved.

The ways in which these usages derived from practice will be examined in Chapter 5, but it should be stated here that the term 'drama-documentary' comes directly from television. British television professionals tend to disallow any other term. Ian McBride told me: 'I don't think most viewers, or most people, can handle the distinction between "documentary drama" and "drama-documentary". I think the distinction is completely lost.' Over a period of thirty years the drama-documentary has become celebrated as a format of British television programming that tends to challenge received (and would-be received) wisdoms about controversial subjects. Its period of maximum effectiveness began in the 1960s, and it should be seen as being distinctively of that mould-breaking period. The socially critical edge of the drama-documentary earned it a kind of dragon-slayer reputation, particularly in Britain. This issue-based genre has consistently taken on controversial topics and has often pressed rulers to explain themselves to the ruled. It is not just co-production companies who 'buy into' this reputation; audiences endorse and support it too.

Common usage

Most attempts to define mixtures of drama and documentary begin by taking the drama for granted and concentrating on examining the relationship with the documentary. This has become the kind of opening gambit that we cannot ignore. There have been relatively few attempts to assess the relationship of the form with drama. Such an assessment has now become of the utmost importance in my view, because the dramadoc/docudrama seems increasingly to be a form that is 'preoccupied less with the factual than with the meaningful'.[5] It has become more and more a dramatic form in recent years, its documentary element being buried ever further outside and below the surface of its performance.

Although disputes about the form have classically revolved around questions of value, where the worth of the resulting programme is judged in both aesthetic and informational senses the formal values have become concentrated within the realm of the dramatic. What we are beginning to see on our screens is indistinguishable from other television drama. But paradoxically, the standard of the debate surrounding the facts and information has been rather more sophisticated and interesting than the discussion of the drama has ever been.

In a constantly evolving area of programming the relatively new development heralded by 'dramatic reconstruction' is especially interesting. The perceived need to reconstruct indicates a desire on the part of media institutions and their audiences to get ever closer to lived reality. This fits with the recent shading of news and current affairs towards 'docutainment' and 'infotainment', *Court TV* and *Video Diaries* formats being particularly prominent. It is yet another development in television's dual mission to weld the twin aims of education and entertainment into one.[6]

The usages are, it is true, slipshod in their imprecision, but only in the way common usages have to be in order to become common. The easiest way forward is to say that in drama-documentary the dramatic element is controlling the documentary and diverting the programme into structures and rhetorics associated with drama (rehearsed and 'staged' action, recognisable characters, coherent plots, selected camera shots, clear and directed sound, dialogue-based scenes that both illustrate character and develop plot). We must add that this kind of style is routinely labelled either 'dramadoc' or 'docudrama' – hence my elision of these words.

In past examples of documentary drama, on the other hand, it has been possible for the documentary element to exert more control, diverting the programme more clearly into documentary structures and rhetorics. Formal features have included 'wildtrack' and/or live sound, improvised camera-work with hand-held instruments, improvised acting (sometimes using non-actors), real locations, plentiful captioning and other documentary visuals (graphs, charts, etc.). Finally, I would claim that 'documentary drama' is a variant that existed for only a brief period *ca* 1965–75, that it is unlikely to re-emerge in the future, and that it should not be confused with 'docudrama'. If anything, it had something in common with the American 'faction' in its substitution of fictional for actual personalities. Formal features like those mentioned above have today been largely sacrificed because they tend to disrupt dramatic realism, and a 'documentary style' more than ever refers to look rather than substance.

Critical tools

Phrases incorporating the words 'drama' and 'documentary' have been used loosely, to say the least – as have 'dramadoc' and 'docudrama'. But I want to use the two commonest historical terms – 'drama-documentary' and 'documentary drama' – as critical tools in what follows. The persistence of such phrases in critical writing has meant that it has become axiomatic to define them in two particular ways – either to call attention to the institutional base of a programme (linking it to the discursive priorities of an entertainment/drama or a news/documentary department) or to analyse a programme's formal properties (locating them in modes of address that emanate from, and are comparable to, those of drama or documentary 'pure'). Thus, a news and current affairs department, by making journalistic use of dramatic structures and techniques to 'get where the camera can't go', produces a drama-documentary. John Corner's insistence on the phrase 'dramatised documentary' makes clearer this construction of adjective-modifying-a-noun and draws attention to the likely processes of production (1995: 92).

Meanwhile, a drama department, by making use of various kinds of documentary 'look', produces a documentary drama – again taking 'documentary' as an adjective modifying the noun 'drama'. Leslie Woodhead made this similar-but-different process clearer by using the phrase 'documented drama' in his BFI/*Guardian* Lecture in 1981. Drama departments have used such techniques in the past to bring a qualitatively different level of seriousness to their entertainments at the point of production. At the point of reception audiences have often been prepared to acknowledge the serious documentary as a manifest contribution to the drama (as, for example, in the case of the 1966 *Cathy Come Home*).

In performance a drama-documentary will tend to use the names and identities of real historical individuals, and its plot will stay close to the pattern of (relatively) verifiable real-life events – as I suggested in Chapter 3. Its use of these elements will, perhaps, be closer to its surface. A documentary drama, on the other hand, will tend to use fictional constructs, such as an invented plot and characters composited from several real-life originals. Its factual base will, like the mass of an iceberg, be located below the surface of its action, in the research that has informed it. Within the essential fictionality complex elements of verifiable factual precursors and real-life situations may be incorporated, however, and may show through as in a palimpsest. It is to some extent a matter of available structures – in drama-documentary the drama diverts the documentary element into dramatic structuring; in documentary drama the documentary diverts the drama into documentary structures.

Both forms make use of the visible and audible evidence that we associate with 'authentic' documentary – news and current affairs footage, still photography, the visual rhetoric of graphs, charts and statistics, the aural rhetoric of location sound, commentary and interview/witness statement. But in the drama documentary the use of this kind of evidential material is always likely to be incorporated within the parameters of naturalistic believability in performance. In the 'hierarchy of discourses' (or the spectrum of ways in which the programme communicates, arranged from most to least important) 'drama' is above 'documentary'. A use of dramatic action in montage with non-dramatic, documentary signifiers (captions, oral testimony by talking heads, newsreel footage, graphs and charts) is likelier in the documentary drama of British television's golden age. This form broke from naturalism and used documentary material non-diegetically more often than any other fact-based form (see Chapter 7).

John Corner is surely correct in saying that, as a means of categorisation, the two terms 'documentary drama' and 'drama-documentary' usefully mark out what he calls 'clusterings of work with a sufficient level of internal commonality' (1996: 31). It is equally true, however, that we have become accustomed to certain kinds of performance on our cinema and television screens – we have become 'acculturated' through repetition, in television and other dramas, of an acting style that covers a relatively small range of predominantly naturalistic techniques. 'Serious' styles contrast quite markedly with the more melodramatic styles of the soap and the serial, which are more heightened but usually just as naturalistic.

The acting styles found in single-play drama on television seem to be more 'real', if only because they are, so to speak, ratcheted down in terms of performative display. *Goodbye My Love* (see Chapter 1) showed how the claim for the real in acted performance is now secured by doing less, not more, on screen – a tendency exacerbated by the trend towards the minimalism of film dialogue. In Chapter 5 I shall examine again the broader historical antecedents of dramadoc/docudrama within the 'moment' of documentary film itself and to trace the practical origins of some of the theoretical dilemmas encountered so far.

Practitioners of the form both past and present have nearly always argued that dramadoc/docudrama acquires authenticity through its special relationship with its documentary elements. Commentators, meanwhile, have cast doubt on this, and are now even doubtful of documentary's originary claim of authenticity. Both wrestle with notions of documentary and drama, of fact and fiction, which were the subject of this chapter. The next will focus on the link – in an image-dominated century – between developing technologies of vision and our changing visions of the real as the effects of film on the early television industry are explored.

Blurring the boundaries

'Judicious fiction'

The common end-of-century view that many things that were once clear are now blurred means that easy assumptions can no longer be made about the ways in which media represent reality. Once, television was seen as a 'window on the world' and seeing was believing; now, theorists routinely cast doubt on both these propositions. Arguing that the Gulf War was only meaningful as a media event, for instance, Jean Baudrillard has suggested provocatively that sophisticated societies are so heavily dependent on the media that they can now only operate with and through 'simulations' – sub-realities constructed by the media representations themselves. For some, this is an indication of the rarefied, and useless, world inhabited by the intellectual.[1]

Theorising is not without its use value, however, particularly when it can show that documentary has always constituted a very particular kind of seeing. A good deal of the power of dramadoc/docudrama stems from the 'judicious fictions' of the Griersonian documentary film tradition, problematic though it undoubtedly was.[2] Grierson it was who formulated the ubiquitous definition of documentary film: 'the creative treatment of actuality'. It is more than curious how often this phrase has been misremembered (as shown in Judge Pollack's words quoted in Chapter 2). Only the definite article and the preposition have been safe: 'creative' sometimes becomes 'imaginative', 'treatment' often turns into 'interpretation' or 'use', and 'actuality' is sometimes changed to 'reality'. In *Imagining Reality: The Faber Book of Documentary* even specialist editors exemplify this tendency to garble the phrase: 'Grierson famously defined the documentary film as "the creative use of actuality", a phrase so broad it is almost meaningless' (MacDonald and Cousins, 1996: 93). One of the reasons for meaninglessness, perhaps, is the kind of presumption that, through misquotation, blithely erases the original context of Grierson's pronouncement.

Vagueness about the phrase has been exacerbated by the tendency of Grierson's own colleagues to embellish it.[3] The words first appeared in *Cinema Quarterly*, an Edinburgh-based periodical edited by Grierson himself in the 1930s. He offered the definition in an essay, almost as an aside: 'Documentary, or the creative treatment of actuality, is a new art with no such background in the story and the stage as the studio product so glibly possesses' (Grierson, 1933: 8). It is interesting to note the paradox of the full sentence. Grierson simultaneously opposes documentary film to what he unproblematically takes as the inferior products of stage and studio (note the force of the adverb 'glibly'). The 'creative' dimension to what is seen as a 'new art' is an integral part of his conception. Griersonian documentary film actively embraced an artfulness that was always likely to be at odds with 'actuality' (which is always more than simple 'reality'). The apparent rejection of 'story' is thus countermanded in the parenthetical phrase that has achieved such notoriety (via the force both of 'creative' and of 'treatment'). The sub-text implies that (human) agency without which there can be no 'art'.

The definition thus first celebrates documentary's splitting-off from fictional forms, then binds documentary practice to invention of various kinds. This quasi-philosophical move aimed to legitimise the technologically inevitable. There was little practical choice but to reconstruct in the 1930s and 1940s, given the nature of the camera/microphone technologies used by the Grierson-influenced Empire, GPO (General Post Office) and Crown Film Units. 'Fiction' was an indispensable line of approach to the documentary subject for crews wrestling with primitive cameras and, for many years, lacking location sound altogether.

In the following issue of *Cinema Quarterly* the producer H. Bruce Woolfe eagerly advocated the use of fiction in documentary practice, as did most Griersonians. He wrote: 'I believe that the addition of judicious fiction may increase both the aesthetic value and the point of a film that in the main deals with a non-fictional subject' (1933: 96). The word 'judicious' brings documentary into line with its own legal provenance (see also the discussion of 'Key-word 2' in Chapter 4). During the formative phase of documentary the protesting of documentary's difference was a rhetorical move designed to distinguish it from its 'significant other' – Hollywood fiction film. While it depended methodologically upon 'judicious fiction', it protested its seriousness and its difference rhetorically.

The 1938 film *North Sea*, sometimes described as a 'semi-documentary', is a good example of the mix of fact and fiction that the pre-war British documentary movement bequeathed to post-war British television. Ian Aitken offers the view that it was heavily influential in its integration of 'documentary techniques and methods into a format derived from the feature film' (1990: 145). Brian Winston puts forward a convincing case that the liberal/non-interventionist politics of the documentarians made for conservative practice (1995). Always prepared to compromise politically, they leant more heavily towards Hollywood than they were prepared to let on. But it must be said that even a film maker in Winston's pantheon, Joris Ivens, did not eschew the 'semi-documentary', using judicious reconstruction in his 1933 film *Borinage* (on police violence during a miners' strike in Belgium).

The narrative turn that the emergent cinema medium took early in the twentieth century had the effect of making all new forms reactive to the dominant narrative feature film associated with between-the-wars Hollywood. This realist movie went about its business to entertain through the interaction, in a more or less linear plot, of key characters with whom the spectator was encouraged to identify. Encouragement was organised, as has been often noted in film theory, through realist *mise-en-scène*, continuity editing and naturalistic acting. In such fictionalisations the believable in terms of performance constituted, and continues to consititute, the credible in terms of reception.[4]

In the 1920s and 1930s it was necessary to 'fake-tionalise' an actuality that was denied to the cumbersome camera and microphone equipment then available. In Grierson's own 1929 film

Drifters the ship's cabin had to be mocked up; in the GPO Film Unit's famous 1935 film *Night Mail* a mail-truck's interior was constructed in the studio, leaving one side open to the camera. This 'set' was rocked from side to side to simulate the motion of the eponymous mail train the camera and the microphone could not fully access. A script also had to be written. In this regard, *Night Mail*'s set was different in degree but not in kind from the elaborate layout in Granada's Studio 12 that was described in Chapter 1. The American documentarian Robert Flaherty, the Griersonians' role model, was known to fake action in all his works.[5]

When the documentary movement went into wartime service, it continued to develop the look of the feature film. Andrew Higson calls the style of the Crown Film Unit 'a particular de-dramatised naturalistic form' (1986: 76). The restraint in performance that was the stock in trade of these understated films sorted well with a generally stoical British wartime mood. The 'documentaries' produced by the Griersonians and funded by the Ministry of Information were more often than not, as Higson points out, 'documentary-dramas' (1986: 79 – and note the hyphen). In America there was a much more direct incorporation of realist narratives because of the drafting in of Hollywood directors like Frank Capra and John Huston (see Barnouw, 1993: 155–64). But the style was also, relatively, restrained. The appeal to identification with characters worked just as usefully in the fiction feature as in the documentary at a time when stark contrasts between life and death constituted day to day reality for many people.

Two good examples of 'character-ised' wartime documentary are Harry Watt's 1941 *Target for Tonight* and the original *Memphis Belle*, directed by Hollywood's William Wyler in 1943. Both were 'windows on the world' of the long-distance bomber flying missions over Germany. Watt had always preferred his own notion of 'dramatisation of reality' over the Griersonian creed, and he studied flight logs for his script. Scenes of briefing and debriefing were then acted, but by actual participants in the bombing war. Using assumed names, they 'repeat[ed] their roles for the benefit of the camera.'[6] These non-actors now seem stilted and impossibly 'stiff upper lip', but their performance was probably read at the time as understated and restrained. However their performance is viewed, 'characterisation' is a major signifying technique in Watt's film.

Writing of directors of American war films, Bruce Crowther notes that 'most settled for the small unit which represented all the other small units which made up the whole' (1984: 134). This metonymic method was the classic way in which the nation at war (whether British or American) was represented. So, in *Memphis Belle*, for example, the crew of the eponymous aircraft come from all over the USA (white USA, that is). Their hometowns are rehearsed for us in voiceover. The bomber crew 'characters' in *Target for Tonight* are regionalised in a similar manner.

The Griersonian documentary moved steadily away in such practices from its early techniques of montage 'collision' editing (which drew on Soviet Russian film making practice[7]) towards the styles and values of the American-dominated film industry. The Second World War was mediated to the contemporary movie-going public on both sides of the Atlantic either in this 'fact–fiction' mode or in newsreel form. The big difference between *Memphis Belle* and *Target for Tonight* is in pace and style. In both respects the British film gives far more ground to the documentary. As a result, it is close to being unwatchable for a modern audience; the Wyler, though dated, mobilises sufficient current cinematic codes and conventions to be acceptable.

The mixture of fact and fiction did not produce much heart-searching, either in the 1930s or during the war; Eric Barnouw has noted: 'There was little public discussion about the validity of such techniques' (1975: 131). After the war Italian neo-realist films swung the feature film in the direction of the 'un-dramatised' and understated, bringing the force of social observation to the seductive power of the individualised narrative. Television was not well placed to capitalise on these developments during its studio-bound early post-war history, but in the 1950s it shared the earlier lack of concern about the propriety of mixing fact and fiction (see Chapter 6 for further detail).

In one of the last interviews he gave Grierson had some interesting views on the post-war synergy between the documentary film and television. 'You must see the BBC in Britain', he admonished

Ernest Betts, 'as taking over the documentary film movement which I directed in the thirties'[8] (see Hardy, 1979: 320–1). He argued further that television inherited not only a journalistic 'Fleet Street tradition' but also 'some of the traditions of show business' (including what he called 'the tradition of Western European theatre').

Griersonian television

The drive towards a mode that would fake action in order to claim the documentary real began, then, very early in the history of the new form and swiftly became part of its territory. The dramadoc/docudrama simply extends one aspect of the documentary that has always been inherent in the form as practised. The Griersonian notion of 'the creative treatment of actuality', the defining principle of the early film documentary, already enacted the willingness to dramatise.

As documentary film became culturally more visible in the 1930s and 1940s, various institutional bodies tried to describe and define it. From a distance, this looks like a doomed effort to limit the parameters of the faking in which film makers were already constrained to indulge. Partly as a result of the success of the documentary during the war, an organisation was formed post-war with the grand title 'World Union of Documentary'. At its 1948 conference in Czechoslovakia it agreed that documentary should be permitted a certain amount of 'sincere and justifiable reconstruction'. It also acknowledged, importantly, that appeals 'either to reason or [to] emotion' were equally necessary

> for the purpose of stimulating the desire for, and the widening of, human knowledge and understanding, and of truthfully posing problems and their solutions in the spheres of economics, culture and human relations. (see Barsam, 1974: 366)

'Sincere and justifiable reconstruction', like 'judicious fiction', was obviously important to the film makers of the 1930s and 1940s, but it became less so as camera technology improved. However, it constituted an enabling rubric for the making of documentary proper in television for the following two decades. The cumbersome television equipment of the 1950s made the junior medium appear a lot like pre-war film. Both cinema in the 1930s and television in the 1950s were thwarted technologically in their desire to 'go with the flow' of events (a desire now so surfeited that it is taken for granted).

In Britain the synergy achieved through the Griersonian inheritance can be illustrated very clearly: Paul Rotha, one of Grierson's protégés, was put in charge of a 'Documentary Unit' at the BBC in the 1950s. Rotha was 'less than enthusiastic at the conventional mixture of studio-reconstruction and film-inserts' on which the television documentary magazine programmes of the time depended, as Norman Swallow recalled (1982: 87). During his short tenure at the BBC (1953–56) Rotha was especially irked by dramatic solutions to technical deficiency. He preferred film because of its growing promise of access to reality via portable cameras and sound equipment. Reconstruction, however 'sincere and justified', could be eliminated altogether by these means, or so it seemed, and he believed this would increase the social impact of documentary film.[9]

Rotha's disenchantment with television was evident in his disparaging comments on BBC staff; he accused them of 'envy of the professional skill already attained by film people which television in its infancy ha[d] yet to acquire' (1956: 13). Yet Rotha had a symbolic importance for the fledgling BBC documentarists. Norman Swallow, a key figure in post-war television documentary, wrote of 'the sense of excitement that followed the announcement that Paul Rotha was to become the Head of our new Documentary Department' (1982: 86). Elaine Bell observes that 'all Unit members had seen documentary films, were enthusiastic about their integral social conscience, and assumed that television could – or must – perform a similar role' (1986: 71), Ironically, by the late 1950s the real potential for documentary work was to lie in television. Kenneth Adam, director of BBC Television in the immediate post-war period, reflected:

> After the war there was nothing left for the documentary film-makers but amiable and diffused sponsorship to which the survivors attached themselves. It was left to television to pick up the pieces and to assume the social responsibility. (Swallow, 1966: 86)

This remark is a fair reflection on the destination of the 'documentary conscience' post-war.[10]

The penetration of documentary film by fictional, narrative rhetorics can be read in almost all industrial pronouncements on documentary. The acceptance that necessarily existed at a technical level was philosophically sufficient for most practitioners. To distinguish the form from the newsreel and the news broadcast practitioners made space for both 'judicious fiction' and 'sincere and justifiable reconstruction'. Even the Academy Awards rules on documentary state:

> Documentary films are defined as those dealing with significant historical, social, scientific, or economic subjects, whether photographed in actual occurrence or re-enacted, and where the emphasis is more on factual content than entertainment. (Jacobs, 1971: 276)

Playing with purpose

Nevertheless, documentary continued to try to define itself as separate from fiction film by claiming documentary purity of various kinds. A purity unachievable technically was often finessed into social purpose, and documentary films undoubtedly claimed a social use value. Willard Van Dyke, who made the 1939 US film *The City*, and was the camera operator on Pare Lorentz's *The River*, remarked: '[the documentary] cannot be a re-enactment. The social documentary deals with real people and real situations – with reality'. This hard-line documentarist statement grounds itself in a declared social purpose within which the possibility of the dramatic is evident. He continues: 'the elements of dramatic conflict [in documentary film] represent social or political forces rather than individual ones.' The drama of the social, rather than the personal, has been a key feature of the dramadoc/docudrama too (Barsam, 1974: 367).

Whenever documentary practitioners have tried to argue for a special relationship of their work to reality, they have often imported such ethical notions of intention or purpose. This tendency was especially marked amongst the pioneers. Basil Wright, for example, invoked the educational purpose of documentary, claiming: 'documentary is not this or that type of film, but simply a method of approach to public information' (Barsam, 1974: 367). His colleague Stuart Legg contended: 'Documentary is very much influenced by outside events. It is an instrument of information, of propaganda, and to that extent it's dependent on needs of communication' (Sussex, 1975: 203). Harry Watt, in BBC2's *Arena* programme on Grierson in 1983, observed that Grierson's own preference was for the 'instructional and educational type of film'. The playing of purpose against representational shortcoming has proved a useful trope in justifying the documentary ethically. What Griersonian thinking always supplied was an ethics, allied to a rhetoric of artistic restraint; this became its aesthetics. The historical role of the documentary film was to function as the conscience of the film industry.

Dai Vaughan, with the twin perspective of theorist and practitioner, has perhaps best summed up the double-bind of the documentarists' wished for one-to-one relationship with reality and their actual, inevitable, position of adjacency to fact. Documentary is, he says, 'one of those terms which refer not to an entity which may be definitively described but to an ideal, attainable or otherwise, perhaps even self-contradictory, to whose fulfilment we aspire in our specific uses of it'. Many concepts of value are like this – ideal rather than real. 'Objectivity' and 'truth' are other examples of terms that resist definition but which represent ideals that could ill be spared from human affairs. As aspiration, such concepts have a significant part to play in the history of dramadoc/docudrama. Documentary-as-aspiration can be protected from its 'self-contradictory' claims to the real relatively easily because, as Vaughan adds, 'common to all forms so designated has been the appeal to an anterior truth'. This appeal has provided documentary and its derivative forms with their most significant and permanent stock in trade (Vaughan, 1976: 1).

As with the historical play, the appeal to 'an anterior truth' or 'a prior referent' is, at the very least, a useful means of drawing attention to a piece of work and alerting potential audiences to its 'known-ness', its existence in the realm of the actual rather than the virtual. This has often been a matter of rhetorical assertion: for example, the film maker Lindsay Anderson baldly stated: 'It isn't a question of technique, it is a question of the material. If the material is actual, then it is documentary. If the material is invented, then it is not documentary' (Lewin, 1971: 66). There has always been an acknowledgement that 'documentary' simply designated a means of representation. W. H. Auden, who supplied the famous verses for *Night Mail*, said:

> The only genuine meaning of the word 'documentary' is true-to-life. Any gesture, any expression, any dialogue or sound effect, any scenery that strikes the audience as true-to-life is documentary, whether obtained in the studio or on location. (Mendelson, 1977: 355)

Between the pro-filmic event and the set of codes and conventions that help an audience to accept a piece of film as 'true to life' lies documentary's continued claim for attention.

The academic debate

The academic debate, like the history of the dramadoc/docudrama itself, can be split into two traditions. In the American academy, as Alan Rosenthal remarks, the docudrama was 'virtually ignored' for many years (1988: 16). Commentary in book form mainly occurred in writings on the documentary proper or on the institutional bases of American television (see Chapter 6). Docudrama's claim to documentary status was often challenged and usually dismissed. However, Andrew Goodwin's two books on drama-documentary for the British Film Institute (1983 – with Paul Kerr; 1986) mark out a very different British critical tradition in which there is a clear acknowledgement of the cultural importance of the dramadoc. John Corner's investigations both of 'public drama' (1995) and of documentary (1996) are similarly central to a theorisation of the dramadoc form that is not replicated in book-length American theorisation of docudrama. The situation began to change in the USA in the 1990s, especially with the input of feminist criticism (see Chapters 7 and 8).

The efforts of practitioners to define and describe their activities pre-date the entry of academics into the debate, but both have had to face the fact that drama with a capital 'D' (rehearsed and performed drama) is always excessive in comparison to drama with a small 'd' (real-world drama). By 'excessive' I mean that the pro-filmic is different in both degree and kind in acted performance from the pro-filmic in documentary proper. In dramadoc/docudrama, whether factual material is in the foreground or the background, the performed drama will always be an 'excess', if only because it has been added to what happened. The justification for the added element constitutes the theoretical battleground of proponents and opponents alike.

Some critics, especially in newspapers, have picked up on this excess and constructed it as a gap in credibility. They have focused on and opposed the drama's attempt to be more-than-just-fictional. Journalists have habitually preferred, and continue to prefer, to find programmes either bad documentary or bad drama, or both. This view has wide currency: the notion that documentary is somehow more honest is at the heart of the hostages' tacit claim in their letter (see page 11) that some subjects just should not be treated as drama at all. The belief that the audience is being manipulated and/or mis-led through the drama is still a feature of newspaper critique (and of sensitivity in the industry).

By contrast, academic writing has been more conscious of the audience as active negotiators of meaning. Academics are necessarily more aware of (or perhaps more inclined to take seriously) the tradition of audience research in media studies and to argue less often for the danger of a duped audience. There have been famous occasions when audiences have been duped into believing that something fictional was really happening. These rare occasions have in every case depended upon acts of bad faith on the part of broadcasters, in which codes and conventions have been imported from one area of broadcasting into another without warning. Sometimes this has had a comic purpose, at other times it has been the result of an artistic overreaching rather than any conspiracy to defraud. Examples demonstrate very clearly to broadcasters that they cry wolf at the peril of forfeiting their overall credibility. [11]

It is worth taking seriously Pierre Bourdieu's observation that the popular audience is always likely to prefer the uncomplicated and direct. If we are to believe the evidence of schedules and viewing figures, audiences seem to prefer, as he remarks, 'plots that proceed logically and chronologically towards a happy end' and 'simply drawn situations and characters' (1984: 31). His conclusion: the innate conservatism of a popular audience is all of a piece with a widespread social suspicion of vanguardist ideas of all kinds. Commentators (myself included) have often recommended innovative formal experiment as a potential way forward socially and politically (in the sense that experiment offers new 'ways of seeing'). This view is rarely taken seriously outside the academy.

Bourdieu's view is in fact uncannily similar to those of most television executives. The conservatism of programme makers at one end of the chain of communication extends to the conservatism of popular audiences as they view. This is not necessarily to argue pusillanimous conduct on the part of executives or lack of sophistication on the part of the audience, but it does suggest that the acceptance of codes and conventions is hard-won at the levels both of production and of reception. A wish to regulate, and legislate for, the dramadoc/docudrama in part reinforces this impression – the mere suggestion of confusion induces a conservative reaction.

Andrew Goodwin points out that 'clashes and connections... between television's factual and fictional discourses' are part of the representational territory (1990: 8). In the debate that Goodwin and Kerr highlighted in their key text of 1983 this clash/connection is the single most important feature of the on-going development of the dramadoc/docudrama. If the debate has had any effect at all, the periodic rejection of connection between the two discourses has reduced dramadoc/docudrama's access to the handling of serious issues, and has diminished the form's documentary presence in its present phase of development.

When the British drama-documentary first started to become a media event in the late 1960s and early 1970s, there was a good deal of effort to understand what was happening conceptually. The English writer Paul Ableman, for example, expressed a representative ethical belief that 'for television to remain a force for mental expansion and greater understanding, it is vital for the distinction between the real and the simulated to be kept sharp and clear'

(1972: 48). This view (which is still seen and heard) exists alongside and in spite of the growing awareness that the bleeding into each other of the real and the simulated is now so far advanced that it is itself a fact of post-modern (mediated) life.

Early reflections on the British dramadoc include an influential essay by the practitioner Jerry Kuehl in 1978. Like Ableman, Kuehl was uncomfortable with the ethics of the exercise, feeling that 'factual claims... [were] compromised by the very existence of the dramatic elements' (1978: 3). But he acknowledged a 'legitimate province' for the drama-documentary in subjects that 'resist exploration by the methods of classic documentary film-making'. His answer to the problem of dramatisation was prescient if we consider the current legal situation discussed in Chapter 2. He advocated what amounts to a footnoting methodology, suggesting that 'precise descriptions of the sources for each scene and each line of dialogue' be made available, which 'do not necessarily have to be transmitted' (1978: 7). Returning to the debate in *Sight and Sound* in 1981, Kuehl had become less sanguine, saying the form's 'inauthenticity' was 'inescapable' (1981: 274).

In the USA the work of Bill Nichols (especially in 1981 and 1991) has been particularly influential in defining and describing the nature of the documentary mode, but his brief observations on the 'docudrama' suggest that he sees it as existing outside what he calls the 'discourse of sobriety' (1991: 160). A particular kind of seriousness, inscribed within documentary, stands in contra-distinction to fictional discourses of entertainment. Defining docu-drama as 'stories based on fact but performed by actors and scripted from both documents and conjecture', he suggests it lacks even a subjective documentary's grip on real-world pro-filmic events. The docudrama must ultimately be located, he says, in an 'essentially fictional domain'.

For Nichols the docudrama, like the historical drama, is excessive, whereas the documentary is in one sense insufficient. Docudrama works through 'a body too many' – actors (in themselves) being manifestly beyond the realm of the history they depict. In documen-tary, by contrast, there is 'a body too few', because it is not the real body that is present but its photographic index. If reconstruction is used, a film 'trade[s] documentary authenticity for fictional identification' (1991: 250); you cannot logically have both in one. The American docudrama is thus a contemporary-historical fiction, its fictional excess manifest in the 'body too many' of the performer impersonating the absent real-life individual. Another American writer, Michael Renov, concurs with this theoretical view: 'At the level of the sign, it is the differing historical status of the referent that distinguishes documentary from its fictional counterpart' (1993: 2).

Some American theorists have followed practitioners in making an approach through function and purpose rather than analysis of the sign. Richard Barsam follows the Willard Van Dyke line, claiming: 'The documentary is distinguished from the factual film by its sociopolitical purpose, its "message"' (1974: 369). Such a view has been echoed more recently by William Guynn, who claims that documentary films 'seek to account for actual occurrences in the phenomenal world' (1990: 13), and by Paula Rabinowitz, who says that 'the implicit meaning of documentary is not only to record but to change the world' (1994: 102). The explanatory and the campaigning aspects of documentary, in other words, can be argued as having a use value, irrespective of the status of the reality depicted.

It is here that the British dramadoc has an advantage over the American docudrama tradition. Its ethical fit with the documentary is almost seamless. If its reality status can only ever be under challenge, its bids over the years to intervene in historical situations have given it credentials drawn from the discourse of sobriety. This is very clear in ITV Network Centre's 1994 *Statement of Best Practice*. The opening paragraph reads:

> ITV is proud of its record in factual drama. Programmes such as *Who Bombed Birmingham?*, *Shoot to Kill*, *The Life of Phillip Knight* and *Fighting for Gemma* have used journalistic methods and drama techniques to bring important issues of public policy to the widest audiences. Series such as *Crime Story* and *In Suspicious Circumstances* in part fulfil a documentary tradition of throwing light on the human condition, as well as presenting popular programming. (See Corner and Harvey, 1996: 253–4)

The whole emphasis here is on the dramadoc's manifest 'discourse of sobriety'.

The mixed form, then, has been dominated by questions surrounding its representation of the documentary. In the late 1970s and early 1980s the real academic debate about the form began, and the distinctions between documentary, drama-documentary and documentary drama became important to practitioners and theorists alike. A seminal article by John Caughie in 1980 contributed to a growing view that there were in fact two dominant forms in operation: 'dramatised documentary' and 'documentary drama'. The article was framed by an ongoing discussion about 'progressive drama'; this posed the question: which (if any) fictional representations on screen were likely to lead to changed political awareness in the audience.[12]

Caughie's two categories separated out rationalist/documentary (what Nichols was later to call the 'discourse of sobriety') and aesthetic/dramatic ('discourse of entertainment') intentions arising principally from the department of the broadcast institution from which the programme in question emerged. Discursive origins were therefore evident formally in the cinematic 'looks' mobilised in the finished product and could be read off the product. Drama-documentary, in the Caughie taxonomy, was a convergent form emerging from an investigative, journalistic imperative; its audience was encouraged to think of itself as moving towards the truth of a specific situation. Documentary drama, meanwhile, was a divergent form, its audience being encouraged to move outwards from a representative fiction in the direction of generalisable, but still 'documentary', truth. Both forms in this British tradition could be used to campaign for something and in that sense carried the seriousness of purpose of the documentary. However, Caughie concluded that practice which was formally disruptive was more likely to lead to a kind of questioning response in the audience. Overly naturalistic styles would be more likely to lead to acceptance of the *status quo*. The argument derived, in part, from Brechtian theatrical concepts aimed at producing the 'active spectator' through performance and from Marxist theory.[13]

The view that dramadoc was a form that 'blurred boundaries' emerged fully in the 1980s, in critical writing as much as in institutional practice. The view of Bennett *et al.* in 1981, for example, can stand as a representative example:

> While the broadcasting institutions would strictly demarcate between documentary series and drama, this distinction has recently been blurred by various hybrids of drama-documentary, which lay claim to greater historical accuracy because the sequence of events depicted (and, in some cases, the dialogue spoken) is in some fashion authenticated by archive sources. (1981: 285)

The British tradition regards facts and information as some kind of key that can unlock a closed social situation and lead to action in the wider political world. This is what Oliver Goodenough calls the 'fact-rich British tradition' (see Chapter 2). American writers have endorsed this view; Bruce Crowther, for example, believes that the presence of British personnel on the 1983 Anglo-US co-production series *Kennedy* brought a 'detachment' to proceedings that helped to make it 'the most thorough examination of the Kennedy era so far brought to the screen' (1984: 160–7).

While there has been a good deal of havering between 'documentary drama' and 'drama-documentary' in British circles, the term 'docudrama' has been used consistently in American writing. Robert Musburger (1985: 93) quotes a 1951 definition of docudrama: 'a program presenting information or exploring an issue in a dramatic fashion, with story emphasis usually on the social significance of the problem'.[14] As this quotation indicates, there has been less emphasis in general on the 'fact-rich' approach in the American tradition. In 1924, at the very beginning of his career, Grierson himself had been struck by the American journalistic penchant for the 'story' over the 'report' (see Winston, 1995: 99), and the force of individualised narrative has always been in evidence in the docudrama. Hoffer *et al.* (in Rose, 1985: 182), for example, describe docudramas as 'accurate re-creations of events in the lives of actual persons.' This definition completely ignores the issues of 'public policy' on which the British tradition has rested. Todd Gitlin too offers discourse of entertainment as a provenance for fact-based television drama, calling it: 'melodrama whose stereotypes...sometimes disclose the point of view of historical victims' (1994: 162).

The American documentary tradition, in film and theatre, made much greater use of the victim and 'Little Man' concept – individualising social concerns from a very early stage. The 'Living Newspaper' theatre productions of the 1930s New Deal era, for example, specifically used the character of the Little Man to demonstrate the vulnerability of the 'ordinary citizen' to failures in social systems with primary duties of care.[15] Gitlin notes the similarities between the docudrama and another liberal American cultural phenomenon, 'the social problem movies that Warner Brothers produced in the thirties and forties' (1994: 170).

The tendency towards melodrama noted by Gitlin is part of this individualising national cultural trait, displacing social debate into the tropes of victim and villain, hero and antagonist, crisis and rescue, which are part of 'trauma drama' or, in Jane Feuer's words, 'the eighties version of the "sociological film" or "public service drama" [which] resolved the traumas of the American family in a rejuvenation of public institutions by the people, the same promise that got Reagan elected' (1995: 13). Gitlin sees a psychosocial function in the docudrama: 'it exists not to comprehend but to document, to authenticate the validity of surface detail, to establish that this really happened' (1994: 162). Feuer, by contrast, takes the view that the trauma drama is the end-game of American public service television, denoting a 'massive loss of faith by individuals in [public] institutions' (1995: 18).

The trauma drama is thus part of society's ongoing testing out of reality – of what can and cannot be deemed true-in-the-way-of-belief. It gives expression to a belief that society's major institutions will do you down – unless you stand your ground and fight. The trope of the 'Little Man' extends in the 1980s trauma drama to include the 'Little Woman' as demonstration of the institution's ability to move (eventually) with the feminist times. The resultant movies, however, still structure their narratives insistently through individual-in-crisis, against-the-odds stories. I will return to this topic in Chapters 7 and 8.

Paula Rabinowitz believes that docudrama as a form is dependent on documentary cinema in one further respect. She sees both documentary and docudrama 'pictur[ing] history through vivid characters who live in families' (1994: 137). To an extent, the primary American myth of the white European family hacking out 'civilised' territory from the wild (in opposition to wild peoples who do not live in families) persists. The new frontier is in a quotidian reality of citizens who are routinely failed by institutions that were set up to 'look after' them and rely instead on more individualised communities. The late capitalist world of privatisation thus inscribes itself indelibly upon its (factual) fictions. In their reliving of the 'trauma' the dramas offer comfort and hope but little in the way of overt practical assistance. They do not, on the whole, promote the idea of facts as keys to locked doors; in this tradition the facts of a situation provide templates to confirm the possibility of individual action.

The British playwright and essayist David Edgar set out the basic rules of engagement for both the dramadoc and the docudrama in a series of important contributions to the subject that began in the early 1980s. 'What sets drama-documentary apart from the mass of public plays', he said in 1980, 'is not the employment of facts but the theatrical use to which those facts are put.' 'Theatrical' is possibly the most important word here; his notion was that the 'credibility' of performance was enhanced by facts (1988: 52).[16] Edgar is one of the very few people to take serious account of the role of drama in the mixed form. His highlighting of 'credibility' (rather than 'believability' or 'trueness to life') is important. In invoking the documentary in their dramas, whatever the order of the two words, writers and programme makers seek more than just dramatic justification for belief. Only audiences can ultimately judge the success of the claim. More recently, Edgar noted:

> In drama-documentary, our interest is in the rights and wrongs of what is being represented …, or the credibility of the argument … In documentary drama, on the other hand, the doc is merely a means to the dram; specific events are used as a source for treatment of general questions, in the same way as Shakespeare drew on real history, historical myth and his own imagination for plays that dealt with essentially similar themes. (1989: 13)

Like Nichols, he places one form in the realm of the historical fiction; unlike Nichols, he retains space for a form that can still *intervene* historically, whatever its provenance.

Pointing out

All televisual forms and genres offer resemblances/explanations of elements in a society and culture, some of which are problematical. As well as offering a resemblance between what is depicted and some aspect of an anterior reality dramadoc/docudrama offers an intertextual relationship between two forms that elsewhere are kept separate. The programmes, crucially, 'point towards' their anterior realities in an altogether more urgent way than either the contemporary drama or the history play of old. Additionally, we can see them as suggesting an equivalence between drama and documentary that is provocative in audience terms (asking, sub-textually, in what ways any drama can be 'documentary' and any documentary 'drama'). This is the basis of their negotiation with an audience. They offer a form (not-documentary, not-drama) through which we are challenged to reconstruct our mental model of the real by means of codes both documentary and dramatic.

The two areas can be contrasted through the matrix opposite. This is intended to help rethink the dramadoc/docudrama as an intertextual form, negotiating (and provoking or encouraging negotiation) between the documentary and the drama columns. A particular example of practice will sometimes be closer to one column, sometimes closer to the other. An awareness of both might lead to the kind of positive reappraisal of the form that is much needed in the light of routine denigration.

The notion of intertextuality has been a popular and useful one to students of literature and the media. From the reader or viewer's position it means that the more texts you know, the more likely will diverse texts 'show through' the particular text with which you are dealing at the time. This is useful because it connects texts with one another in a relationship that is more than a simple one of similarity/dissimilarity; it articulates a way of viewing the world through texts. Thus we look not so much for originality as for

RETHINKING THE DRAMADOC/DOCUDRAMA: TABLE OF 'DOCUMENTARY' AND 'DRAMA' FEATURES

Documentary	Drama
Theoretical categories	
Realm of 'non-fiction'	Realm of 'fiction'
Heavy emphasis on 'fact'	Light emphasis on 'fact'
Cool medium	Warm medium
Sobriety	Entertainment
Reason/the rational	Imagination/the intuitive
Authenticity	Credibility
The prior referent	Imitation of an action
Objectivity	Subjectivity
Particular truth	Essential truth
Content	
Data/information	Feelings/emotions
Current affairs issues	'Human condition' issues
Public over private	Private over public
Institutions	Individuals
Practice	
Research/accuracy	Invention/creativity
The journalist/researcher	The writer/creator
Unrehearsed pro-filmic events	Rehearsed pro-filmic events
Real-world individual	Character
Behaviour	Acting
Commentary/statement	Dialogue
Exegesis (for example, captions)	Diagesis
Montage	*Mise-en-scène*
Location/non-design	Setting/design
Natural light	Key light
Location (messy) sound	'Balanced' (clean) sound
Audience	
Belief	Suspension of disbelief
Convergent thinking	Divergent thinking
Consideration of issues	Identification/empathy
Comprehension	Apprehension
(through the mind)	(through the senses)
Distance	Closeness

confirmation that certain structures of representation are still helpful in making sense of our lives.

For practitioners there is also a use in intertextuality, even if they might regard the term suspiciously. It means that he or she can count on an audience that is not likely to be at all fazed by intertextual reference to other texts. Leslie Woodhead remarked to me:

> I feel a lot more confident of the audience's abilities to decode what it's getting. It seems to me that an audience that can read *Hill Street Blues*, or a rock video, or can respond at the same speed with which popular drama now hits them, is well able to deal with notions of dramatic re-creation.

The academic world's investigation of the qualitative act of reading/spectating (through so-called 'reader-response' and 'reception' theory) is potentially as useful as quantitative longitudinal studies of 'audiences'.[17] The dramadoc/docudrama retains an intertextual relationship to the documentary in its active 'pointing to' an anterior circumstance in a dissimilar but comparable way. At a functional level the dramadoc/docudrama and the documentary proper share territory rather than dispute it.

The dramadoc/docudrama is an inherently indexical form: it points more insistently towards its origins in the real world than other kind of drama. In another context, Richard Maxwell observes that the very act of pointing first 'draws attention to the pointer', then diverts it towards that which is pointed at (1992: 183). So, in dramadoc/docudrama we are always more immediately aware, as it were, of the dramatic pointing than of the place-pointed-to. But the latter enters our consciousness at 'second looking' in the same way that we look past an actor representing, say, John F. Kennedy, to the historical original. This gives the form its campaigning edge at times. From its 'moment of presentation' in fictional, dramatic form dramadoc/docudrama points beyond the realm of fiction to a realm of non-fiction that is always already-lived. In one sense, all drama, all fiction, aspires to this condition, but this kind of drama, by pointing at an explicit rather than an implicit reality, 'indexes' that explicit reality in ways that are difficult to ignore even if we deny them.

Thus, so far from pointing out from itself towards a universalised, generalised 'reality', the drama-documentary seeks to overlay the

Stanislavskian emotional equivalence of 'As If' with a documen-
tary-indexical 'See This!'. The relation to reality claimed in the
solely dramatic 'as if' through equivalence and parallel is asserted
in dramatic documentary mode through the repetitions of recon-
struction/re-enactment (these words/actions, in this place – with a
gesture back to 'that time'). Where one set of actions is in parallel to
the real, the other is an attempt to superimpose, to fit as with a
template, an acted 'reality' on film on to a previous, unfilmed one. A
time lag manifestly ruptures the pro-filmic moment of production
and the filmic moment of reception in all films, of course, but these
features surely mark out the dramadoc/docudrama as different
from either the documentary or the drama 'proper'. This strongly
indexical possibility exists in both American and British traditions
but is stronger in the British as a result of the gravitational pull of
Griersonian film practice. As Andrew Higson notes, this constituted
'a radical challenge to … the decade of the dream palaces [or Hollywood cinema]' (1986: 74). It continues in some ways to authenticate the seriousness of British television art over American.

Unique television

Fact–fiction forms are a special preserve of the mass medium of television. The dramadoc/docudrama is in effect part of the repertoire
of a late twentieth-century culture that is highly dependent on the
television medium. Although variants exist in the theatre, on radio,
on film, in the novel, or even in poetry, only the dramadoc/docu-
drama has reached a mass audience, with all that that implies.
Experimentation in television has never been as radical as it has,
say, in the theatre and the novel, but the special 'take' on mixtures
of fact and faction in television is what has made the dramadoc/
docudrama programme a known quantity in modern culture.

For more than fifty years the form has been a kind of 'public
service' in itself, and in Chapter 6 I will show how academic
analyses fit with the practices of two similar-but-different traditions
of practice. In the Introduction I remarked on the range of drama-
doc/docudrama subjects: the form has dealt with social problems
(housing and poverty in *Cathy Come Home*, 1966), contemporary
history and international affairs (Soviet foreign policy and the Cold

War in *Invasion*, 1980). In the USA, in its 'made-for-TV movie' form, it has similarly approached aspects of American history in series such as *Roots* (1977) and 'difficult' human issues, such as cancer (*Brian's Song*, 1971) and AIDS (*And the Band Played On*, 1993). Watching the dramadoc/docudrama, however it is labelled, can mean confronting (if not resisting) dominant ideologies.

Television programmes that mix fact and fiction are now so commonplace throughout the world that everyone reading this book will have seen many examples, if not those given above. To attempt to list even those made in the UK and the USA since the genre acquired its status in the 1960s would be a large task indeed. Andrew Goodwin and Paul Kerr attempted to provide some basic information of this kind in 1983, as did Alan Rosenthal in 1995, and a useful American reference book (*Movies Made for Television* by Alvin H. Marill) was published in 1987. But as Goodwin and Kerr acknowledge, 'the chronic lack of documentation in this area makes it unlikely that a fully comprehensive list of drama-documentaries could ever be compiled' (Goodwin and Kerr, 1983: 39–53; Rosenthal, 1995: 231–6).

Audiences are still drawn to the dramadoc/docudrama in numbers significant enough for it to remain part of television scheduling. Although these numbers may be small in relation to the big battalion television genres (soaps, sitcoms and cop and hospital series), the form has great 'TV talk' power, especially when it is controversial. The Independent Television Commission's Research Monograph *Television and the Public's View* (1992) employs 'drama-documentary' as a separate category in two of its chapters ('Viewing habits and preferences' and 'Impartiality') even though the types of programme with which it is being compared are much more frequently transmitted. In the chapter on 'Impartiality', for example, the other four categories are news, current affairs, drama, and entertainment. As Ian McBride observed, drama-documentary 'makes large numbers of people talk…about something they wouldn't otherwise have talked about.'[18]

The transmission of a dramadoc/docudrama, as I argued in the Introduction, can easily turn into a media event. Martin McKeand, producer of the 1980 ATV documentary drama *Death of a Princess* recalled it being 'one of those programmes everyone had an opinion about, even if they hadn't actually seen it.'[19] What McBride calls the form's 'power and particular quality' is a power that has often gone beyond that of most documentaries or most dramas. The material effects hoped for are sometimes uncertain (as the makers of *Hostages* found out), but, as Alan Rosenthal says, many writers enjoy 'the ability to break free of the limitations of documentary, and yet still aim to change the world' (1995: 229).

But Paul Kerr is surely also right to point out that controversial dramadocs/docudramas have always been the exception rather than the rule: 'such programmes are not always so explosive – and that fact is far too easily forgotten in the wake of whatever is the latest "controversy"' (1990: 74). Mostly the form treats fairly anodyne topics, and George Custen draws attention to the ways in which the kind of fame deemed suitable for dramatic treatment in docudramas differs from that associated with the subjects of the 'classic' biopic of the 1930s and 1940s (1992: 216). Television fame looks at ordinary people, he says. Like Ian McBride, he is concerned about the replacement of 'hard' with 'soft' news in the current television climate. With the 'Tabloid Famous', Custen says, 'notoriety has…replaced noteworthiness as the proper frame for biography; short-lived, soft news has replaced the harder stuff, history'. Television fame is necessarily even briefer than biopic film fame, for it is domesticated rather than public. It has become a cliché, but Andy Warhol's 1960s *bon mot* about everyone being famous for fifteen minutes looks more and more prophetic, except that the time allowance looks rather generous as time goes on.

However, the dramadoc/docudrama still has a capability to be controversial, because it sometimes concentrates discussion of issues in the public sphere in a unique way. These two somewhat contradictory aspects of dramadoc/docudrama can be focused further through a consideration of the institutional histories of dramadoc/docudrama on British and American television. In the Introduction I drew attention to 'three phases' in the development of these forms. An account of these phases (in Chapters 6 and 7) will give a firmer historical base to this simultaneously contentious and bland form of contemporary television and allow the focus to shift away from cinematic antecedents on to the history of television itself.

6

Histories

The three phases of development

The history of British dramadoc and American docudrama can be split into three phases: the post-war period 1946–60, the following two decades up to 1980, and the period up to the present. At first the documentary was the all-important element and, in the era of what I called 'Griersonian television' in Chapter 5, was little doubted. Later, the 'debate tended … to concentrate more on the doc than the dram' in the sense that the documentary claim was interrogated (Edgar, 1988: 23). Now the 'doc' has receded while the 'dram' has become ever more important in practice. A form that started out as a response to real-world events in documentary has become primarily a response in filmic drama.

In the pioneering first phase television drama's synergy with contemporary theatre was at its strongest, and mixtures of drama and documentary were effected principally for technical, operational reasons. During the second phase specific practices consolidated into a programme category that would be recognised for the rest of the century even if its definition was problematical. A new fluidity – the result of accelerating technical innovation – increased experimentation with form. Two traditions of practice emerged with differing documentary and dramatic priorities, the results of markedly different cultures and institutions on either side of the Atlantic. In the period from 1980 to the present day the American docudrama tradition has become dominant, but 'public-service' British dramadoc is not without continued influence. The values of the fiction film have currently become dominant (but have not necessarily prevailed).

British television has always had a more developed role in public service than American television. Brian Winston argues that over its lifetime the BBC has managed to sail pretty successfully between 'the Charybdis of American commercialism' on the one hand and 'the Scylla of ... Western European state control' on the other (1994: 38). However, the technological revolution of cable and satellite television channels threatens the demise of this essentially European institution, born of the liberal state. The American system has always dominated economically, the British system being regarded as a model for responsible, non-commercial broadcasting.[1]

The USA has 'lacked even a cultural reservation, an institutional home (like the BBC or a national theater) for a segment of popular culture empowered to owe allegiance to standards beyond the marketplace' (Gitlin, 1994: 29). PBS has only survived by adapting to the commercial environment in which it found itself and to which it was partly abandoned in the 1970s. It is important, however, not to claim simplistically that American television lacks a public service imperative altogether. Les Brown observes that the networks have provided 'a unique and valued service as the central meeting place for the nation', as well as an 'influence, for better or worse ... throughout the world' (1995: 284; 259).

The lack of a dedicated public service network can be attributed to the USA's status as the major capitalist nation of the early twentieth century. To read accounts of the wheeling and dealing that brought first radio then television to American households is to marvel at the ingenuity of the capitalist mind (or – and it comes to the same thing – to marvel at the lengths to which people will go to make a buck).[2] The cultural difference can be marked by personalities. British broadcasting culture had Lord Reith as a founding father – sober, responsible, suspicious of popular taste, pre-eminently a colonial-style élitist administrator. The USA's equivalent figure might be David Sarnoff, head of NBC in its early years. Known within the company as 'The General', he was at once industrialist, entrepreneur, populist and visionary exploiter of new technologies. His honorific military rank (jealously guarded once conferred) is a fitting badge of his militant commercialism. The national American predilection for entrepreneurial activity virtually ensured that broadcasting would, like other human endeavours in the USA, be commercial in orientation.

In the two national television systems the key post-war determinants that shaped the British dramadoc and American docudrama forms were economic, historical, cultural and political. They followed templates already laid down in other media. What Hoffer, Musburger and Nelson say about the roots of American docudrama is equally true of British modes: the uses of drama-in-documentary and documentary-in-drama are to be found 'in theater, motion pictures, radio, newspapers, and books' earlier in the century – as are their founding practitioners (1985: 183).

UK – the 'dramatised story documentary'

The 'dramatised story documentary' (a phrase coined by Caryl Doncaster in the first phase) was the first development of factual drama in British television. Programmes were based on the journalistic practices of pre-war BBC radio, which already had a reputation for mediating factual material through drama. 'Radio features' in the 1930s used documentary material in dramatised form in order to make subjects of public interest accessible.[3] BBC television's post-war dramatised story documentary was built upon the twin foundations of this work and the Griersonian documentary film. Dramatised story documentaries in the late 1940s and early 1950s were essentially 'documentary dramas' according to my definition in Chapter 4. They explored a documentary subject dramatically and were focused either on some public service institution – hospitals, the police, the probation service – or on individuals and their achievement of professional status within such institutions.

In the late 1940s television personnel shared an intellectual reach with their radio and film colleagues but they lagged far behind in technical grasp. Radio and film had the advantage of a twenty-five year start in technical development. Getting the television cameras of the time outside the studio required the kind of logistics needed to get medieval armies on the march. Set-piece outside broadcasts (sporting and royal occasions, for example) were possible from the outset, but studio-based approximations were the necessary norm for other subjects. In the early, innocent, period such approximations were accepted as inevitable by the industry and, in the absence of a real alternative, seem to have been unquestioned by audiences. As a result, rehearsed re-enactments and simulations of situations based on research took the place of an actuality filming that was to become the natural element of television as a medium.

To educate the audience documentarily about some matter of public interest 'the cameras stayed put while the actors and researchers went out into the world to gather a faithful record that could be recreated in the studio' (Goodwin, 1986: 3). Illustrative film sequences were often inserted into live studio action as a means of providing authenticating documentary film and as a visual escape from the studio. But the live format was paramount, and practitioner Arthur Swinson could even define the difference between television and film in terms of 'a "live" as opposed to a recorded medium' (1963: 28). For audiences, the novelty of a new kind of seeing – taking place in their living rooms – vastly outweighed any ethical questions concerning the means of representation or any doubts about the status of the reality being represented. The main difference by comparison with reconstruction used in radio features was that a realist *mise-en-scène* was now required. The 'look' of reality inevitably became an issue for a medium that has always, in one sense, been less free imaginatively than radio.

Key personnel included Robert Barr (a former journalist), Duncan Ross (a former film maker), Michael Barry (a former theatre worker) and Caryl Doncaster (a former teacher). Barr's dramatised story documentary *It's Your Money They're After* (1948) was unproblematically described as the 'first ever "documentary series"' by Norman Swallow (1982: 86). As it was entirely acted, some would have difficulty in regarding this programme as a documentary at all. But the pioneers did not see dramatisation as a second-best alternative to location filming; this was the perspective of a later phase. They saw dramatisation as their means of controlling the documentary material editorially and technically. In other words, because their focus was on the documentary not the drama, they seem to have been blind to the representational shifts that are inevitable when something is acted.

Doncaster picks out Ross's 1950–51 *The Course of Justice* as the path-breaking series.[4] She claims that he 'found a method of translating complex social problems into human terms' (1956: 44). In many ways this is the classic defence for mixing documentary and drama: in dramatising documentary material you both humanise it and sweeten the bitter pill of fact, allowing audience identification (which makes for something entertaining). In a 1951 memo Barr wrote to his head of department, Cecil McGiven: 'Documentary is concerned with...the dramatization of facts, reconstruction of events, and it uses any dramatic device to make its point' (see Briggs, 1995: IV, 705). The willingness to dramatise at virtually any cost to the nature of documentary as actuality could hardly be more evident, nor the Griersonian link plainer.

'The facts of life so [dramatically] presented', Doncaster writes, 'get across to a much wider section of the public than the straight talk...One appeals to the intellect, the other to the emotions' (1956: 44). This very 'common-sense' approach has not gone unquestioned in the twentieth century but is still widespread today. We can trace it to the 'keywords' themselves and their cultural assumptions about works of the head and of the heart. Doncaster's 'straight talk' is a less attractive proposition in this taxonomy, even if it is accompanied by illustrative visual material.

On the other hand, Doncaster makes it plain that, in spite of the emotional appeal deriving from drama, the dramatised story documentary differs in degree and kind from 'straight drama'. She even concedes it to be less-than-drama in certain respects, observing that writers must discipline themselves to cope with the restrictions on their freedom of expression that result from the programme's research base. The necessity for documentary objectivity (this is a given) can easily produce 'unwieldy intractable material'. She warns that there may be 'a temptation for the writer...to include too many facts in the draft dialogue' (1956: 46). Her advice – when in doubt to cut the facts and go for the drama – is still a classic formulation (see, again, Sita Williams' remarks in Chapter 3).

In her own programme *Return to Living* (a 1954 story documentary about the re-emergence of ten prisoners into the outside world) Doncaster's start-point was 'an outline giving the progression of action, number and type of characters, sets and film sequences required'. She submitted this outline (effectively, her 'treatment') 'to all interested parties so that minor inaccuracies of fact or emphasis [could] be corrected and any major points of disagreement thrashed out'. A dramatic skeleton of action and characters provided a narrative structure that could be agreed as factually representative in a situation in which no real historical individual was being named. Here again, the dramatised story documentary resembles the documentary drama more than it does the later drama-documentary. A dialogue script was developed from the outline and, after minor amendments, became the rehearsal script (Doncaster, 1956: 45ff).

The writing process, unlike the usual process of writing drama, was clearly subjected to a rigorous régime of interrogation, yet Doncaster still talked, just as producers do today, of her particular relish of 'the characters...coming to life' during the polishing of the dialogue script. The enabling conventions of the dramatised story documentary were emphatically dramatic – and naturalist/social realist at that; this was a given of post-war practice. 'Television drama', as J. L. Styan sagely remarked, 'leans hard on characterisation in the naturalistic vein: the age of Freud and the Method is ripe for this medium' (1962: 189).

The pieces were documentary dramas that used composite characters and plots invented to typify anterior realities. At the level of information a position of authority was established by research, but at the level of performance credibility of the action was all-important. Doncaster felt that the actors in this kind of programme should not just underplay (already perceived as a necessity for television by comparison with theatre): they must, she states flatly, '"be" the person [they are] portraying'. For his role in *Return to Living* Thomas Heathcote (a well-known British character actor of the 1950s) 'spent many hours talking to an ex-inmate of Dartmoor to get the feel of his character'. The artistic aim was: 'so that he might stop acting and become an ex-prisoner himself' (Doncaster, 1956: 45ff).

Folding the identity of an actor into that of a character is a frequent feature of Method-inflected screen acting. Over the years this seriousness of attention to real-life models has proved powerfully reassuring to dramadoc/docudrama programme makers, writers and actors. It is a symptom of anxiety at the level of dramatic credibility made inevitable by a documentary absence. The mantra-like claim of equivalence based on research is neurotically necessary at some level for an audience too. Acted performance, after all, is only ever based on conventions to which an audience can assent to by believing or deny by disbelieving. Any kind of naturalistic acting is, at best, a leap in the dark justified by the hope or belief that an audience will endorse it. The fusing of actor and real-life protagonist is as much as anything a rhetorical appeal to belief made in the hope of an affirmative response.

A mix of drama and documentary is, and always has been, more vulnerable to audience doubt than any other form of realist drama. Despite their best efforts at painstaking research, performers who impersonate real people (and who are often cast because of physical resemblance) and film makers/writers rely on their audience to square the circle. As a result, pre-publicity for the dramadoc/docudrama still asserts equivalence between real-world experience and its reconstruction. Doncaster's observation that Thomas Heathcote talked to his real-life model for 'many hours' is a classic example. Why 'many hours'? Because it says more than, simply, 'he talked to him' or 'he met him'. The rhetorical insistence is part of a claim to authenticity that can only ultimately be secured by audience belief but which actively solicits that belief prior to the event of performance.

A recent example is that of Colin Firth's description (at the *Hostages* press preview) of being mummified in adhesive tape and put in a 'coffin' underneath a lorry (*Daily Mirror*, 19 September 1992). This method of transportation around Beirut was employed by the captors of John McCarthy, his 'character', from the middle of 1987 and was central to the torture and traumas suffered by the hostages. In Alasdair Palmer's treatment for the film 'Camera tape and suffocation' is mentioned seventh in seventeen key 'Elements in the story'. 'It was an appalling experience,' Firth is quoted as saying, 'even though we were trussed up like that for just a couple of hours.' In the metonymic relation of his 'couple of hours' to the repeated experience of his real-world model lies the rhetorical claim of the dramadoc at the level of performance. Doubts about what anything is 'really like' may haunt the realist mode, but they bedevil the fact-based drama to the extent that such simulation becomes *de rigeur*.[5]

It is also worth considering Doncaster's 'experts' and their right of veto. These people were called in for the final few days of rehearsal of the dramatised story documentary. For *Return to Living*, she recalled: 'I contented myself with a Home Office official and a representative "ex-lag" – whom we invited to visit us on different days!' There is no mention of a lawyer's involvement. As I argued in Chapter 2, the increased level of such input today is an index of greater cultural doubt and anxiety and an emblem for fears of television's increased social power. Doncaster's trust in the figure of the 'expert' is a vivid blast from the innocent post-war past. Her confidence in the notion of documentary authenticity is underwritten by research and the assent of experts. There is a deference to these experts and to documentary 'objectivity', which not only guards against drama's excess but also acknowledges a superior status for facts and information. There is also a culturally learned deference towards 'straight' drama (implied, for example, in Doncaster's statement: 'I am not suggesting...that the production of a story documentary is more difficult than that of a drama'). She says revealingly: 'These productions are popular with actors because they often graduate from them to drama proper' (Doncaster, 1956: 47–8).

It is easy to see why Doncaster's somewhat clumsy construction 'dramatised story documentary' did not subsequently gain currency, but it does have the virtue of some degree of precision: it describes a documentary (category of origin) made for television by dramatising (methodology) a story (journalistic, rather than literary, product). Pressure of usage simply shortened this first to 'dramatised documentary', then 'drama documentary' and finally 'dramadoc'. But this 1940s/1950s form is better termed 'documentary drama' so that it does not become confused with the different practices of the second period. At the time, as now, both phrases were routinely used in the industry. For example, Duncan Ross termed 'documentary drama' the same programmes Doncaster called 'dramatised story documentary' when he was writing in the *BBC Quarterly* in 1950 (see Goodwin and Kerr, 1983: 12).

Arthur Swinson, another early practitioner, illustrates in his work the development of terminology in Britain. His *Writing for Television* was first published in 1955, went into a second edition in 1960 and then was partially rewritten (as *Writing for Television Today*) in 1963. In the earlier editions he used a shortened version of Doncaster's term 'dramatized documentary' (1955: 78; 1960: 80), and in a new chapter ('Present trends') in the second edition he noted: 'The dramatized documentary has moved closer to the play; and the actuality documentary has moved closer to the dramatized form' (1960: 138). In 1963 he replaced, significantly, 'dramatized documentary' in every instance with 'drama-documentary' (though he still referred to Barr, Ross and Barry as 'the three men who evolved the dramatized documentary' (1963: 116)). Amongst other notable shifts of emphasis, he altered the earlier advice that all documentary programmes needed 'several stories and one theme' (1955: 87) to make space for the developing emphasis on the single story in the late 1950s (1963: 123). Over the eight-year period of these books the industrial trend to single-story drama-documentary can plainly be seen.

Swinson defines three kinds of documentary production in all his writings: 'dramatized documentary'/'drama-documentary', 'actuality documentary' and 'magazine documentary'. He subdivides the first category into studio programmes and what he calls 'the built O. B.' (outside broadcast). On the former, he says (1955: 80; 1963: 118–19):

(a) It is played by actors who give, as far as possible an accurate interpretation of the people they represent.
(b) It is produced 'live' in the studio, with the help of film sequences.
(c) The locations in which the action takes place in life are copied and reproduced in the studio.
(d) The stories are true in the sense that they are taken from life with as little modification as possible, bearing in mind the demands of the medium.

Once again, the innocence inherent in the confident proposal of so many questionable notions ('accurate interpretation', 'locations…copied and reproduced', 'as little modification as possible') should not blind us to the fact that these rubrics are still in use. What has changed, arguably, is the willingness of an audience now to agree to, and become complicit with, such proposals of equivalence between art and life.

With the 'built O. B.' those who appear on screen are not actors, they are people 'acting the parts they played in real life and in the real setting. The "thoroughly scripted and rehearsed" programme' has them 'speaking lines they had learned by heart and performing movements worked out by the producer' (Swinson, 1963: 120). In his earlier book Swinson says: 'The technique of getting people to "act" their own jobs is becoming so well established that in television the gap between an actor playing a surgeon and a surgeon playing himself is being considerably narrowed' (1955: 53). The restraint of British documentary's underplayed style, so well known to all the television workers, narrowed this gap further.

This technique caused the first public debate about the ethics of such mixes on television. British television's days of innocence might even be said to have ended when Maurice Wiggin, the respected television critic of the *Sunday Times*, unwittingly used a 1954 programme about the National Health Service (*House Surgeon*) as a stick with which to beat the studio-based dramatised story documentary. He compared studio work (which he found stilted) to what he took to be the greater documentary authenticity of *House Surgeon* (see Swinson, 1955: 82–3; 1963: 120–1). But Wiggin 'did not, as he imagined, see "the real thing" at all; what he saw was a reality created by artifice'. The programme was a 'built O. B.' in which its maker, Bill Duncalf, had extended the remit of the dramatised story documentary: 'He argued that if interviews could be rehearsed, then dialogue could be rehearsed, as in a dramatic programme using actors.' The suspicion that the audience is in danger of being fooled, now endemic in newspaper criticism of fact-based drama, can be traced back to that early experience when (as Swinson innocently acknowledged) Wiggin 'was deceived' about *House Surgeon* (1963: 207).

Deceit was perhaps more excusable in those early days because of television's profound need for the real at a time when it was establishing its social *bona fides* as an institution both diverting and useful. Audiences, who were becoming accustomed to television as a major source of both information and entertainment, completed the communication circuit willingly enough, but a residual doubt opened up between programme makers and audiences. It can probably never be stopped, however great the search in the aesthetics of the 'real' for new means of claiming a one-to-one relationship between the real and the constructed. At times of controversy it is precisely this gap which continues to be exploited and finessed (especially by journalists and politicians).

From this early period confusion between the various labels is all too evident. Three phrases – 'dramatised story documentary', 'drama-documentary' and 'documentary drama' – are used to describe the same thing: researched dramas which attempt to supply information. ITV's Annual Report 1959/60 (see Goodwin and Kerr, 1983: 3) proudly proclaimed the development of 'two established documentary drama series *Emergency – Ward 10* and *Probation Officer*'. They were, in effect, documented soap operas. Antony Kearey, producer of the former, drew attention at the time to the research dimension of his series, saying: 'A panel of special advisers is permanently on call' (*ca* 1958: 7). The ITV Report even includes in its list of documentary dramas a programme (first transmitted in 1960) that went on to become British television's longest-running soap opera – Granada's *Coronation Street*. It may be hard now to imagine it as in any way 'documentary', but early episodes had a realist, 'kitchen sink', orientation derived from contemporary theatre and film.

At the end of the 1950s the BBC was also searching for grittily realistic contemporary drama. It developed the police series *Z Cars*, which (again, relatively speaking) provided a new take on police work in the suddenly fashionable north of England. Today, one of *Z Cars'* two original writers, Allan Prior, is clear on one major point: he believes that the makers of dramatised story documentaries

virtually invented the Studio Play: they were making documentaries but the techniques were to remain the same to this day... These men's names may be half-forgotten now, but they made the rules of television-drama, rules that remain, even now, in place. (Prior, 1996: 5–6)[6]

The documentary aspect of such programmes lay in two related areas: first, their seeking of a socially realistic look; and second, their incorporation of a new social extension in subject matter. In retrospect, this can be seen as all of a piece with the drive in the late 1950s to make space for new voices and locales in British culture, which was most often evident in the seeking of working-class subjects and protagonists and a 'documentary' visual style (made increasingly possible during the 1960s by the new portable sound and image recording equipment).[7]

USA – the 'documentary-drama'

The different imperatives of American television in this early period produced the 'documentary-drama', a different kind of programme from the documentary-based 'dramatised story documentary' and one that was influenced both formally and institutionally by the film industry. Formally, it was led by the narrative practices of the feature film. Institutionally, the 1948 Paramount judgement heralded an adjustment in the film industry to new, post-war industrial conditions that had a profound influence on the television networks. In the area of fact-based drama this influence was to become almost total.[8]

In US culture there were some similarities with pre-war British film and radio practices. The Griersonian film documentary was paralleled (but not quite mirrored) in the work of such directors as Robert Flaherty, Pare Lorentz and Willard Van Dyke. But America's pioneering of the 'photo journal', through which actuality photographs were turned into a popular art form, was also influential. From the founding of *Time* magazine in 1923 US journalism's address of the real was energetically focused through the still camera lens.[9] When NBC and CBS radio expanded their drama output during 1928–29, some of it was sponsored by the photo-journals; for example, *Time* magazine developed *The March of Time* for NBC. From its inception in 1931 the radio version used actors; their voices provided further illustrative input to a mode that was

essentially narration in direct address to the audience. Impersonation by actors of real-world individuals was, in other words, a
staple technique. There was also CBS's *True Story*. Sponsored by
Macfadden Publications to boost sales of a magazine of the same
name, this populist drama series was 'based on magazine stories,
neatly bowdlerized and dressed with strangely literate dialogue and
philosophizing' (Barnouw, 1966: I, 224). Barnouw described it as
'both lurid and respectable enough to be a smashing 1928–29
success' (1966: I, 224). The lineaments of the modern American
docudrama can be clearly discerned in these early journalistic
reshapings of the documentary project.

When *The March of Time* became a film series in 1935 it was a
newsreel with a difference. It was the first in the visual field for the
illustrative re-enactment that is now so beloved by the tabloid end of
reality television. William Bluem remarks that in the radio version
the enforced absence of any authorising image made it a technique
that was easy to absorb at the point of reception as well as to
organise at the point of production; it enabled the editors to make a
key decision for the film version: to use fewer stories than competitor
newsreels, but to treat them in more depth (1979: 36).[10]

The judicious mix of drama with actuality film in their programmes helped secure this editorial decision. Bluem notes:

> This expansion of time in the reporting process was important chiefly
> because it permitted a journalistic style in which emphasis was divided
> between the inherent drama of an event and a dramatic technique of
> presentation. (Bluem, 1979: 36)

The March of Time ordered and indeed plotted its news items,
enabling a structure that 'mov[ed] toward a dramatic climax which,
in turn, dictated a unified continuity' (Bluem, 1979: 36). These are
the terms of classic Hollywood realism. A socially responsible
dimension to the project was evident: 'The journalistic documentary was designed to inform great audiences of the immediate
conflicts and crises of the age' (Bluem, 1979: 40). The format was
eminently exportable, and *Time* magazine opened offices in Canada
and Britain. Granada, with its distinctive dramadoc methodology in
World in Action, is the British heir to this tradition.

The 1950s were the golden age of the live 'dramatic anthology series' on American television. Dramas for anthological programmes such as *Philco Television Playhouse, Goodyear Television Playhouse* and *Kraft Television Theater* were produced from a large studio in New York. Such writers as Paddy Chayevsky achieved reputations as pre-eminently dramatists for television, and a supply of cheap new acting talent fresh from Lee Strasberg's Actors' Studio was readily available. Tino Balio notes that in the 1953–56 heyday of anthology drama 'the networks broadcast 20 such programs a week' (1990: 17). NBC's *Armstrong Circle Theatre*, in which John Cassavetes, Robert Duvall and Telly Savalas made their television débuts, was one such series.

Armstrong Circle Theatre began to base its dramas on factual material in 1955. The year is a crucial one because movie studios had started to sell off their back catalogues to television. RKO (one of the 'Big Five' pre-war film studios) did this in 1955 as part of a complete withdrawal from film production. The emergent television network ABC made an agreement with Warner Brothers in the same year, but Warner was not being terminally 'downsized' like RKO; the agreement was a prelude to their active participation in television production. As film fictions past (from back catalogues) and present (from new television film production companies) were about to flood the market and anthology dramas came under pressure to move with the rest of American television from the east to the west coast, the producers of *Armstrong Circle Theatre* elected to stay in New York and to move into original, fact-based, teleplays.

Armstrong Circle Theatre used fact-based material because it was both readily accessible to a viewing public and unlikely to have already been seen in Hollywood's back catalogues, which were notorious for their tentative approach to subjects of social significance. Its plays were, in effect, pre-sold to their audience as a result of the prior existence of their stories in the wider news media. The teleplays were, broadly speaking, socially responsible in terms of content but may be contrasted with British dramatised story documentaries of the same period in two respects: (a) their strategic objective was commercial; (b) their priorities were dramatic not documentary.

Armstrong Circle Theatre's producer Robert Costello

> worked toward a format which offered two basic methods of dramatisa-
> tion. In certain cases it was found advantageous to deal directly with a
> real person, and in others it was found best to create a purely fictional
> character which represented several real people or a shared attitude
> (Bluem, 1979: 193).

Costello's commitment to public service was evident: 'We can't use
an idea only or a news story only, we must also be able to present
some potential solution, some hope for our citizens to consider, to
think about' (Bluem, 1979: 193). The team that produced *Armstrong Circle Theatre* had backgrounds mainly in drama, but expert
consultants were employed to establish a documentary base (see
Hoffer *et al.*, 1985: 182). A journalist/narrator supplied narrative
continuity (as in the modern reconstruction programmes featuring
the emergency services).

Armstrong Circle Theatre 'specialized in dramatizations of actual
events' (McNeil, 1991: 53), utilising approaches of both drama-
documentary and documentary drama. Bluem and others label the
resultant teleplays 'documentary-dramas', and it seems likely that
this term and the shortened 'docudrama' were in use in the 1950s
(see Musburger, 1985).[11] When the programme was taken up by
CBS (1957–63), its shift away from documentary towards drama
became more marked. In 1961 CBS 'eliminated Douglas Edwards
from the narrator's role', thus bringing the series into line with the
filmed dramas that were already beginning to dominate the networks (Bluem, 1979: 165). Significantly, Bluem concludes that the
demise of this programme in 1963 was due to the constricting
nature of documentary-drama as developed by *Armstrong Circle
Theatre*; it was

> neither fish nor fowl...its commitment to the faithful duplication of
> events and people limited its freedom as drama...[but] the use of actors
> and theatrical conventions deprived it of any validity as documentary.
> (Bluem, 1979: 163)

This succinct summary of the problems of the form (in terms of the
perception of the critics) could stand today. With hindsight, the
series can be seen as a prototype for the made-for-TV movie.

A good example of an *Armstrong Circle Theatre* play based on fact is *Freedom Fighters of Hungary*, which was transmitted on NBC on 22 January 1957 in prime time (9.30–10.30 pm).[12] Written by Art Wallace and produced by Costello, the play is a treatment of the 1956 Hungarian uprising. The programme is introduced by a news anchor (John Cameron Swayze) in a newsroom set. He frames the story ideologically, telling the audience that the historical event is evidence of 'the complete brutality and inhumanity of Soviet oppression'; archive footage of Soviet tanks in the streets of Budapest follows these words. This opening is, however, a kind of continuity announcement, for an advertisement break follows. (All the advertisement breaks in the programme, in the common practice of the time, are for the sponsoring company's products – Armstrong in this case).

The play proper mixes archive newsreel exteriors with acted studio set interiors, very much in the manner of the British dramatised story documentary. There are several representative characters: a boy celebrating his twelfth birthday with his family; an officer in the Hungarian army and his girlfriend, whose father runs a pavement café; and a group of students, one of whom lives with a grandfather who remembers Hungary's proud and independent past. There are three or four room sets, and the camera-work mostly closes in on the characters in one- and two-shot arrangements. The *mise-en-scène* is basic by comparison with the practices analysed in Chapter 1. Because both studio shots and newsreel footage are in black-and-white, the frequent cutting from documentary to drama works fairly seamlessly. The studio lighting helps by making greater use of chiaroscuro effects than is common now. So, when a sequence following the first advertisement break mixes archive footage of street fighting with studio shots of the students taking cover behind café tables, the continuity of the narrative is not affected in any Brechtian way: it is unlikely to be experienced as an 'interruption' to the story.

Swayze in voiceover sets and resets the scene frequently, giving dates and times and recapping situations, which are illustrated with newsreel action. The drama meanwhile portrays the human dimension: the father and his son die in the uprising, as do the army officer's girlfriend and one of the students. The mother (Anna), son, students and officer finish up in Anna's flat, defiantly continuing to fight the perfidious Russians. The acting style, viewed today, appears very overstated, very theatrical. The writing, too, telegraphs the main points and goes in for self-consciously theatrical repetitions. For example, the collectivity of the Hungarian people against their oppressor is figured regularly through a repeated question-and-answer sequence. Sandor (the army captain) asks several of the characters: 'Do you know how to handle a gun?' All reply: 'I can learn.' This exchange is repeated with the girl student, the twelve-year old boy and the boy's mother. On each occasion someone has died (a male student; the father; the boy) and that dialogue signifies heroic continuity in the struggle. Finally, the bereaved Anna speaks the line as the last words of the play.

A further, documentary, dimension is achieved in the casting of Eva Soreny as Anna. Billed in the cast list as 'the First Lady of the Hungarian National Theatre' and announced as such by Swayze, Soreny does a piece to camera as the programme's final extra-textual word on this great historical moment of the twentieth century. She speaks with the authority of someone who lived through the period between 23 October 1956 – when the first demonstrations took place in Budapest – and 4 November, when the insurrection was brutally crushed. She has the additional authority of someone who then escaped to the USA. In her own person she speaks briefly but movingly of a still-living 'spirit of Hungary', which she herself represents both in and out of the action. The emotional effect would almost certainly have been heightened by the play's transmission only two months after the events depicted.

First-phase practices – 'public goods' and 'public good'

Some distinctions based on differential Anglo-American practices in the fact-based drama of the first historical phase can now be proposed. Initially, in the American commercial model, television drama series used factual material to develop a form that pre-sold itself – this *documentary-in-drama* approach became the 'docu-drama'. It took its colour from early series like *Circle Theatre*, whose priorities were essentially dramatic. In the second phase, this form

developed into the 'made-for-TV docudrama' and the 'faction'.
Finally, it led in the third phase to the 'trauma drama' (see
Chapter 7).

In contrast, in Britain the concept of 'public service' led to the
development of a *drama-in-documentary* approach, which eventually
became the journalistic 'dramadoc' associated with Granada TV.
This developed from the 'dramatised story documentary'. British
documentary-in-drama also existed, in the form of serious dramas
dealing with social realism (see next section on the second historical
phase). British forms took their colour in general from the discursive
priorities of documentary and the discourse of sobriety.

In the USA synergy between the film and the television industries
gradually increased the dramatic priorities in made-for-TV docudrama, moving them away from investigative journalism; in Britain
a weak film industry could (and did) influence visual styles, but the
journalistic link between documentary and drama remained as
stronger endorsement of documentary claims. In the USA an entre-
preneurial concept of 'public goods' predominated over the ethical
concept of 'public good'; in Britain the emphasis was reversed.

In 'public goods' programme making, public 'wants' are upper-
most at the point of production; conversely, public 'needs' are upper-
most where 'public good' is the consideration. As Vance Kepley Jr
puts it: 'advertiser-supported commercial television is an example of
a public goods industry…[in which] the public good label refers only
to the industry's economic qualities' (1990: 42–3). Thus the max-
imising of a product's sales potential is the key consideration; it
must and does come before everything else. The made-for-TV movie,
emerging in the mid-1960s, was an ideal vehicle for such a scale of
priority.

Second-phase practices – projecting truth

During the second phase live studio drama was gradually superseded thanks to technological change. This had implications not
only for drama departments, but for political/current affairs, arts
and science departments too. In Britain 'documentary drama' and
'drama-documentary' practices achieved parallel development in

the period, some departments leaning towards informational, documentary priorities and others towards recreational, dramatic ones.

It is not necessarily the case that the more informational the department, the more documentary will be the method. Roger Silverstone has pointed out the reasoning behind the BBC Science Department's pressing need to incorporate drama into its largely explanatory programmes: science relies on 'non-scientific narratives to legitimate itself' for lay audiences (1986: 82). Drama offers a dialogical framework through which an intellectual 'other' – representing as often as not those forces which doubt and oppose the advances of science – can provide an antagonist for the scientific protagonist. The BBC's science programme *Horizon* (broadcast from 1964), for example, has routinely used what we can now recognise as 'drama-documentary' practices. Silverstone calls attention to the generally 'agonistic', dramatic, nature of such presentations.

The work of Ken Loach provides an illustration of the contrasting potential for documentary styles by drama departments in the same period. A crucial factor in British culture has been the bringing in from the margins, through the direct agency of the liberal state, of radical commentaries on contemporary society. This kind of commentary has often acquired the 'documentary' label because it has used factual material to critique, accuse and oppose the *status quo*. Using contemporary material – the 'only just past' – the documentary drama as practised at the BBC by Loach and his associates (producer Tony Garnett and writers Jeremy Sandford, Nell Dunn and Jim Allen) was classically issue-based. Loach has acquired a deserved reputation for films that traverse the point at which the documentary could be said to turn into the drama. He himself has talked of his belief that his films 'really cut through the glass wall that separates fiction from fact' (Hood, 1994: 199). In this sense, all his work is 'documentary drama' as defined in Chapter 3.

Loach's status as *auteur*-director has been ironically confirmed by his later move exclusively into film. During the early 1980s he became such a controversial figure that he could not get any of his work screened in the cinema or on television. Now he has acquired international success with films such as *Ladybird, Ladybird* (1994), *Land and Freedom* (1995) and *Carla's Song* (1996). His television documentary dramas of the 1960s – *Up the Junction* (1965), *Cathy Come Home* (1966) and *In Two Minds* (1968) – were made for the BBC's *Wednesday Play* series (1964–69). This programming strand for new television drama was the brainchild of the Canadian producer Sydney Newman, and it was calculated to capitalise on the new taste for realistic social drama through 'agitational contemporaneity' (see Sendall and Potter, 1982: I, 338).

Loach's early films bear trademark features: a pronounced social critique at the level of content, usually focused through 'underdog' protagonists; filming techniques that place a premium on immediacy (from which authenticity can be inferred); and acting styles that stress the underplayed and the improvisational. Performances are thus shifted away from any hint of the theatrical, and Loach has frequently used non-professional actors to access this 'unconscious' quality in performance. His favoured professional performers, too, have an unstudied quality on screen that is the ultimate refinement of Strasbergian focus. Compare *Cathy Come Home* (1966) with *Ladybird, Ladybird* (1994) and these features are still evident in the later film.

Loach's major preoccupation, which links all his work, is 'to give a voice to those who are often denied it'; this democratic ideal animates all his films.[13] His current working practice is to shoot a film in story order (i.e. chronologically and not for organisational convenience) and to deny the actor any overview of the script (revealing the script, so to speak, one page at a time). Loach's methods, like those of Mike Leigh, another British film director with a similar *vérité* style, are warmly endorsed by actors because they avoid the danger of 'playing the result' (something that actors must guard against). Robert Carlyle, who was in *Carla's Song*, said: 'Ken makes it easier to become real...You're not projecting a character, you're projecting a truth' (*Guardian*, 31 January 1997).

Cathy Come Home is the prime example of a golden age documentary drama that 'projects truth'. Widely regarded not only as 'a representatively "classic" piece of British television', it is also 'a piece of "essential television"' (Corner, 1996: 90). In some ways *Cathy* was simply a film whose time was right. Loach says it was 'by and large approved because even Tory politicians got on the bandwagon and said: this is helping to solve the problems of the homeless' (Hood, 1994: 196–7). It gave due prominence to a 'public good' and attacked the public conscience very effectively. *Cathy Come Home* is that rare creature, a television programme that is not ephemeral: it registered with audiences at the time and continues to do so on both the documentary and the drama scales. Modern students are ready enough to transpose the supposedly dated factual material into their own times and they still respond to Cathy's human dilemma at the level of dramatic identification. It is for this reason the British charity Shelter continued to use the film as a consciousness raiser long after the particular facts embedded within it became out of date. *Cathy Come Home* must surely be the most repeated drama on British television.[14]

Is *Cathy* documentary drama or drama-documentary? John Corner puts it in 'the camp of documentary-drama rather than dramatised documentary' because it 'opens up documentary space around the storyline' (1996: 106). Although its writer Jeremy Sandford described it as 'dramatised documentary' in an article in 1973, this was surely a matter of the preferred industry-usage. The interdependence it achieves between the two elements is probably no longer possible. Jeremy Sandford said to me: 'Perhaps *Cathy* could only be done once. It was part of TV's "Age of Innocence".' Loach concurs with this view, saying in 1994: '*Cathy Come Home* had quite a strong impact because the audience were much more innocent at that time.' [15]

Cathy Come Home was a fiction film that emerged from a drama department but that had a strong documentary element in two regards: the script was the result of research and the film style echoed contemporary non-fictional works that relied on new camera technology. These two elements ensured its sharp cutting edge in terms of social criticism. Loach and his producer Tony Garnett smuggled their contentious subject matter through an institution that was always likely to be resistant to challenging ideas; he considers that *Cathy* was made 'despite the powers that be rather than because of them'.[16]

In truth, *Cathy Come Home* is unique in the way it has been able to transcend a classification that is muddled and compromised by institutional and cultural histories. It is this quality that ensures its continuing debate for as long as mixtures of drama and factual material are found problematical. What *Cathy* emphatically possesses, and which is seen even now, so many years after its first transmission, is what Garnett calls 'life in the frame' – a level of authenticity conferred by a style of film making that appears (like the acting) to be improvised. This style, which derives to some extent from the hand-held techniques of 1960s documentary, was sometimes derided as 'wobblyscope' by camera operators schooled to aim for the technically perfect image. The documentary element of Loach's directorial style was made possible by this new equipment, which was widely used in both documentary and anthropological film making. The dramatic component was born of a combination of the naturalism favoured by the Royal Court Theatre and the realism of television drama that followed Sydney Newman's lead.

The documentary element of *Cathy Come Home* is mediated through a sophisticated series of looks and sounds that offer to the implied audience a variety of spectator positions. Sometimes we witness in an omniscient, surveillant, 'objective' way; at other times we see and hear emotionally and viscerally, through Cathy herself.[17] The documentary and the drama of *Cathy Come Home* pull us to different angles of vision, which are complementary in the way officialdom is seen as neither competent nor sympathetic in the face of human misery. Like his style, Loach's view of the provision of social services in Britain has changed little in the twenty years between *Cathy* and *Ladybird, Ladybird*.

Writing in 1962, J. L. Styan commented:

> the slice-of-life drama is never better received than when it is written and presented in the mood of topicality, when we are aware of the camera following the actors a little raggedly, when the actor is spotted groping for a word, and when there is a *commedia dell'arte* spirit of improvisation in the studio. (Styan, 1962, 188–9)

The look of fiction film contrasts with the documentary look, and the documentary drama avoids it. In fiction film the visual element is generally uncluttered and clear – action is 'staged' to achieve this. The documentary drama, meanwhile, seeks the 'natural' clutter and confusion of documentary filming as its guarantee of authenticity. On one side there is 'perfection in the frame'; on the other, 'life in the frame'. Spectators drawn into Loach's world could (still can) see their experience as part of a continuum that includes action in the real, phenomenal, political world. This kind of experience is, importantly, not just entertainment; there is a seriousness, a 'sobriety', to use our earlier word, which is both authenticating in respect of the viewing experience and self-validating in terms of the pleasure offered to a viewer.

Made-for-TV movies

In the USA in this same period the second-phase shift to the docudrama 'made-for-TV' contrasts culturally, institutionally and formally with middle-period British documentary drama. Virtual mirror-image forms emerged: the American more constrained to accept the world as it was, the British trying very earnestly to question and challenge that world through formal experiment and provocative subject matter.

If the American fact-based drama ended its initial period with the demise of *Armstrong Circle Theatre* in the late 1950s, it reconfigured itself through the made-for-TV movie in the 1960s. Gary Edgerton proposes three categories for this genre: the telefeature, the docudrama and the mini-series. In whatever form, all made-for TV movies capitalised on 'the intrinsic topicality of the TV medium itself' (1985: 152). The progenitors of the docudrama are to be found in the Hollywood biopic and the kind of socially aware fiction film that Warner Brothers went in for from the 1930s. Edgerton emphasises the aesthetic turn of the docudrama; although it seems 'to blend essential aspects of both the fictional and the documentary film... the narrative form has usually dominated in its subsequent execution on American television to date' (1985: 152).

Nonetheless, its proposal of public issues qualifies the docudrama as a post-war development of the 'public service drama'. Like all made-for-TV movies, the docudrama has always had a dependence on fiction film techniques that has attenuated its relationship with documentary. Todd Gitlin comments acerbically: 'Television docudrama abhors what it considers polemic, didacticism, speechifying. Convention clamps a tight frame round the story. It doesn't want the larger public world leaking in' (1994: 175). The low-concept docudrama certainly downgrades the abstract and the contentious; it is what could be called 'a very American genre'.

The idea is to have socially relevant themes, but to deliver them to your audience well wrapped in individually focused stories that deflect discussion to an experiential rather than a political level. The public is rendered principally through the private, the factual claim ('based on a true story') simply supplying an authorising rubric – 'Yes, this really happened.' Elayne Rapping claims that docudramas 'never use actual footage of historical events and interviews with real people' but rely entirely on 'actors, staged settings and dramatically written scripts' (1987: 142). A whole generation of American scholars has alleged that the made-for-TV movie is, lineally, the descendant of the despised B-movie of the 1940s and 1950s.[18]

Gary Edgerton takes the view, however, that the comparison with film is misguided and that meaningful comparison can only be made within the television institution itself. The emergence of a production system for these made-for-TV movies in the late 1960s, he claims, has had some cultural benefits. He sees such films as 'the "televisionization" of contemporary American interests, affectations, and obsessions' (Edgerton, 1985: 167). The cultural landscape of middle America can be discerned quite clearly, especially in what he calls the 'high-concept' docudrama (Edgerton, 1991). This manifestation of seriousness of purpose in American television drama should alert us to the danger of dismissing the form too easily. Edgerton argues that the made-for-TV movie as a whole has always been allowed greater latitude by the networks' Broadcasting Standards Departments (which we encountered in Chapter 3). Their 'greater freedom in [the] handling of controversial topics' comes about through the genre's 'noncontinuous format and because of the TV movie's special quality and higher status within the sphere of nighttime programming' (Edgerton, 1991: 124). This more nuanced view certainly fits the Anglo-American co-production work of the third phase and the interventions of feminist critics (see Chapters 7 and 8).

American writers vary on the question of which were the first of the made-for-TV docudramas, but high-concept subject matter is evident in all the examples cited, as is broad agreement on the early 1970s as being the key period. By the mid-1970s all three main networks were regularly screening made-for-TV movies and the 'docudrama' was recognised as a subdivision of the genre (Gomery, 1983: 126). Hoffer *et al.* (1980) claim *Brian's Song* (1971) as the first purpose-made docudrama, whereas Edgerton (1985) cites *The Weekend Nun* (1972). The former, the story of a football star's battle with cancer, was a drama-documentary that used real names and verifiable places and events; the latter was a documentary drama based on the life of a nun, Joyce Duco. Both films offer serious treatment of a serious subject; both use a realist film-style; both are called 'docudramas' by Americans.

American practice branched out further in the 1970s with the so-called 'faction'. It would seem that the cultural reasons for America's interest in factual drama in the 1970s were to do with a bicentennial mind-set, in which there was an almost valedictory attempt to get to grips with its past and present. This can be compared to Britain's cultural attempt in the 1960s to get to grips with similar concepts. Key examples are: ABC's 1974 *The Missiles of October* (a docudrama on the Cuban missile crisis of 1962);[19] ABC's 1977 *Roots*, one of the most successful network series of all time (which explored the history of Black America in a researched drama); and Paramount's 1977 *Washington: Behind Closed Doors* (a 'faction' that probed the latter days of the Nixon administration). In 1979 the docudrama was sufficiently well established in American network programming for a symposium on it to be held by the Academy of Television Arts and Sciences.

The publicity potential of 'fact' continued to be a powerful persuader for the adoption of the mixed form at this time and was borne out by the success of these and other examples. Free trails from already existing news and current affairs sources, both inside and outside the television institution, were the trump card. James Monaco gave this summary:

> Trading on the striking identity between fiction and reality that characterizes the television experience, program executives developed the so-called 'docudrama', a made-for-TV film based more or less loosely in

current events and history, dealing with subjects already well known to viewers and thus in a sense presold. (Monaco, 1977: 380)

ABC's *Brian's Song* was not only hugely popular on first transmission, it was much repeated. The American docudrama is relatively cheap to make, and when successful has 'long legs' (achieving multiple repeats across many channels over long periods of time). It was so successful that there was even a cinema release (very unsuccessful – presumably because so many people had already seen the film!). Frequent repeats are possible because the folk memory associated with unusual current events and individuals in unusual situations is a rather better trigger than a journalistic, theme-based programme tied, like the daily papers, to the news. In a marketplace that is always likely to become more not less competitive the public's fondness for individualised narratives will probably ensure that the American docudrama continues to enjoy a built-in advantage over the more event-specific British dramadoc. HBO, however, was still repeating the 1990 Granada dramadoc *The Tragedy of Flight 103: The Inside Story* (known as *Why Lockerbie?* in Britain) in September 1997.

A very British genre

By 1980 the dramadoc was as well established on British television as the docudrama was on American. Granada TV provided strong continuity in this development through *World in Action*. This current affairs magazine programme began mixing dramatic reconstructions with documentary footage almost from its inception in 1963 in a practice that links backwards to *The March of Time* and forwards to *Rescue 911*. Its founder-producer Tim Hewat made programmes on the Portland Spy Trial and the Great Train Robbery using what Leslie Woodhead now terms 'dumb show' dramatisation. Look-alike figures re-enacted actions to voiceover commentary, sometimes in very brief fragments of illustrative film. Jeremy Wallington, a former journalist on the *Sunday Times*, who came to Granada in 1967, was also a key influence in the search for what Woodhead calls 'visual equivalents for that torrent of verbal information you got in [*Sunday Times*] "Insight" features'.

Woodhead recalls that he came to *World in Action* primarily as a film maker:

> I was very engaged by the texture of Loach, the way he visualised things, where he placed the camera, the documentary stillness with which he framed things. I was very interested in the aesthetic turn Loach was exploring.

Peter Watkins' 1964 BBC film *Culloden*, with its news broadcast dynamic and *cinéma vérité* visual aesthetics, also excited and influenced Woodhead, as did the Richard Leacock/Robert Drew documentary film work of the time.[20] He was, he acknowledges, less aware of the Doncaster/Swinson dramatised story documentary of the 1950s.

Woodhead believes that Granada's first drama-documentary was Mike Murphy's *The Pueblo Affair*, transmitted early in 1970. His own *The Man Who Wouldn't Keep Quiet*, which is sometimes cited as first in the field, was transmitted later that year. Woodhead's film was based on the diary of a Russian dissident, Major-General Pyotr Grigorenko, which was smuggled out of the Soviet Union. Woodhead described the film in 1976 as having been 'nurtured and matured inside the *World in Action* set-up' (see Goodwin and Kerr, 1983: 25). With *World in Action* a style of drama-documentary emerged that Woodhead describes as even now being 'very careful and rather puritanical'. There were from the outset, however, mixed visual approaches, and John Wyver describes the documentary and the drama 'looks' of the 1980 *Invasion* as rather going against 'the producers' statements of rigid asceticism' (1983: 33).

Woodhead's view is that the drama-documentary had, and still has, a very particular set of responsibilities towards its audience. A key component of the 'cool' style of the Granada dramadoc was the deliberate selection of film crews with documentary backgrounds. Woodhead claimed in 1976 that this ensured 'visual understatement'. David Plowright, who was to become Granada's managing director, says that he 'welded together the skills of the investigative journalists and the filmmakers at Granada' during the 1970s, and this sustained the dramadoc (Goodwin and Kerr, 1983: 26).

For Woodhead, there are 'special responsibilities [in] impersonating living individuals' that can only be accessed through the research and skilled performance. He offers the picture of the actor Leslie Sands preparing for his role (as Edward Gierek, the First Secretary of the Polish Communist Party) in the 1976 *Three Days in Szczecin* 'by detailed study of film of Gierek' and learning an important speech 'under the watchful eye of a photograph of the real Mr. Gierek pinned on his study wall' (Goodwin and Kerr, 1983: 28). The reliance on research as an authorising rhetoric makes a conservative style of performance inevitable; Woodhead is certainly sceptical about formal dramatic experiment.

Woodhead places special emphasis, as all Granada staff tend to, on the use of captions to supply the provenance of the information from which the programme develops. He sees them as a primary means of declaring intention and avoiding the risk of misleading an audience as to the status of the programme. Their principal function is to narrow the choices available to an audience and cause an indexical relationship with factuality. This 'pointing towards' the facts is what pushes the form away from the looser constraints of fictional drama. He talks of the 'passionate obligation' he felt at the time to 'labelling and telling the audience what game [the film makers] were playing, to let them know at the outset that this was not a conventional documentary'. Referring to the lengthy exposition at the beginning of the 1981 *Strike*, he said to me: 'These days that would be regarded as an Andean barrier to audience sympathy!'[21]

By 1980, the techniques of the Granada dramadoc were so well established that producer David Boulton described them in a Granada publication as the 'Woodhead doctrine'. This was:

> to recreate as accurately as possible history as it happened. No invented characters, no invented names, no dramatic devices owing more to the writer's (or director's) creative imagination than to the implacable record of what actually happened.

Crucially, he adds: 'For us, the dramatised documentary is an exercise in journalism, not dramatic art' (see Goodwin and Kerr, 1983: 29).

World in Action's 'Iron Curtain' dramadocs had an almost Amnesty International campaigning edge to them.[22] Paul Kerr has characterised second-phase dramadoc as based on 'reporter inaccessibility', for the most famous examples were located in a

Soviet bloc to which Western news and documentary television crews were not admitted until the Velvet Revolutions of the late 1980s (1990: 82). In retrospect, examples like the 1980 *Invasion* (about the destruction of the 'Prague Spring' by the Soviets in 1968) can be seen as evidence of the first chinks in the collapse of the various satellite Soviet régimes, and they were welcomed by Western establishments.[23] Ian McBride observed to me: 'Nobody ever argued that dramadoc was a deeply flawed and suspicious form when we were in shipyards in Gdansk, or psychiatric hospitals in the Soviet Union!'

Media events

By the end of the second phase the dramadoc/docudrama had also shown its potential to become a 'media event' by being controversial as well as worthy. If 'Woodhead doctrine' drama-documentaries about the Soviet bloc were perceived as being usefully critical of communist régimes, documentary dramas such as Peter Watkins' anti-nuclear film *The War Game* (BBC, 1965), Loach/Garnett's *Days of Hope* (BBC1, 1976) and Antony Thomas's *Death of a Princess* (ATV, 1980) were more contentious, and even seen as dangerous. Watkins' controversial film was banned and remained untransmitted for twenty years; *Death of a Princess* caused widespread diplomatic panic in terms of Britain's relations with its ally and trading partner Saudi Arabia.[24]

These programmes illustrate the fact that controversy always results from issues about content, not form. When factual treatments stray into areas of political tension and anxiety, problems begin to occur, as they did with Thomas's treatment of the gap between Middle Eastern and Western societies. The film was self-reflexive in its foregrounding of the difficulty of accessing 'the truth' of any situation. Thomas dramatised his own search for the truth about the execution of a Saudi princess in 1978 by placing himself in *Death of a Princess*, thinly disguised as 'Christopher Ryder'. Situating his audience within this subject position he hoped to clarify the essentially illusory nature of any documentary claim to objectivity.[25]

The self-conscious attempt to make points about the nature of representation marks a kind of 'coming-of-age' of the dramadoc/docudrama. *Death of a Princess* is the televisual equivalent of 'meta-theatre' (theatre that takes as its subject the making of theatre). It also illustrates how little such a formal strategy protects against the wrenching of a programme into a 'media event' moral panic. Controversy is the price paid when the outer public world has yet to come to terms with the content of a programme, whatever the inner-world intentions of its makers. As Ian McBride says: 'When you're dealing with something which has got a political resonance...that's when these kind of arguments take off.'

The dramadoc/docudrama became established in the second phase as one of the primary means by which the public world could be represented and, at the same time, as a highly suspect mode. By the end of this phase both the US Academy of Television Arts and Sciences (in 1979) and the British Film Institute (in 1981) were able to debate the programme category's characteristics and terms of reference on the basis of examples of significant practice. In the third phase of development, to which Chapter 7 turns, the synergy is increasingly to be found in co-operation and co-production between television cultures.

High concept/low concept – the modern trauma drama

The third phase

Todd Gitlin's notion of the 'leaking in' of a 'larger public world' is fundamental to developments in the third phase. Without the public world there would be no prior referent and no opportunity to pre-sell product. There are, however, differences in the degree of leakage and different contexts in which programmes leak. Much low-concept American docudrama (the main object of Gitlin's disdain), apparently lacks either an issue of public policy or an obvious social focus. Instead, he says: '"docudramatists", simply by accepting the conventions of their form, are committing a kind of self-censorship' (1994: 175). The argumentational line is by now a familiar one: the realism of the individualised stories destroys all abstract analytical potential in the subject proposed.

However, as Jane Feuer points out, there are dangers in readings that 'proceed from thin description to condemnation' (1995: 147). She argues that the 'trauma drama' is culturally interesting in the sense that it is a populist articulation of a widespread social frustration. Trauma dramas, she claims, have frequently given voice to popular doubts and suspicions that have been growing for some time about social institutions. She gives as her first key example ABC's *Friendly Fire* (1979). The film is about 'ordinary' American parents forced to investigate their son's 'accidental' slaying by his own side in Vietnam. The very title of the film throws back at the military its own ghastly newspeak euphemism, the product of a war of 'body counts' and 'pacification programmes'. On the same film, however, Robert Sklar took the Gitlin view, saying that Peg and Gene Mullen of La Porte City, Iowa, were 'universalize[d]' by the producers, who 'thereby...neutralize[d] them' as actual agents in a historical situation (1980: 187).

Feuer takes issue with this formalist dismissal. She lists eight structural points to trauma drama (1995: 25–7). All focus dramatically on the very self-help individualism that got Reagan elected in 1980 (and that Reaganism sought to exploit but could not ultimately control). Trauma drama 'opens up documentary space', to borrow John Corner's phrase, in its 'outing' of official cover-ups and thereby mimics the actual experience of individuals forced to act on their own behalf. The mendacity of authorities actually engaged in covering up such deaths – their failure of responsibility – is what triggers individual actions in the real world. In their turn, these crusades refute the claims of the officials that they care about those in their control. It is with this classic official versus individual trope that the trauma drama operates. The form's shaky re-assertions of normality (point eight of Feuer's structure) can be read as the clearest evidence of a profound ambiguity. The troubled moment of closure often illustrates that, as Feuer says, 'the stability of family life is fragile indeed' (1995: 34). The trauma drama is one of several forms through which, to borrow the punning title of Feuer's book, people were 'seeing through the eighties'.

More obviously journalistic investigations of 'public policy' were still possible through 'Woodhead doctrine' dramadoc, which developed into co-production in the third phase. This occurred via a revival at Granada, presided over by Ian McBride and Ray Fitzwalter, which renewed the form's potential for controversy. I have argued that the dramadoc is an 'occasional' form, which distinguishes it from the more regular made-for-TV docudrama. The 'occasionality' of late 1980s dramadoc was achieved by shifting the focus from Communist to Western societies and acknowledging a similar global suspicion to that which animated the domestic trauma dramas of the USA.

Such programmes as *Who Bombed Birmingham?* and *Shoot to Kill* asked the question: How sure can we be about our democracy? The question mined an uncertainty at the heart of British society that was eminently transferable to other developed capitalist ones. The new dramadocs had detached themselves progressively from their *World in Action* base and, standing alone, had much in common with American practice. By the end of the 1980s the two traditions – trauma-docudrama and journalistic dramadoc – were fused through economic necessity. Transatlantic co-operation was not new, of course. Leslie Woodhead points out that 'from the mid-1960s *World in Action* had a New York office with an American crew...They had a much more free-wheeling approach'. *Death of a Princess*, too, was a co-production between ATV and WGBH (Boston), Telepictures (Holland), Seven Network (Australia), and Eastern Media (New Zealand). The losses and gains of such arrangements can be gauged through a comparison between two major players in third-phase co-production: Granada and HBO. Granada brought the dramadoc tradition to such deals; HBO brought a willingness to fund high-concept docudrama into a new television era.

Granada TV and HBO

Leslie Halliwell waspishly described Granada as 'more intellectual than the other ITV companies' (1986: 326). An 'original' franchise-holder (winning in the first commercial television franchise bids of 1955), it has demonstrated a 'public service' awareness on a par with that of the BBC but has always been more populist in orientation. Granada's location in Manchester is important to its history; the city has had a particularly independent voice in national affairs ever since the nineteenth century. Granada built on a tradition of populist radicalism, which it continues to uphold. It was founded by Sidney Bernstein in 1955, and from 1964 its managing director was Denis Forman. Both had connections with the documentary film movement – Bernstein in the Films Division of the Ministry of Information during the Second World War, Forman at the pre-war GPO Film Unit under Grierson. They 'introduced Grierson's ideas into the heart of the contemporary media establishment' (Aitken, 1990: 4). Granada's commitment to 'social purpose' has been spearheaded by *World in Action* (Sendall and Potter, 1982: I, 346).

Like the work of Grierson, this has always followed a reformist political line (believing that access to information will lead to general societal improvement and the raising of mass consciousness).

World in Action's house style has always included dramatisation. Colin McArthur points out that Stephen Heath and Gillian Skirrow began debating the implications of this in *Screen* in 1977 (1980: 14–15). Granada personnel believed (and still believe) that abstract issues become more accessible by their being personalised. Forman himself acknowledged as much in 1966, noting that experts 'are seldom interesting unless they disagree emotionally. Intellectual disagreement is generally better expressed in the written word' (see Swallow, 1966: 217). The *World in Action* documentary tradition is almost identical to that which emerged in the BBC after the war and which I examined in Chapter 6.

HBO, in contrast, is a very modern media organisation. Launched in 1972 as an American cable television network, it is a division of Time Warner Entertainment. It had eighteen million subscribers in the USA in 1994 and has subsidiaries in South America, Asia, Scandinavia, Turkey and Eastern Europe. It also has agreements with national television companies both via network subsidiaries (for example, Granada International and BBC Lionheart in Britain) and with independents (such as Britain's World Productions). HBO's New York office, run by Colin Callendar, has been the prime mover in buying into the British dramadoc.

Todd Gitlin says scathingly that 'pay cable, dominated by Home Box Office, seems most interested in circulating Hollywood movies and their derivative forms' (1994: 329), but HBO has acquired a reputation for serious programme making through its documentary output and from its *Showcase* and *Saturday Night* slots. It was the first cable company to win an Oscar for a documentary, *Down and Out in America* (1987) and has attracted Emmy awards regularly. Cinemax, a division of HBO, produces made-for-TV movies and mini-series, and the company's commitment to the high-concept docudrama can be seen in such films as *The Simon Wiesenthal Story* (1989) and *And the Band Played On* (1993). The former was about Simon Wiesenthal, the famed Nazi-hunter who brought Adolf Eichmann (amongst others) to trial; the subject of the latter is the AIDS epidemic. HBO 'took over the project after NBC rejected it' (Horenstein *et al.*, 1994: 156). The company has also made films about Kennedy's assassination and the Vietnam War, both crucial markers of seriousness in American popular culture and history. When Home Box Office struck its 1990 co-production deal with Granada International, the agreement was one of its most extensive to date, eight co-productions being planned for the *Showcase* slot.[1]

1990s co-production

Dramadocs were revived at Granada because, as Ray Fitzwalter says: 'We believed we could do more popular subjects...and tougher subjects, things that were closer to home.'[2] As resources tightened, co-production facilitated the treatment of large-scale, ambitious subjects. Collaboration with HBO began in 1987 on *Tailspin* (US title)/*Coded Hostile* (UK), which was Granada/HBO's take on the shooting down of Korean Airlines flight KAL 007. 'This was very ritzily made,' its producer Leslie Woodhead says. 'High-profile actors, driving score – but it retains for me all the journalistic priorities which I'm completely comfortable with.' The Woodhead doctrine of journalistic priority was evident, too, in the 1990 *Who Bombed Birmingham?*, the story of the 'Birmingham Six', six men from Northern Ireland who were jailed in the UK in 1974 for allegedly perpetrating the IRA bombings in Birmingham the previous year. (HBO re-titled the film *Investigation: Inside a Terrorist Bombing*.) Taking up the research of Labour MP Chris Mullins, *World in Action* campaigned from 1985 for the men's case to be reopened, and the dramadoc built on all these layers of serious investigative journalism.[3] The men were eventually released by the Court of Appeal in late 1990. Clearly, the campaign that led to their release was multi-faceted, but the broadcasts themselves were a distinctive part of that campaign.[4]

Ian McBride, editor of *World in Action* at the time of the 1985 documentary, was himself impersonated in the drama-documentary by the actor Martin Shaw – an unusual occurrence for someone 'behind the scenes' – while Chris Mullins was played by John Hurt. A framed poster for the film on the wall of McBride's office at

Granada, signed by the grateful members of the Birmingham Six, is an emblem of the wider potential significance of the drama-documentary. Those who made *Who Bombed Birmingham?* at least have reason to believe in the power of '(re)trial by television'.

McBride, 'Head of Factual Drama' following restructuring in the 1990s, shares the journalistic background of the majority of Granada's dramadoc personnel. By contrast, *Hostages* producer Sita Williams, who was on the executive team in the early 1990s, had a training and background in drama. As a result, she focuses on the increasing importance of drama in the era of co-production:

> Essentially what you are striving to do is present something on the screen which is dramatically coherent, and is a story told through character...You can't make drama-documentary just with the journalists – people suggest all sorts of stories to me, and they're good stories, but there has to be a key. Not every good journalistic story can be translated into a piece of drama. Drama-documentary starts out in news broadcasts, something in the public domain. We have to see if it has 'documentary legs' – something new and different to say. More importantly, to justify its existence, it must have 'drama legs' too.

Five key questions have to be resolved before the drama-documentary format can be justified, in Williams' view:
1 Is it a viable [journalistic] story?
2 Can it be created out of the available material?
3 Is there documentary/is there drama?
4 Will simplifying produce a legal problem?
5 Will the amount of information produce a problem for the audience?

Answering these questions successfully, she says, demands 'a skill for knowing how the drama and the documentary will marry'.

Finding the 'story' is the province of the producers. The concept of 'the available material' highlights the practical roles of the producers as editorial controllers as well as production co-ordinators. They sort through material sourced from information retrieval systems elsewhere in the Granada organisation (including electronic and 'hard copy' archives only available to Granada researchers and journalists). Williams tellingly describes the knowledge acquired as 'real short-term memory stuff, like revising for an exam.' Research material is thus prepared for the dramatist, who receives it with some initial indication of narrative shape and a pre-assessment of the material.

One could argue the case of the dramatist in such projects in two contrasting ways: either they derive benefit from work previously done and acquire ownership of it as they shape it further; or conversely they are a kind of 'hired hand', lacking real ownership of the material. Whichever way one argues, dramatists are expected at the very least to familiarise themselves with the research material very quickly. There is no time to do much by way of their own research. Michael Eaton's case on Yorkshire Television's 1990 *Shoot to Kill* is instructive here. When he joined the project the journalists on the team had already done three years of research into the Stalker affair. It was his job to synthesise what was there. 'We are', Michael Eaton says of his fellow writers, 'structuralists rather than dramatists – producers want us to supply form and structure.' It would be fair to say that some writers enjoy the constraints that this inevitably induces, whereas others find them irksome.

The legal aspect, as we saw in Chapter 2, is becoming increasingly important. Leslie Woodhead can recall no legal problems on earlier Eastern European subjects, but that situation changed as soon as domestic subject matter was involved. His first legal problem was, significantly, with *Collision Course* (a 1979 reconstruction of a 1976 mid-air collision over Zagreb).

> We'd used the flight recorder for the last few minutes of the British Airways flight. An injunction was served by the [British Airline] Pilots' Association, whose representative was Norman Tebbit [later to become a Conservative cabinet minister],

Woodhead recalls. 'They took us to the High Court to ask whether we should use this tape, which was the copyright of BA. They lost.' But from this time onwards, all personnel confirm that legalling became more and more important. In the transformation of research documents into drama, Eaton notes drily, the writer can argue points with the journalist/researchers and even win occasionally, but in any argument with the lawyers 'the lawyer always wins'.

With the fifth of Williams' question, of course, we are in the realms of aesthetics. The journalistic imperative is clearly still fundamental to the Granada dramadoc tradition, but the demands of drama are now impacting strongly. In the new dispensation the shift to filmic discourse carries the danger of edging out discursive documentary elements. Richard Kilborn (1994), John Corner (1995 and 1996), and Julian Petley (1996) have all drawn attention to the present structuring of the form through templates drawn from fiction film: for example, the use of the 'international thriller' and 'disaster movie' genres in *Why Lockerbie?* (1990) and *Disaster at Valdez* (1991). (In the USA these films were titled *The Tragedy of Flight 103: The Inside Story*, and *Dead Ahead: the Exxon Valdez Disaster*.) *Hostages* was at times a buddy-movie with a documentary difference – at the outset nobody knew whether Butch and Sundance would survive – but it was also structured like a political thriller. Both McBride and Williams acknowledged the provenance of *JFK* and of *LA Law* in the making of *Fighting for Gemma* (a main storyline involving lawyer Martyn Day and his three associates in a legal firm). The BBC advertised *Hostile Waters* at its press preview in 1997 as 'a submarine action thriller, inspired by a true story' (the 1990 *Hunt for Red October* has a comparable structure).

British 'golden age' documentary dramas (*The War Game*; *Cathy Come Home*; *Days of Hope*; *Death of a Princess*) and drama-documentaries (*Invasion*; *Strike*) aimed for filmic 'looks' too. But it was the values of the documentary film, as well as its look, to which they primarily aspired. With fiction film genres driving the dramadoc towards the docudrama as never before, David Edgar (1993) has challenged the view that the documentary contains the originary power of the form:

> I have some doubts about the Granada team's insistence that they are, in fact, not plays but works of journalism carried on by other means. This could be taken to imply that journalism operates in the realm of pure and objective fact, as opposed to the supposed vagaries and subjectivities of drama, which seems to give television journalism a credit that almost no journalism is due. More profoundly, it also implies that people read drama-docs as docs rather than as dramas, whereas it seems to me that the power of the drama-documentary is in what precedes rather than follows the hyphen.

The detailed account of *Hostages* that follows will illustrate this comment.[5]

The example of *Hostages*

Because the story of *Hostages* centred on American captives in the Middle East as well as those from the British Isles, there was every reason to expect large audiences in the UK, the USA and, indeed, wherever the programme could be sold after its airing in the home countries of its producers. Not only did the film deal with a public issue, the very notion of 'ordinary' citizens being taken as unwilling representatives of their governments touched a very real fear in Western populations at the time.

Finance from HBO almost inevitably followed the selection of this high-profile, international subject. Colin Callendar, HBO's executive in charge of the *Hostages* project, said of the arrangement with Granada: 'We have never told Granada what they should make, or how they should make it. They come to us with a list of things they are going to do, we invest in the things we think are right for us' (*The Times*, 22 September 1992). Ray Fitzwalter commented to me that making drama-documentaries in Britain 'was less expensive for [HBO] than making [them] in America. All the company provided was half the finance and some editorial expertise.' HBO's funds offered additional flexibility, but Fitzwalter notes that 'making a drama-documentary was still about four times the cost of an equivalent documentary on the same subject'.

The hostage crisis had troubled Western governments ever since Muslim terrorist groups began using the tactic of taking hostages in 1980 and can be seen as one aspect of the wider, historical 'Middle East problem'. At the end of the 1980s a resolution of the crisis seemed no nearer. Although no television programme can be expected single-handedly to change the course of history, there was no reason why *Hostages* should not have become a major contribution to an honourable tradition in British television. At one stage during pre-production pretty well everyone directly involved in trying to get the hostages out (excepting governments) was agreed that the programme offered potentially useful publicity. The release of people who had been held captive in some cases for nearly ten years was the paramount consideration. Western governments, inclined like Margaret Thatcher to deny 'oxygen of publicity' to terrorists, were not so helpful; but then this too came with the *World in Action* territory of crusades for public information against the tendency of twentieth-century governments to be 'economical with the truth'.

Hostages was conceived by Alasdair Palmer, who started work on it in 1990 (Sita Williams recalls him doing 'all the initial research'). The 'natural' drama of Brian Keenan's press conference in Damascus on his release in 1990 was Palmer's starting-point: it had riveted him just as it had many who watched it. He developed a treatment and the process of production began. '*Hostages* started out as a campaigning film to get them out of Beirut,' Sita Williams recalled. Then, according to Ian McBride,

> it became clear that it might well be misunderstood by those holding them, and cause immense anguish and perhaps continued incarceration. So we put the whole thing to one side, with the occasional piece of 'care and maintenance'.

Palmer, who had personally invested a great deal in the project, took a break from it until December 1991, by which time Terry Anderson had been released.

Palmer had been with Granada since graduating from Cambridge in 1987. He worked as a journalist on *World in Action* and first experienced the drama-documentary as a researcher on *Why Lockerbie?* In 1990 an article in the *Guardian* convinced him that 'it was a natural thing, to write about this relationship between Brian Keenan and John McCarthy. And you couldn't do it as a documentary, you had to do it as a drama because John was still in captivity'. Palmer therefore wrote a treatment, a four-page document the essence of which was a character-based drama that made use of potential event programming (as hostages continued to be released). As a keen student of film he was alive to the generic possibilities of the project.

The most intractable problem was dramatising the situation in which hostages found themselves; they spent much of their time in darkness and boredom with, literally, nothing to do. Palmer recalled the initial reaction of the producers as one of uncertainty, their question being: 'How do you make two hours of darkness viable?' The answer effectively came from the research process itself. Denied access to one of the protagonists by circumstance (McCarthy was still incarcerated when the project began) and to the other (Keenan) by his antipathy to the project, Palmer felt 'you could come outside, where the women were doing this incredible work'. Further research opened different plot-lines, so that the hostages/captors/ Middle East plot was mirrored in a relatives/governments parallel plot. Action by the relatives, and orchestrated inaction by the governments, supplied vital contrasts and, crucially, female characters for the drama. Williams summarised the multiple appeal of the *Hostages* project:

> *Hostages* is not only the story of John McCarthy, Brian Keenan, Terry Anderson, Tom Sutherland and Frank Reed. It is also the story of how their friends and families fought to bring their plight to the attention of the world. And their fight was not principally against the hostage takers, theirs was a fight against governments who, like the British Government, said: 'We do not negotiate with terrorists' and did not; the American Government who said they would not negotiate and then were found to be trading 'Arms for Hostages' and in the case of Brian Keenan the Irish Government, the least powerful, and probably because of it, the most successful in negotiating his earlier release (Williams, 1994: 209).

The research process meant that Palmer and, later, Williams consulted widely over 'eighteen months of painstaking research' (Williams, 1994: 21). In addition to assistance from the normal agencies Palmer had help from the Irish Foreign Office, which facilitated a meeting with the Iranian ambassador in Bonn, who had been responsible for the release of Brian Keenan. He also met the Lebanese who arranged the release of the French hostages, with whom he also spoke. Jean-Paul Kauffman, one of the hostages he interviewed, had already appeared in a *This Week* documentary in 1988. This programme had reconstructed the 'mummifying' method of transporting the hostages around the Lebanon (see Chapter 6). Most important of all, he met the campaigning groups of relatives.

Campaigns had been launched, with varying degrees of public prominence, by Jill Morrell (John McCarthy's girlfriend) in Britain; by Peggy Say (Terry Anderson's sister) in America; and by Brian Keenan's sisters, Elaine Spence and Brenda Gillham in Ireland. Palmer contacted the campaigners, who were interested and prepared to help. At this point (1990), although Reed and Keenan had been released, Sutherland, McCarthy and Anderson were still in captivity. All the interest groups made warm noises because there was a strong possibility that the programme, if made, could help the cause of release. Palmer had direct contacts with Jill Morrell and the 'Friends of John McCarthy': 'I had to make a presentation to them. They were wonderful. Very dedicated people.' Jill Morrell herself followed up Palmer's initial approach to Keenan's agent. The agent, says Palmer, 'was quite interested', but his client was not. By this point, Keenan's opposition was becoming evident.

In many ways, Palmer's meeting in Boston with Frank Reed in late 1990 takes us to the heart of the difficulties likely to be encountered when drama-documentary anchors itself in portrayals of real people:

> Frank was half an hour early for the meeting, arranged by his agent, and we talked. He was very interesting about John. Then the agent arrived, and said, hold on, switch off the tape recorder, we've got to do the deal first! I explained it was for a television drama-documentary, and that Jill Morrell wanted to do it, and that we could buy Frank's time but no more than that – I mean we just don't buy people's stories, that's not what we're about. The agent said, we're looking at bids in excess of $1 million for this story. So that was the end of the meeting! But I had got a lot of interesting stuff about Brian and John, and about Frank's relationship with John.

In microcosm, this is what happened to Palmer subsequently with almost everyone, as the hostage crisis moved towards its conclusion in December 1991. As the historical process bore down on the individual protagonists of this international news drama, everyone was being drawn into a situation where their (bitter) experience was, ironically, becoming their major asset. Protection of this asset caused *Hostages* to cross the cultural line between worthy campaigning film and controversial invasion of private rights.

I have already mentioned the agents of Keenan and Reed; as time went on, all the protagonists acquired agents to protect their capacity to market their stories. So, Peggy Say, to whom Palmer talked in Washington, was initially helpful before her book. Then he 'ran into the same problems with her agent, too'. After McCarthy's release in August Jill Morrell facilitated a meeting with Palmer in London in December 1991: 'He talked very freely and openly and so did Jill... It was great to meet him and get a sense of him.' Palmer felt that both made it clear at the meeting that, although they were not in favour of the film and were unwilling to back it, they did not intend to take action to oppose its transmission. But then the ex-hostage's agent Mark Lucas began to try to win a veto on the *Hostages* project by threatening legal action. He sought (and obtained) disclaimers from those 'Friends of John McCarthy' who had already spoken to Palmer (who found it 'all very unpleasant, because I knew and liked these people').

The project was by now locked into the Granada/HBO co-production deal. It had a writer (who was busy drafting scripts) and a director, and the casting process was well under way. From the point of view of the people mainly concerned with the project, two years' worth of work was already at stake. The impetus towards production was substantial by this time, and it was certainly enough to carry the film to completion. Resources had been committed; *Hostages* had reached a point of no return. Palmer continued with the research; there was another meeting with Frank Reed in America and in the New Year a four-hour interview with Tom Sutherland in Scotland:

> He was just out. It was like someone who had just had enormous pressure taken off him. In a way he was the most helpful of all because the experience was very fresh and he'd been with all of them, and he was one of the last to be released.

McCarthy, understanding all too well the strain of post-traumatic stress, worried about Sutherland's co-operation with Granada :

> I was... very disappointed when Tom, eager to accommodate all-comers, spoke to Granada, after all. I was deeply troubled that he was taking the attention and adulation too much to heart. I tried to explain to him that

while all the warmth and affection was quite genuine, it wasn't based on who we really were, but on the symbolic value which we seemed to have acquired. (McCarthy and Morrell, 1994: 613)

Hostages writer, Bernard MacLaverty, incorporated the Sutherland material into his final draft, and the company met for a read-through in Manchester at the end of March 1992.

An impressive cast was assembled by Sita Williams. The subject and the script had attracted Americans Kathy Bates (Peggy Say), Harry Dean Stanton (Frank Reed), Josef Sommer (Tom Sutherland), and Jay O. Sanders (Terry Anderson) – all actors with international reputations. Williams remarked: 'The scales between cinema and television are quite different... I wouldn't have got Kathy Bates and Harry Dean Stanton for the kind of fee I did if *Hostages* had been a feature film.' *Hostages* cost in the region of £1.5 million to make, at least partly because of the presence of 'Oscar-winner Kathy Bates', as the tabloids tended to refer to her. English actors Colin Firth (John McCarthy) and Natasha Richardson (Jill Morrell) and Irishman Ciaran Hinds (Brian Keenan) completed a cast that, if not precisely 'star-studded', certainly represented the very best in Anglo-American film acting. Hinds had already worked for the Granada team, playing Richard McIllkenny in their 1989 dramadoc *Who Bombed Birmingham?*. Firth too was familiar with portraying living people, having played Robert Lawrence in Charles Wood's film about the Falklands War, *Tumbledown* (BBC, 1987).

Hostages was rehearsed over a seven-day period in March and April, then filmed in Manchester and Israel between 7 April and 12 May 1992. Post-production continued through the summer, and the programme was transmitted in the UK in September 1992 and in the USA in February 1993. Meanwhile, Mark Lucas in Palmer's words, 'never let up... I could understand why he was doing it – it was financially driven. He thought, I can't sell the film rights to this book if they've done a film without [those rights].' For his part, Lucas claimed, that Granada's motives were similarly pecuniary: 'It's been a cynical, fiscal exercise by Granada in getting the story before anyone else, doing its own version and not paying anyone for it' (*Sunday Times*, 20 September 1992). McCarthy sent his own letters to Granada requesting withdrawal of the film and said: 'I have made my opposition clear to Granada and I am saddened they are still going ahead' (*Daily Telegraph*, 19 September 1992).[6]

McCarthy first went public with his opposition on 2 February 1992. An article in the *Sunday Times* (headlined '"Exploited" McCarthy seeks ban on TV hostage drama') quoted Keenan's agent, Antony Howard, as saying that Keenan was 'uncomfortable and unhappy' with the project. He also claimed that Mike Beckham (producer-director of *Why Lockerbie?*) had made false statements about Keenan's alleged co-operation. Beckham himself denied this. Ray Fitzwalter refuted the notion that the project now lacked credibility: 'We have done a great deal of work over many months and are entitled to bring it to conclusion ... We have had the co-operation of a vast number of people.'

All the controversy culminated in the letter quoted in the Introduction (page 11), in which McCarthy, Keenan, Waite and Anderson accused Granada of 'grossly misleading the public'. Their major contention was that 'of the six hostages portrayed in the film Granada ha[d] spoken to just two, Frank Reed and Tom Sutherland'. This being so, there could be no 'legitimate basis on which to claim that they ha[d] a "full story for the first time" [as pre-publicity stated]'. The letter goes on to make one emotional and one somewhat naïve but ostensibly rational appeal. First, emotionally, the signatories wonder 'how Granada and HBO can think they have the right to produce a story, reporting [*sic*] to be true, before those at the centre of it have come to terms with it themselves'. Second, they make a distinction between a researched/factual and a 'true' story, saying *Hostages* 'is only partly factual': 'We feel Granada and their American co-producers must explain this to their audiences and also make plain that we four have no part in the film's production.'

There is, perhaps, one further aspect to a crisis of this type. Just as individuals find themselves in a 'slowed down' state after a traumatic event, like a traffic accident for example, so something similar seems to occur in a national collective consciousness after an event that cannot be readily assimilated or comprehended. Dramadocumentaries are the visible evidence of this state in a culture. All dramadoc/docudrama, by this definition, is 'trauma drama' – by which collective guilt, paranoia and vicarious suffering is picked over and examined and anxiety about it quelled. This concept is key to an understanding of the new generation of dramadoc/docudrama. It explains why *Hostages*, even for those who did not watch it, became such a *cause célèbre*.

UK – 'Drama out of suffering'

All the publicity had a very direct effect on the reception of the film. During the week of transmission, many newspapers in Britain carried the story of the hostages' opposition to *Hostages*. The *Independent* of 19 September summarised the main difficulty: 'The moral question: should McCarthy's life have been seized again by Granada TV for the purposes of entertainment?' All the national newspapers that week wrestled with this dilemma. On 22 September the *Independent* condemned the television company in a leader article – 'Drama out of suffering' – which alleged that Granada was 'guilty of distressing insensitivity'. Interestingly, the tabloids were less censorious, the *Daily Mirror* telling its readers on the day of transmission (23 September): 'Some may think it simply turns the victims' dreadful experience into entertainment. Judge for yourselves.'

On the same day the Granada production team – Palmer, Williams, McBride and Fitzwalter – replied to the hostages' letter, again in the *Guardian*. Much of their reply is taken up with refutation at the level of fact: there was, for example, no evidence that Reed and Sutherland were misled ('as Mr Reed's lawyer...can confirm'); most of the factual material had 'entered the public record' and was uncontentious; the disclaimer demanded was already in the film. The writers counter-claimed that they had never stated that *Hostages* was the 'true story'.[7] The producers concluded with their own questions:

> The issue is: exactly which account will be the 'true' or 'full' story? Will it be Brian Keenan's, to be published the day after our film is transmitted? John McCarthy's? Terry Anderson's? Terry Waite's? Who will reconcile the inevitable differences? And how? Could any account, written from a specific standpoint, be the 'full' story?

It is interesting, incidentally, that it was the producers (rather than the writer or the director) who took responsibility for defending the film.

As might be expected of someone with a good deal of experience of (re)presenting living people in performance, Colin Firth had some interesting reflections on these matters. English newspapers of the week of transmission quoted extensively from his remarks at a fairly hostile press preview of *Hostages*. In the *Daily Express* Firth defended the film: 'I think John McCarthy has become something of a folk hero...He captured the public imagination, because a man who emerges from a horror with such immense charm is inspirational to thousands of people' (19 September 1992). He went on to claim that it was actually 'the most balanced account of the events because we're independent collectors of information'. In the *Daily Telegraph* he said: 'We are dealing with a very interesting and public story which in a way held us all to ransom, and we want to understand its effect on us' (19 September 1992). *Hostages* generated enough attention for the same edition of the *Daily Telegraph* to say elsewhere: 'The row will undoubtedly boost audience figures.'[8]

This should have been the case, for, as Ian McBride says, 'Dramadocumentary's power has to do with whether the audience are attracted to the subject.' But advance publicity for *Hostages* seems to have convinced the audience that it should not be attracted to this subject. The private view of the producers is that *Hostages* underperformed precisely because of the intervention of the real hostages and the resulting furore. In Alasdair Palmer's view:

> The effect was very much to stop people watching it. We were all very disappointed in the viewing figures. I think it was two things: partly the 'anti' campaign, also something to do with it being very tough viewing in midweek.

Sita Williams recalls: 'there was a huge amount of press interest...I've never worked on a programme which created more press and media interest. I was never off the phone'. And yet the publicity was, she is convinced, 'a turn-off factor'. *Hostages* was watched by an audience of 6.7 million (representing a twenty-nine per cent audience share). By contrast, *Fighting for Gemma* (shown a

year later in the same *World in Action* slot – Wednesday, 8.00–
10.00 pm), had an audience of eight million and a share of thirty-
five per cent. Both Williams and Palmer pronounce themselves
proud of *Hostages*, even if the viewing figures did not go as high as
they had once hoped.

USA – 'Struggles…in a larger context'

To Williams, the American press and media reaction was 'entirely
different…[from] the mealy-mouthed knocking we got here'. The
film was received in the USA with more openness, some enthusiasm
and very little concern about media intrusion into the lives of
private citizens. *Hostages* was first transmitted by HBO on 20 February 1993 (a Saturday) and was repeated six times during the following three weeks of February and March. February is an important
month in US television, for one of the yearly 'sweeps', in which
ratings are calculated, takes place then. Networks often seek to
boost their viewing numbers by screening programmes with known
rating value or that will be easy to publicise. *USA Today* welcomed
the film as 'an HBO specialty: the investigative docudrama' (19 February 1993).

Whereas four hostages had condemned the film in the UK, HBO
found one to endorse it at their press showings. Tom Sutherland was
widely quoted in the American press, saying: 'The movie is stark
and realistic' (*USA Today*, 19 February 1993). In the *Boston Herald*
on the same day he said: 'it comes as close as is humanly possible to
showing what we went through', and in the *Fort Lauderdale Sun-
Sentinel* he went further: 'Frankly I was kind of shocked at the
reality of it. I watched in amazement. To see somebody re-creating
what we had been through so vividly and so accurately, I was
kind of blown away' (19 February 1993). Terry Anderson, a co-
signatory of the *Guardian* letter, also approved, or so Sutherland
claimed in an interview with Tom Feran of the *Cleveland Plain Dealer*
on 20 February:

> When I saw this movie, I thought, 'My God, that's really well done.' So
> I called [Anderson] and said, 'Have you seen it?' He said no, so I sent

him a copy and called back. He said, 'I just talked to my agent at NBC a couple of minutes ago and told them, 'You guys have to come up with a good movie because you've got a damn good one to beat here.

In the *Washington Post* Sutherland tempers all this praise some-what, noting that the requirement of compression can increase the drama to a level that was not present in the real situation (it was, he says, 'just boring and frustrating as hell'), but it is clear that he sup-ports the film generally and gives it his 'blessing' (17 February 1993).

A fascination with the documentary values of the Granada team's style can be found in virtually all the American reviews pub-lished in the week of transmission, and this contrasts interestingly with the British press's obsession with the contaminating presence of the drama. *USA Today*, for example, praises the film's 'astringent objectivity', while the *Seattle Post-Intelligencer*'s critic (19 February 1993) praises the 'careful, ethical approach'. In her lengthy article for *New York Newsday* on 18 February Diane Werts contrasts the America docudrama unfavourably. She observes that, while Ameri-can network television 'might try hard to personalize the situation – using long scenes among the hostages to have us identify with one or more of them', the Granada programme 'goes a more complex route… Instead of a few expansively telling moments, we're given hundreds of brief snapshots with which to piece together our own understanding of the situation.' John J. O'Connor in the *New York Times* echoes Wert's praise for previous HBO co-productions with British drama-documentary makers and notes the care with which the script 'keeps placing the struggles of the hostages in the larger context of Mideast and world politics' (19 February 1993). In *Weekly Variety* Todd Everett finds a cryptic tabloid formulation for all this: 'The gripping production cleverly mixes news footage with topflight thesping' (17 February).

The American tabloid press connects the cast list quite frequently to their major movie successes: Kathy Bates to her Oscar-winning role in *Misery* (1990); Jay O. Sanders (Anderson) in terms of *JFK* (1991); Josef Sommer (Sutherland) to *Witness* (1985); Ciaran Hinds (Keenan) to *The Cook, the Thief, His Wife and Her Lover* (1989); Colin Firth (McCarthy) to *Valmont* (1989); and Natasha Richardson

(Morrell) to *The Comfort of Strangers* (1990). Even Conrad Asquith, who plays Terry Waite very briefly in the film, is mentioned in connection with his part in the film *White Hunter, Black Heart* (1990). Harry Dean Stanton (Reed) is described in *Entertainment Weekly* (14 February 1993) as a 'veteran character actor' (while *Weekly Variety* pronounces him 'able to communicate more with his back to the camera than many actors can in several pages of script').

Some reviewers did raise criticisms similar to those voiced in Britain. John Engstom remarked: 'If "Hostages" falls short, it may be because it follows so many characters through so many years' (*Seattle Post-Intelligencer*, 19 February 1993). The 'under-use' of the women was remarked upon both in *USA Today* and in *Entertainment Weekly* (which called Bates and Richardson 'peripheral figures'). Only Jeff Jarvis of *TV Guide* (20–26 February) seemed troubled by the furore that dominated the British press, noting that the film was 'not the authorized story of any single hostage'.

The *Hostages* crisis

The film's shortcomings as drama are probably what limited its appeal in the USA, but the failure of *Hostages* in Britain followed its crossing into forbidden territory. John McCarthy's and Brian Keenan's opposition to the making of *Hostages*, in marked contrast to Tom Sutherland's enthusiasm, was clearly crucial. In popular culture they were hero/martyrs; their records of personal experience (part historical record, part personal therapy) were received almost with reverence. This is evident in Colin Firth's respectful handling of his relationship with his real-life other:

> I thought about getting in touch with John but it boiled down to asking for some sort of absolution. I wanted to say to him, whatever control you want over this film, just tell me. You develop a sort of love for the character you play, but in this case it was a scorned love. (*Daily Telegraph*, 19 September 1992)

The Granada film unwittingly interfered in this private (and public) process – and it paid the price.

All the hostages' accounts – in very different ways – are vivid documents, and none more so than Keenan's 1992 book *An Evil Cradling*. But Keenan maintains a silence about the film and its reception. McCarthy, however, in *Some Other Rainbow* has an account of what might be termed 'the *Hostages* crisis'. In his part of the book he first alludes to it on page 585, implying that Keenan's opposition to the Granada project virtually compelled his own as a result of two factors. First, after their release he and Keenan still needed each other's support. Second, there was 'a decision we had all made in captivity...not [to] get involved in any dramatic representations of our years as hostages until we were all free'. McCarthy's decision to oppose the film, whenever it was taken, clearly reinforced Keenan's (and Keenan's implacable dislike of *Hostages* showed McCarthy that he 'wasn't the only one with worries'). For McCarthy, the most painful part of all this was the fact that Keenan was opposed to something Morrell and Chris Pearson (of the 'Friends of John McCarthy') had once approved: 'I was trying desperately hard to reconcile the world I now lived in with the world I had lived in as a hostage, yet my greatest friends from those two worlds were divided by a misunderstanding.'

McCarthy refers to the film as 'a recurring irritation' (McCarthy and Morrell, 1994, 612). Morrell, giving her account, acknowledges her part in the early plans for the film, but claims:

> When John was released...I believed that the situation had changed so dramatically that the film would be redundant. Chris [Pearson] told Granada that we would no longer be involved, and we believed that the film would not go ahead. (McCarthy and Morrell, 1994, 616)

She also tries to discredit *Hostages* by criticising the way McCarthy is 'curiously transformed from producer to reporter' in the first scene (see Chapter 3, page 71).

Sita Williams not only refutes his charge of inaccuracy (again, see the account in Chapter 3), she feels that:

> it's really neither here nor there, what was important was the irony, that was much more interesting. The irony that he was doing a report about Brian Keenan just before he was kidnapped and he then ends up

in captivity with him! I think that's what that scene is about. And it was fact that he submitted this report.

Williams has no time for what she calls the 'slippery slope argument' (by which critics want one wrong detail to discount everything). In her view the clear focus in this scene is dramatic not documentary, and to argue otherwise is perversely to miss the point.

Morrell's difficulty with the film – indeed the whole 'inner circle' view of it – is probably best summed up by her frank acknowledgement: 'I felt guilty that I had contributed to something that was putting [John] under such strain; our correspondence with Granada, the stories in the press and the prospect of the programme itself cast a shadow over us until the film was shown' (McCarthy and Morrell, 1994: 616). On Granada's side there was no such 'guilt', the producers believing that the film, as 'a dramatisation of events which illustrate[d] circumstances and attitudes and show[ed] context', still had a part to play in public understanding of the hostage crisis, and that: 'No one ha[d] an exclusive right to a story which [was] in the public domain' (Williams, 1994: 210, 212).

By contrast, in July 1992 a play called *Someone Who'll Watch Over Me* by the Irish playwright Frank McGuinness opened at the Hampstead Theatre Club in London. It was strongly endorsed by Keenan. Set in an unnamed but clearly Middle Eastern country, it depicts three men – the Englishman, Irishman and American of popular joke and mythology – chained to the walls of an undifferentiated cell. Its link to the Beirut hostages was evident and, like *Hostages*, its marketing when it transferred into London's West End depended upon its proximity to real recent events. Unlike *Hostages*, however, it used fictional names for its protagonists – Adam, Michael, Edward.

Before the play was produced at the Abbey Theatre, Dublin, Keenan himself supplied an Introduction to what was effectively a new edition set up specifically to incorporate his endorsement. He explains: 'Though he had no information on which to base his play, I could see that he had the touchstones of emotional truth' (1992b: 1). Keenan's warm regard for the play is clear; indeed, the prose blazes with his feeling for it – like the writing in his own memoir. Equally clear is the value he sets upon the imaginative truth of

Someone Who'll Watch Over Me. Although he never mentions *Hostages*, the film is in the background of Keenan's endorsement of 'emotional truth' (over 'information') and most evident when he says that the play 'touched wellsprings that moved the drama out of its vague topicality and sang to Everyman' (1992b: 2).

The essence of Granada's claim to the hostage story, however, was that it had an overview unavailable to those directly involved in events in Beirut. From the outset the *Hostages* team had tried conscientiously to cover this angle. In his treatment Alasdair Palmer does examine the general context; on the first page, he writes:

> The aim [of the film] is not only to depict the culture of terrorism. It is also to provide insight into an alien but crucially important aspect of Muslim/Iranian psychology – an aspect the people and governments of Britain and America have so far totally failed to comprehend.

The production team's own admission that the documentary claims of multiple narrative interfered with the potential of the drama offers a corrective to Keenan's view on emotional truth. The problem for the programme *Hostages* was that the historical hostages came to represent an excess in Bill Nichols' terms: 'If excess tends to be that which is beyond narrative in fiction films, excess in documentary is that which stands beyond the reach of both narrative and exposition' (1991: 142). Excess in *Hostages* was evident in both the documentary and the drama; it was in the history itself, which can exceed representation precisely because it is not, as postmodernism would have us believe, simply narrative.

The reaction to *Hostages* in Britain caused by the exchange of letters of 21 and 22 September 1992 fatally affected the transmission of the film on 23 September. This exchange had the effect of locating the film within a discourse of what might be called the 'privacy of suffering'. The campaigning film of the producers' intentions had been dragged unwittingly into the arena of discussions about the intrusiveness of television. Here its promise of insight into cruel captivity had been superseded in its truth claim by the witness discourse of the hostages themselves. Some of this can be perceived in Hugh Hebert's review of the film in the *Guardian* (24 September).

First of all, Hebert praises the programme's conscientious setting of the hostage crisis in its political context and notes that this aspect 'was almost totally lost in the emotional bonfires lit by the carefully graduated release of the captives'. But he goes on to claim that '*Hostages* misses on what television drama ought to be able to do, get inside the heads of its characters. The more you stick to known facts, the more difficult that becomes'. This is echoed elsewhere in the British press response to the film. Sita Williams believes that the critical move that constructs a programme as bad documentary or bad drama (or both) is not as evident in the tabloid press as it is in the broadsheets. This claim is not borne out in the case of the reviews of *Hostages*; in the *Sun*, for example, Garry Bushell wrote that it was 'more than a play but too full of guesswork to stand as a documentary' (24 September 1992).

The real argument here was not about whether McCarthy and Keenan should be portrayed against their will but about the nature of public sacrifice on a political stage by people who were previously in the habit of regarding themselves only as private citizens. Taken as hostages for political purposes by the proponents of one side of a global ideological argument and isolated as part of the rejection of this tactic by the other (their own?) side in that argument, these individuals became modern martyrs in a global village where any-one might be called to account at any time for the wider actions of the society of which they are a part. As Paula Rabinowitz has noted: 'The invention of the individual witness whose personal story serves as a template for history has been crucial to twentieth-century Western accounts of atrocity and war' (1994: 107–8). And the hostage crisis was, like it or not, part of a war.

No wonder, then, that no one dared criticise these secular martyrs. The quasi-religious idea that only they could tell us about the pain of their experience, and set that pain in an existential context, was very strong at the time. All of them have tried to do these things in their books; Keenan, pre-eminently, has succeeded to an extraordinary degree. What is difficult for all of them, however, is to place their experience in contexts beyond the purely personal. *Hostages*, by its very existence, thrust some unarticulated questions into the public domain in 1992, and this is why it gave offence to so many (when it would have been hailed as a campaigning film had it been transmitted a year earlier). Watching the film began to seem like a violation of the martyrs' suffering – a metaphorical thrusting of hands into open wounds.

The proximity to contemporary events and recent history is, then, simultaneously a strength and a weakness for the dramadoc/ docudrama. It provides the form with its 'pre-sold' element at the economic, and justification at the ethical, levels. Audiences tend to accept programmes if it can be clearly seen that means justify ends. But the opening up of a problem in the real, historical world means that the problem must continue to exist, at least until the time of transmission. Popular genre formats can make dramas more accessible to audiences but complicate documentary claims. The 'tidying up' of plots and compositing of characters demonstrate the incapacity of drama to accommodate to at least some of the complexities of 'real history' and 'real sociology'.

Conclusion

The HBO co-productions also show, if they show anything, not just how the high-concept programme has accommodated to cinema but how it can rival it in terms of production values and in its use of generic structures. Compared with the low-concept, melodramatic US docudrama, these co-productions are, to coin a phrase, 'hand-crafted'. Their budgets may not be big by the standards of blockbuster films, but they are large in comparison with the run of made-for-TV movies. As the American reviews of *Hostages* show, these films have found their market through HBO, and an appreciative audience is aware of both their seriousness and their claim of superiority. The humbler docudrama is likely, in its low-concept way, to exhibit more modest production values; it is the mass-manufactured, production-line, low-budget staple of network television. This is not, however, to dismiss it out of hand. Both dramadoc and docudrama satisfy particular kinds of desire and offer particular kinds of pleasure. Chapter 8 will examine the pleasures of third-phase dramadoc/docudrama, and consider possibilities for development in the twenty-first century.

Futures – only one way to tell it?

'Competitive fictions' – theorising the third phase

'No other way to tell it' is still a useful phrase in terms of justifying the access sought by television journalism to real-life events, but now that American drama practices dominate the co-production aesthetic, 'only one way to tell it' may become just as accurate. The major dramatic means of (re)presenting events that were un-available to cameras the first time around remains pretty exclusively naturalism/social realism. I argued in Chapter 6 that the dramadoc is 'a very British' genre and the docudrama 'a very American' one. Today, both are determinedly social realist, but journalistic input into the dramadoc still gives it more claim to documentary power. Current attenuation of the directly documentary, paralleled with increased accommodation to drama, is the clearest sign of the present predominance of the 'docudramatic' over the 'drama-documentary'.

For the latest manifestations of the docudramatic, it is always necessary to look first at American rather than British practice – at trauma dramas, for example: 'domestic melodramas in which private ills are centred in the family' (Feuer, 1995: 31). Rarely offer-ing solutions at a macro-societal level, they articulate what Jane Feuer calls 'social discontent' within micro-situations concerning individuals and/or families. Janet Steiger makes the telling comment: 'One of the most favored effects [of their 'melodramatic structures'] … is tears' (1997: 516). Rod Carveth, on the other hand, believes that the American docudrama now comes in two basic forms. The older form is 'the historical docudrama, a fictionalized re-telling of a period of history', which 'benefit[s]from the perspective of time passage' (in that events depicted within it are widely known). It derives from the historical film and the biopic. The newer form he calls not trauma drama but 'headline docudrama' (Carveth, 1993: 121).

Like the 'Long Island Lolita' trilogy, this kind of film is 'based on events that have occurred much closer to their airing', according to Carveth. Headline docudramas tend to rely on sensational newspaper stories that are transformed into plays and transmitted within a few years of their occurrence. They mimic the headline stories which are their principal source. Everyone who writes on the form comments on the increasing speed and dangers of the docu-dramatic response to news (see also, for example, Rosenthal, 1995: 3, 10–11). Three kinds of ethical danger, according to Carveth, attend headline docudramas: they 'may compromise the legal positions of the principals'; they often 'ignore the social and political forces surrounding an event'; and 'the act of adapting an event to standard narrative formulas changes reality in the process'. Also, producers 'are moving more quickly to secure rights', indulging in what is sometimes known as chequebook journalism (Carveth, 1993: 123–5). Protecting themselves legally by using real-world protagonists as consultants at the point of production, they buy the rights to a point of view rather than subscribing to an older journalistic notion of an 'objective' account of events in the news.

David Edgar has another name for these films: 'competitive fictions'.[1] The 'Long Island Lolita' films illustrate this concept: NBC paid Fisher's bail for collaboration on their film; CBS financed Joey Buttafuoco and his wife to get their 'angle'; and ABC used transcripts of the trial and a rapidly written book. The end-result was three films offering a multiple perspective on this headline story. But the ideal of former times – objective Truth – was arguably not as important to producers as the tabloid 'urban tragedy/sensation' news value of the story. So, NBC's disclaimer (quoted on pages 66–7) admitted that only the protagonists knew the truth; CBS's film simply (and blandly) reminded its audience: 'A Current Affair Reenactment Is Not Verbatim.' ABC's film nods cutely in the direction of a disavowed absolute by observing that there are three sides to the story: 'his, hers and the truth' (as I remarked in Chapter 3, the convention of the disclaimer gets more and more knowing).

The headline docudrama is an eloquent demonstration of the principle that the personal has become the financially expedient: the competitive fiction raises the stakes all round. An individual experience ratified by news coverage is sufficient guarantee of audience interest to put these personal stories into production. In the words of the American executive Mark Sennett, the attraction is in 'stories of people who've been through everybody's nightmare'. John Matoian, CBS executive in charge of made-for-TV movies and mini-series, comments: 'I suppose these are as hard and difficult times as ever, and people are looking for windows into behaviour.'[2]

The HBO co-productions offer a high-concept alternative. Michael Eaton, in his 1996 Birmingham conference paper, put the potential of the dramadoc approach still taken in these films in one sentence: 'In drama-documentary you can throw light into dark places, and show large audiences the way power is exercised.' 'Drama-documentary', in Ian McBride's polished phrase, 'takes the camera where the camera, seemingly, can't go,' and in so doing gives privileged access to events. The viewers may not even need to be convinced that a film shows exactly how it was, but if they are drawn to the programme at all, and even partially convinced by a 'new light' claim, then they will be drawn into ongoing public debate. Leslie Woodhead believes that this democratising method is still working: 'I still take the view after a decade that [HBO's] input has been positive and revitalising. They've surprised me by being even more demonic about information and scripts than we are.'

While acknowledging the vast difference in filmic 'look' over the decade between *Three Days in Szczecin* and *Why Lockerbie?*, Woodhead regards tapping into associations other than those of factual/ current affairs programming as part of the new media territory. He still believes too that, ultimately, the drama matters less than the making of a journalistic point:

Where there is a collision between journalistic values and dramatic values, journalism has to win. If the priority is to bring these things to

the attention of a mass audience, to collide with territories of the twentieth century that they wouldn't otherwise collide with, then it doesn't
matter if the play's bad.[3]

As far as the effects on the dramadoc of Anglo-American co-
production are concerned, Woodhead compared the different
emphases given in Britain and the USA to the final, tragic, section of
Why Lockerbie?/The Tragedy of Flight 103. In the British ending, as
the Pan Am jumbo goes down over Lockerbie, the dot that symbol-
ises it disappears off the radar screen. The film then cuts to roses on
the graves in Lockerbie churchyard and the memorial service. For
HBO producers:

> our ending was too muted. They didn't want bodies tumbling out of the
> sky, but they wanted to feel something about what had been done, so
> they went for about a minute of archive of blazing rooftops and fire
> brigades and policemen rushing round in the night in Lockerbie village.
> It's not a sleazy ending, just a different one, and was a very interesting
> difference of reading of what their audience wanted. It's a kind of cul-
> tural collision, where we can cope with the interiorising of our feelings
> but they feel like they're being short-changed.

It could be on just such a basis that the best in both traditions of the
British dramadoc and the American docudrama will continue to
meet. However, Ian McBride has begun to take the more pessimistic
view that: 'The dramadoc was always journalism of the last resort,
which gave the audience a wide picture of the unglimpsed. But
these "people stories" are journalism of the first resort.'

Good or bad, dramadoc/docudrama remains ubiquitous in the
schedules. Alan Rosenthal notes that forty-three out of 115 movies
shown in the first season of 1992 in the USA and seven out of the
top ten made-for-TV movies of 1991 fit this category. HBO's co-
production agreements are a kind of industry ratification of his
view that 'the public loves docudrama' (1995: 9–10). There is, however, a sneering notion in critical circles that the pleasures of the
made-for-TV movie in all its forms are those of a 'woman's genre',
through which anything serious is first domesticated then trivi-
alised. Laurie Schulze points to the (mostly male) critical move that

unproblematically shifts a negative critique of value to condescending comment on the (presumed female) consumer: 'a female audience is taken to task by popular criticism to strike another blow against what is perceived to be a nonaesthetic and morally defective form of popular culture' (1990: 355). Such a critical move sees documentary as inevitably more important and serious than drama. To borrow from feminist theory, documentary (and its serious offshoot British dramadoc) is a 'masculinised' form; drama (and its trivial offshoot American docudrama) is 'feminised'. Such a move also downgrades any pleasure that might be available to audiences of American docudrama.

Documentary desires/drama pleasures

It is no surprise to find female commentators making more sense of third-phase dramadoc/docudrama than their male counterparts. Seeing docudrama as a trivialising form is a commonplace of much male commentary. In trying to offer a corrective to this view, I will follow Carol Gilligan's use of the terms 'masculine' and 'feminine'. She employs them to: 'highlight a distinction between two modes of thought and...focus a problem of interpretation' (1982: 2).[4] Disparagement of American docudrama tends to mask any potential the form might have by consigning it to the realm of a feminised 'not-serious' (always opposite to a masculinised 'serious'). However, as Schulze remarks, the docudrama nevertheless shows itself as consistently 'capable of pushing at the limits of the controversial without losing its audience' (1990: 364). The nature of this 'pushing at the limits' demands a more nuanced critical methodology than is commonly offered by those who favour documentary and dismiss drama.

Documentary has what Bill Nichols calls: 'kinship with...other nonfictional systems – science, economics, politics, foreign policy, education, religion, welfare'.[5] These serious systems share the 'discourse of sobriety'. Such a discourse has a natural antipathy, he says, towards '"make-believe" characters, events, or entire worlds (unless they serve as pragmatically useful simulations of the "real" one)'. Note that word 'pragmatically': it provides the rubric under which dramadoc/docudrama makes its documentary claim (there being 'no other way to tell it', dramatised forms fill the gap). Although the discourse of sobriety 'operates where the reality-attentive ego and superego live', Nichols is rather reticent on desire for, and pleasure in, sober discourses (Nichols, 1991: 3–4). But I would agree with Michael Renov, who comments that the documentary conscience of ego and superego, in seeking special knowledge or understanding, expresses 'an explicit "documentary desire"' (1993: 5).

Elizabeth Cowie has defined this further as 'the desire for the evidence of our own eyes'. She divides it into two complementary urges: 'the desire for a symbolic or social reality produced and ordered as signification' and 'the desire for the real imaged in film' (1997: 2). Documentary sight claims special insight; it is pointed at in performance, proffered at the point of reception and eagerly embraced by those seekers-after-truth who constitute its audience. The naming of this desire of the seeker-after-truth is an important precondition for reading not only the documentary but also the dramadoc/docudrama.

Pleasures inherent in the sober and serious contemplation of information are what I would term 'puritan pleasures'. There is a seriousness of purpose in such activity before which the concept of mere pleasure, it would seem, must bow and retreat. But the pleasure in seriousness is deeply implicated in pathologies of surveillance and control that reach back into the nineteenth century. There is risk in puritan pleasures, dramatised by Shakespeare through his Angelo character in *Measure for Measure*. Angelo's 'syndrome' is that pathological tendency which, operating overtly with cold rationality and control, covertly desires their warm opposites. It is a suspect, not to say doomed, tendency, as Shakespeare shows very clearly.

Nichols argues that documentary 'spawns an epistephilia', or a reliance on knowledge and on words and language. Its communication circuit involves 'an organizing agency that possesses information and knowledge, a text that conveys it, and a subject who will gain it' (Nichols, 1991: 31). The implied audience for this occupies, in Susan Scheibler's resonant phrase, 'an omnipotent and omniscient' spectator role (Renov, 1993: 136). I believe the puritan pleasures of omnipotence and omniscience are dominantly gendered masculine, if only because the masculine has been the social domain of such surveillance and control in the nineteenth and twentieth centuries.[6] The public service ethic in broadcasting and the arts, which acknowledges both a responsibility to inform and a belief in the ability of human agency to effect social change, is a part of this masculinised domain. Documentary pleasure derives from a social self (part of, but separate from, the private self) that takes pleasure in public duty.

Quite different desires and pleasures are associated with the imitation, simulation and impersonation that result from fictional discourses, such as drama – the imitation of an action intended to connect with a community in a rather different sense. Nichols remarks that fiction, with its interest in unconscious desires and fears, 'operates where the id lives'. The pleasure of a play is in the extent to which an audience can move in and out of belief-in-the-illusion, even while it is unfolding. This feature is inherent in all dramatic conventionalisation. The pleasure that follows derives from an imaginative response to the claim to the 'life-like'. This is an outrageous claim, when all is said and done, but one that retains a formidable psychic power still evident in our regular 'willing suspension of disbelief' as we encounter film and stage fictions. It becomes a supportable claim whenever certain recognised cultural conventions are adequately observed by performers then ratified by an audience in the communal moment of performance. It is always tempting to regard the mainsprings of these pleasures as being in some way universal (hence, Leslie Woodhead's 'discovery' of Aristotelian structure in his favourite dramadocs), but they actually shift with history, technology, culture and fashion.

In psychoanalytical terms, these latter pleasures exist in the domain of the 'Imaginary'. They are often found in discourses of entertainment, and (crucially) exist in a less solipsistic atmosphere than documentary pleasures – they are often shared more actively at the point of consumption. The Imaginary, the 'psychic domain of idealized forms, fantasy, identification, reversible time, and alternative logics' (Renov, 1993: 3), is where we measure how much (and how little) we belong to the social world, rather than how much we might do for it and in it. In television drama, such pleasures are dominantly gendered feminine, if only because they have been accessed historically via a domestic space, and increasingly cate-gorised within dramatic forms which are feminine or feminised.

Some twenty years ago the feminist film theorist and practitioner Laura Mulvey identified 'scopophilia', or a concentration (amount-ing to fixation) on 'looking', as the basis of fiction film's pleasure. She developed from this her influential concept of the 'gaze' in film theory. The gaze is threefold: a camera looks at the performer; characters look at each other within the action; and the viewer looks on (and is accorded the illusion of control by the actual agents of the film's creation). The looker-on derives emotional and sexual power from this privileged looking. Mulvey, and other film theorists using her account of film's 'specularity', concluded that the 'gaze' in Hollywood fiction film was gendered male. (It largely still is.) The female was positioned most frequently in film as the 'looked-at', the desired, the object for someone else's subject.[7]

But spectatorship for film is not identical with that for television. John Ellis has characterised television viewing as based contrast-ingly on the 'glance' rather than the gaze, since attention to the television screen is more likely to be fractured by domestic and other claims (in the cinema, of course, the spectator has gone specifically to look) (1992: 128). I want to argue that television spectatorship involves a subject position that is more dominantly feminine. The looking activity is less about dominance and control and more about self-reflexive questioning and reality-testing. It produces internal dialogue, invites self-questioning, provokes internalised question-and-response.

I shall use my argument as an antithesis to balance Nichols' thesis about documentary's 'epistephilia', or reliance on knowledge (words/dialogue/voices plus sights equals documentary insight). Cowie, talking about documentary film, believes that it 'align[s] the spectator's scopophilic and epistephilic drives, that is, a curiosity to know satisfied through sight' (1997: 5). Television reinforces this 'alignment' through a qualitatively different kind of spectatorship. In cinema film the gaze remains important, because looking has always been so central to the experience. Dialogue, meanwhile, has reduced historically to a minimum and film acting is about showing. In television, a medium with a vital news function, words conveyed both aurally and graphically are still important. In dramadoc/docudrama, as I argued in Chapter 3, even the word-based captioning conventions are structurally important.

As well as the glance, then, the attentive (and inattentive) ear should be remembered in discussion of television drama. When I analysed present practice in Chapter 1, I remarked that an essentially non-realistic sound technique now formed the basis of the hearing through which we engage with distance shots (see note 10 on page 214). The radio microphone, which allows audiences to hear the conversations of distant figures in a landscape (hearing them as though, metaphorically, at their shoulder), was imported from television news and current affairs programming, where its miniaturisation offered additional flexibility to reporters. It is a technological device that derives from television's drive to hear as well as see; in television drama convention, however, it is there to support the visual aesthetics of the real. This is also true of the continued technological quest for privileged seeing.[8]

Carol Gilligan observes that women possess the 'proclivity…to reconstruct hypothetical dilemmas in terms of the real' (1982: 100–1). The serious side of so-called female genres (like the soap) enacts precisely that proclivity, which is not just about internal picturings, but about internal 'dialogue-ing' too. Put simply, the feminised dramadoc/docudrama offers an 'eavesdropping' pleasure in its dramatisation of anterior realities. Far from being disconnected entirely from the documentary, it offers a potentially unique dual perspective on the phenomenal world. The work of the eye and ear are equalised in television dramadoc/docudrama, and words as well as looks have weight.

It would be as well, to repeat a formula I used earlier in this book, to see the ideal spectator for the form seeking to ratify emotionally what he or she already knows intellectually. But the process can be taken a step further now: reversal is also possible, with a (feminised) knowledge being enhanced via affective involvement. The spectator is the witness/looker-on of documentary (looking with a sociological/anthropological scientist gaze) as well as the voyeur of the fiction film. But more than this, the ideal spectator is a looker-and-listener, someone actively engaged in hypothesising the real. This hypothesiser accepts at a fundamental level both the possibility and the provisionality of the form (it might just have looked and sounded like this – or it might not). The ideal dramadoc/docudrama spectator negotiates between levels of reality.

As a result, as Laurie Schulze says:

> Despite critical charges that it does so only to domesticate or depoliticize social issues or emerging ideologies, the TV movie may very well, for some audiences, make a space for progressive or even radical perceptions of the conflicts and fault-lines in American culture. (1990: 371)

Where the spectator of the documentary accepts (indeed, may well seek) imperfection of image as part-guarantee of authenticity; the spectator of dramadoc/docudrama accepts the inherent imperfection of mediation in accepting the form. What both are interested in, in different ways, is the link between what they watch and a pro-filmic reality.

'Relative transferability'

Robin Nelson remarks that, in the generality of television drama, 'authenticating detail can…lend the drama a sense of conviction' (1997: 109). The extra sense of conviction sought in dramadoc/docudrama comes, as it always has, from reference to a prior text – the pro-filmic reality behind the performance. The problem has always been that fidelity to that reality has been doubted more in the dramadoc/docudrama than it has in the documentary. The vexed question of fidelity to a prior reality also comes up in discussions of film and television adaptations of novels, where fidelity to the (prior) text has always been an issue. I think there are some similarities between these apparently distinct areas of television drama and dramadoc/docudrama.

The argument that finds something 'not true to the facts' is, after all, not dissimilar to that which finds a film adaptation 'not a bit like the novel'. Both arguments tend to be part of the experience of the resultant filmed dramas; they have to be at least acknowledged by an audience (and sometimes they prevail on an audience, as probably happened with *Hostages*). In literary adaptation the second argument rarely occurs when the author being adapted is, say, Frederick Forsyth or John Grisham; but the works of Jane Austen or William Shakespeare are very different matters. In film and television adaptation of novels the privileged, canonical text is usually the original one, and a staple élitist argument is the 'not as good as the novel' one. With the 'hypothesisation' of dramadoc/docudrama a greater claim for authority is often ceded readily enough to the documentary (the 'not as true as a documentary' argument – as with *Hostages* again).

Brian McFarlane proposes a notion of 'relative transferability' between literary texts and their adaptations in other media (1996: 13–15).[9] I would like to extend his idea to the dramadoc/docudrama. 'Relatively transferable' in this case applies to the essential elements of a prior event in the real world, without which a subsequent film drama would just not be recognised as being about that prior event. The dramatic narrative that is made around the transferable elements of the event is a different matter. In this 'enunciation' of the essential elements lies the interpretative challenge of the 'story', the narrativisation. However well or badly this is met, some element of intertextuality – the 'showing through' of prior texts into newly-made ones – must occur (otherwise there would be no awareness of a prior referent, and no problem). This showing through of prior referents into drama is a major feature of the novel adaptation, the historical film drama and the dramadoc/docudrama alike.[10]

It is at the point of reception, in the vast collective memory of television talk, that such intertextual forms resonate, cause argument and give pleasure. In the dramadoc/docudrama, what Gilligan defines as masculine pleasures of 'separation' and feminine pleasures of 'attachment' are evident. She uses these terms to describe different, but equally important, ethical positions: 'separation is justified by an ethic of rights while attachment is supported by an ethic of care' (1982: 163–4). The public service 'ethic of rights' has been one of the strongest elements of twentieth-century broad-casting. Like all ethical inclinations it is double-edged: in one sense, profoundly democratic and libertarian, concerned with the creation of the responsible citizen, rationally competent to join in the collective directing of society; in another sense, and just as profoundly, it created a subaltern group, dependent upon an individualised and intellectual élite to facilitate learning, to pre-structure information.

The 'ethic of care', meanwhile, is implicit in the feminised docudrama which invites empathy with the traumas of the Little Person in society. The made-for-TV movie need not necessarily be always inferior to 'the heavy-duty public service ethic dramadoc' (Ian McBride's words). No one would be foolish enough to claim that a classic novel is invalidated by adaptation (though they might assert its reduction). Nor is a real-world event (however relativised) completely erased in either a dramadoc or a docudrama approach. Instead, its proposal of an area of intertextual reference can be seen as a space within which society's 'conflicts and fault-lines' are exposed in culture (Schulze, 1990: 371). This intertextuality calls representation into question without invalidating it, posing questions about what we take to be real – it is a case of 'both documentary/and drama' structures (rather than 'either/or').[11]

Future forms

Janet Steiger says:

> The mixture, the blurred boundaries among the conventions [of docu-drama], and the public discussions caused by these blurrings and mixings, remain central to any full understanding of the practices and the roles of television in contemporary society. (1997: 517)

No institution can entirely escape its history, and I believe 'full understanding' of television will continue to be intimately linked to the way dramadoc/docudrama tries to fulfil television's continuing, but much reshaped, mission to inform and entertain. The idea of the documentary has occupied an important place in a Western culture, with its faith in facts acting as a means of securing an 'ethic of rights'. A distinctively rationalist/forensic cultural imperative is satisfied in the intertext of the dramadoc/docudrama, which is an integral part of Western philosophical as well as cultural history. But the ethic of care is making something of a comeback at the turn of the century.

The most likely future scenario is of adaptation to, rather than erasure by, new technology and its re-inflection of television culture. Since the dramadoc/docudrama is an occasional form, it is likely that it will continue to be a weapon used by television companies in response to important social situations.[12] The 1996 Granada dramadoc *Hillsborough* is a good example of this continued possibility. It was transmitted in the wake of a public campaign that was attempting to revisit a 1989 tragedy – the disaster at an English football ground in which over a hundred people were crushed to death. It was a classic campaigning film, written by arguably the best and most successful television dramatist of his generation, Jimmy McGovern.[13]

The central thesis of the film was that people had died as a result of police incompetence in marshalling the crowd that had gathered to watch an FA Cup semi-final game, and that this incompetence had been covered up by the authorities in the aftermath of the tragedy. The thesis had gained widespread currency over the years since the disaster, but *Hillsborough* offered crucial new evidence. In particular, it refuted a claim by the police that a security video camera's malfunction prevented the availability at inquest of video film of the crowd pen in which the majority of casualties had occurred. Transmission of *Hillsborough* occasioned a renewal of the debate about compensation for the families of victims. Ministers of State were lobbied; there were discussions on radio and television and in the newspapers; and the whole issue achieved renewed public prominence. The dramadoc contributed to this climate of opinion in a major way, providing a focus and an occasion for the kind of 'TV talk' that can change the course of events. Following the 1997 general election the new British government agreed to a fresh inquiry into the events of 1989 at Hillsborough. Most newspaper accounts on the day the new inquiry was announced (29 June 1997) saw *Hillsborough* as a significant element in the families' campaign.

Ian McBride still regards this kind of drama-documentary as special and as an integral part of public service television. 'I would not want the schedules washed clean,' he says, of a form that still occurs, like *Hillsborough*,

> when conventional means of telling a story are denied – usually when the actual participants are either dead or dutifully dumb. The motivation of the 'heavy-duty' drama-documentary remains primarily journalistic, and the dramatist brings to that the ability to tell a story which otherwise couldn't be anyway near as effectively told on television.

Although I have called it a dramadoc, *Hillsborough* can be seen as a trauma drama in Feuer's sense, or as a headline docudrama in Carveth's. Its major dramatic focus was the failure of institutions with a duty of care – the police, to a lesser extent the football authorities, and even the Government itself. It stressed self help as a means to righting public wrongs in its support of the campaigning by the Hillsborough families and, in so doing, kept the headlines on the issue running. This is exactly the sort of orientation in recent American docudrama to which Feuer and Carveth draw attention. *Hillsborough* provided a popular cultural focus on a British society perceived as unable, post-Thatcher, to honour duties of care. Its appeal to feeling was, in an important sense, a refutation of Margaret Thatcher's notorious one-liner that there was 'no such thing as society'. In this kind of political context the new-form dramadoc/docudrama thrives and continues to exercise (or at any rate to claim) the historic function of a 'public service' broadcasting institution.

This kind of response depends in part on there being a social 'marketplace', in the form of a network broadcaster, in which such a discussion can achieve the necessary prominence. The scenario of a continued need for such a forum is, I believe, at least as likely as the scenarios in which television is digitised into a multi-form service (incapable of delivering anything other than niche-market audiences to advertisers). Changes in patterns of television broadcasting will undoubtedly occur as a result of digital, cable and satellite technology, but it seems unlikely that a total shift to 'narrowcasting' will occur. Greater choice, in which niche marketing of programmes is a stock-in-trade, will not necessarily mean the complete elimination of mixed programming on national networks designed for large, collective audiences.

If dramadoc/docudrama is constrained to fit into 'narrowcast' programming, there are obvious problems: as an occasional form, it is not strong enough to sustain its own cable outlet, so would presumably be placed with either documentary companies (like Discovery) or drama/entertainment ones (like HBO). There may even be some call on 'heritage' channels (like 'UK Gold') for reruns of past successes like *Cathy Come Home*. It is more likely that the future of the form is tied to the future viability of national networks. In its favour, it is still relatively cheap.[14]

Another possibility might lie in the development of interactive television. The factual back-up to the dramadoc/docudrama is an untapped resource and lies, like the bulk of an iceberg, below the surface of the drama. Exploitation of the information uncovered in high-concept journalistic programmes like *Hostile Waters*, for example, may enable the old journalistic certainties of the dramadoc to be revisited in the future. The factual base to such programmes, especially if linked to a public campaign, constitutes a resource that is potentially exploitable through computer technology. For a future 'wired' audience the CD-ROM and the Internet may offer possibilities which reconnect docudrama with the dramadoc tradition.

So, if viewers found themselves sufficiently engaged by a programme to join in a public debate, they might through such technology access the facts used by a research team (pre-vetted, of course, by lawyers). Factual material would then be available for the kind of close attention that critics sometimes claim is impossible when a drama is in progress. It might also be possible for an audience, via computer terminals, to enter post-transmission debates and campaigns more directly and more judiciously than is possible in the kinds of ritualistic exchanges that take place in the 'right to reply' phone-in/discussion programme. This would provide a development of the 'extra-textual' and a continuation of the honourable tradition of factual forms in drama (of trying to link up with direct action in the real world). The British investigative tradition would thus extend into a new technological phase.

A recent libel case in Britain in which the ubiquitous hamburger chain McDonalds took two British environmental activists to court already offers an example. Based on John Vidal's 1997 book *McLibel – Burger Culture on Trial*, a dramadoc/docudrama called *McLibel* was broadcast over two nights (18 and 19 May 1997) on Channel 4. This was basically a re-enactment of the trial, linked by a studio talking head. Meanwhile, another more innovative film was being made by producer Franny Armstrong. *McLibel – Two Worlds Collide* is mainly documentary, with drama inserts in which the real defendants Helen Steel and Dave Morris re-enact with actors (Ken Loach directed these scenes). In spite (or because) of its innovative nature the film's transmission has been bedevilled with difficulty. But in May 1997, Armstrong declared her intention to make the programme and its evidence available on the Internet instead. Morris and Steel's supporters already had a website, 'McSpotlight'. The nature of the 'grass-roots' environmental campaign against the corporate giant has made this website very active; as Vidal himself pointed out in the *Guardian*, it has had 'more than 14 million "hits", a figure any mainstream TV executive would love' (16 May 1997).[15]

Unstable genres and hybridisation

Ian McBride notes four 'sub-genres' he mentally consults when planning the 'factual drama' for which he is responsible at Granada:
1 the drama-documentary
2 the dramatisation of a true story
3 the drama based on a true story
4 the contemporary drama

He compares the fourth sub-genre to the single play of British television's past. Like the documentary dramas I described in Chapter 6, the single drama 'often draws heavily on fact', he observes, but allows film makers: 'to play as fast and loose with the facts as suits the dramatic form'. The third category is McBride's preferred formula for 'faction' and those plays whose relative transferability leaves them with little resemblance to any precise factual template.

The second category, according to McBride, has expanded the

most in recent years, and comprises the docudrama end of the 'made-for-TV movie' spectrum. He believes it allows the broadcaster to escape from the 'public policy imperative and desire for journalistic revelation' that are so much a part of the territory of the drama-documentary. This type of film has 'an important place within a television schedule. It could be nothing greater than the celebration of the human spirit, or a triumph over adversity, or a journey through pain.' This is, of course, precisely the affective territory of the made-for-TV docudrama or trauma drama.

While McBride is protective of the first category, the journalistic dramadoc, Julian Petley can only see decline. 'The dramatic look', he says, 'is displacing the documentary one' and the form is 'decreasingly marked out stylistically, from other forms of television drama' (1996: 18–19). But the merging feared by Petley could also be seen as part of what John Corner has called the 'inter-generic hybridization' of television forms (1997: 252). It is precisely this 'hybridization' to which practitioner Leslie Woodhead was alluding when he said: 'It seems to me necessary to go on talking to your audience in a language which they're willing to receive – if they're going to switch off, I've lost!'

There is great potential in the multiplying ways through which television forms trigger intertextual reference, thereby increasing the range of documentary content and stretching the limits of realist dramatic styles in the future. As an 'unstable genre' historically, dramadoc/docudrama has always been an 'inter-generic hybridization', seeking to satisfy the needs of popular audiences both for an intellectual understanding of the phenomenal world and for affective 'windows into behaviour'. Like capitalism itself, dramatic realism might seem capable of infinite adaptation to new circumstances; but (again like capitalism) its ethical dimension is less certain. Technologies of the camera and microphone, and acted performance techniques alike try to satisfy the desire to see more and to see better. But seeing alone is never enough. In the future a return of the documentary (and ethical) repressed should not be ruled out. To adapt Woodhead's words quoted earlier in this chapter, 'collision with forbidden territories' is still likely to be an expressive priority.

At the conclusion of his book *The Art of Record* John Corner states his belief that the future of documentary proper lies in 'a strongly referential and indeed evidential dimension' to the form's 're-imaginings' (1996: 190). Dramadoc/docudrama, in developing a wider range of generic reference than ever in the future, must similarly be tied to a 'referential and evidential' re-imagining of its dramatic project. Anglo-American culture is being seen as moving away, at the turn of century, from the conspicuous consumption of the Reaganite/Thatcherite 1980s (with its 'no such thing as society' individualism) towards a more collective ethic of care. If the move is anything other than cosmetic it will present a huge challenge to the 'meaning makers' of cultural production. In order to shift attitudes and reshape perceptions in a new cultural landscape, the evidential and the ethical will need at least to have parity with the affective in the television dramadoc/docudramas of the twenty-first century.

Notes

Introduction

1 See Victoria Mapplebeck, 'Spoofer's double exposure', *Guardian*, 1 September 1997. In the same article another (unnamed) film maker commented: 'He's broken a taboo and for this he won't be forgiven.'

2 For other summaries, see Corner (1996: 42–3), Kilborn and Izod (1997: 138) and Steiger (1997: 514–17).

3 See Chapter 5, 'The academic debate', 125–34, for an account of the academic writing on the form.

4 Granada has always claimed to use dramadoc as a 'last resort' journalistically. Recently, however, the Granada executive producer Ian McBride has acknowledged that 'first resort' use threatens to become the new norm ('Reality Time' conference paper, Birmingham University, 12 April 1996; see also Chapter 8, where I quote this paper again).

5 The phrase 'no other way to tell it' was first used by Woodhead in his BFI/*Guardian* Lecture (London 1981). I interviewed him (London, 26 October 1994), and have also found useful a letter dated 26 November 1994. All quotations from Woodhead in subsequent chapters of this book refer to these sources.

6 See Chapter 7 for more detail on this case and for the letter of refutation by the producers of *Hostages*, which was published on the following day.

Chapter 1

1 On research, see also Holland (1997: 162–5).

2 The story was recounted to me by *Hostages* producer Sita Williams, whom I interviewed several times in Manchester (on 15 March, 15 April, 27 June and 10 November 1994 and on 31 October 1995). I also quote from her working scripts (*Hostages*, *Fighting for Gemma*, and *Goodbye My Love*). All her quotations in subsequent chapters of this book refer to these sources.

3 Hunter won an Emmy for this performance. In Chapter 8 the term 'headline docudrama' is used to describe such films. The actual 1991 news story which inspired this film also led to another network – ABC – making *Willing to Kill: The Texas Cheerleader Story*. Rosenthal offers an interesting comparison of these two docudramas (1995: 237–44).

4 Leslie Woodhead is one such former Granada employee.

5   For a summary of theories of the audience from a Media Studies perspective, see Tim O'Sullivan *et al.* (1994).

6   Kathy Bates and Harry Dean Stanton in *Hostages*, Rutger Hauer and Martin Sheen in *Hostile Waters*. Sita Williams certainly took this view on costing when I spoke to her, but Kilborn and Izod quote Ian McBride's opposite view: 'They cost as much as full-blooded drama, and more because you have all the journalistic work in advance' (1997: 150).

7   See also Corner (1996: 20–1) on the pro-filmic moment.

8   This book was used by the members of the religious cult 'Heaven's Gate' in preparation for their mass suicide in 1996.

9   The 'key light' convention takes note of the principal light source in any situation but builds around it to optimise definition of the actors' faces. As in the theatre, the face of an actor is even more important as a vehicle of communication than in film (where *mise-en-scène* really comes into its own. Key light is a naturalistic convention. The expectation is that an audience will accept the lighting as 'real-in-the-drama'.

10 Phil Smith, the experienced Granada sound recordist on this film, gave me a telling explication of the essential unreality of the long-shot convention that uses radio mikes to allow an audience to 'overhear' protagonists' conversations while we see them within a landscape. This technology, he explained, was first used in news broadcasting then adapted to the conventions of television drama – the audience's desire to hear always overcoming any doubt about the impossibility of hearing anything over such distances. See also Chapter 8.

11 See Tunstall (1993) and Gitlin (1994) on the television producer as the real power in the industry.

12 For an introduction to theatre semiotics, see Aston and Savona (1991).

13 I interviewed Ian McBride in Manchester on 15 March 1994. He also spoke at the Birmingham University 'Reality Time' Conference in April 1996. I quote from notes made on this paper (to be included in *Why Docudrama? Fact-Fiction on Film and TV*, Alan Rosenthal (ed), Carbondale, Southern Illinois University Press, forthcoming 1998. McBride's essay is entitled 'Where are we going and why?'). All his quotations in subsequent chapters of this book refer to these sources.

14 See Paget (1990: 86–111).

Chapter 2

1   In fact, objections to *Hostages* began to be voiced in the press at the beginning of 1992, eight months before transmission.

2   I interviewed Alasdair Palmer in London on 7 October 1994. All his quotations in subsequent chapters of this book refer to this interview.

3   Both Patrick Swaffer and Oliver Goodenough spoke at the 'Reality Time' conference in Birmingham in 1996; both allowed me to read and make notes on their papers.

4   See also Horenstein *et al.* (1994: 380–1).

5   The company he was referring to was the airline Pan Am, whose jumbo jet had gone down over Lockerbie. Patrick Swaffer, however, was the lawyer involved in the case, and he pointed out to me (letters of 14 March 1997 and 11 September 1997) that Air Malta was the company which actually sued Granada and that PanAm was 'not involved in any legal challenge to the programme'.

6   In Britain in June 1997 there was a renewal of serious debate about press intrusion into private life following the 'James Cameron Memorial Lecture' given by the *Guardian*'s editor Alan Rusbridger. The so-called 'sex/money debate' is about whether industry self-regulation is sufficient to curb tabloid interest in the sexual peccadilloes of the rich and famous, and whether legislation is required to facilitate more serious investigations of financial malpractice. The death of Diana, Princess of Wales, on 31 August 1997 fanned the flames even further and new guidelines from the Press Complaints Commission were issued in September 1997.

7   See Paget (1992: 154–79).

8   Following the 1997 general election, the situation was set to change. The British Labour government pledged to investigate freedom of information legislation and to sign the European Convention on Human Rights.

9   Rob Ritchie was speaking at the 'Reality Time' conference (April 1996).

10 These remarks were made at a British Academy of Film and Television Arts (BAFTA) debate, 'True to the facts', held in London on 3 March 1997.

11 'Flow' is a concept which has itself been much discussed in media studies; see Williams (1992).

Chapter 3

1   The only example I have found is in Feuer (1995: 41, note 2): 'recent drama documentary films such as *Silkwood* (1983).' On an American Internet search mechanism, 'the Electric Library', tapping in the word 'docudrama' (6 October 1997) yielded nineteen recent references; the word 'dramadoc' yielded none.

2   The theoretical term 'suture' usefully draws attention to the way the literal 'stitching together' of film frames by editing almost always guarantees a smooth narrative flow. See Hayward (1996: 371–9).

3   Sita Williams tells an instructive anecdote about this strange situation: the Israeli crew removed Marlboro cigarette packets from the Arab captors' table at one point, believing that these men would not buy a product made by 'the Great Satan'. In fact, this detail had been very carefully researched.

4   Both Keenan and McCarthy present much bleaker pictures of their guards in their memoirs.

5   This is very 'accurate' in terms of the published memoirs – see McCarthy
     and Morrell (1994: 101) and Keenan (1992a: 91) – apart from the mis-
     take in the name of Robert Louis Stevenson's character (Ben, not 'Tom',
     Gunn); Palmer was possibly thinking of the poet Thom Gunn.
6   Michael Eaton was speaking at the 'Reality Time' conference, April 1996.
7   One celebrated American example was Donald Freed's 1970 play *Inquest*,
     which even had displays outside the theatre (see D. Freed, *Inquest*, New
     York, Hill and Wang, 1970: 17).
8   The 'opposers' were Peter Kosminsky, himself a maker of drama-documen-
     taries, Roger Bolton, maker of such documentaries as Thames TV's *Death
     on the Rock*, and Mark Lawson, who was at that time television critic for
     the *Independent*.
9   Lynne Truss's remark (8 July 1996) in her *Times* review of *Killing Me Softly*
     (a dramadoc about Sara Thornton, a woman jailed for killing her husband
     and released after a campaign) is representative: 'With docudrama, two
     types of reality fight it out, and neither wins.'
10   Hutcheon (1988) provides a useful introduction to this difficult area of the-
     oretical debate.
11   Commentators from Caryl Doncaster in 1956 to David Edgar in 1981 have
     made this point; the dramadoc/docudrama (like the talk show, the sitcom,
     the soap opera and the news broadcast) is a televisual form; there is
     nothing quite like it in other media.

Chapter 4

1   For useful definitions of these dramaturgical terms see Hodgson (1988).
2   See Ellis (1989) on documentary films in developed and undeveloped
     nations.
3   See Chapters 2 and 3 of *True Stories?* (Paget, 1990) on the techniques and
     significance of 'documentary theatre' and 'theatre of fact'.
4   The history of documentary theatre demonstrates that the form lacks
     continuity, being essentially a 'guerrilla' form. Although a 1946 play,
     Documentary Drama, indicated that documentary theatrical techniques
     were well known in Britain, the new generation of 1960s playwrights had
     virtually to relearn them. Van Erven (1988; 1992) shows that, although
     Third World practitioners often have some knowledge of Brecht, for
     example, they also tend to find documentary theatrical techniques out of
     pure political necessity.
5   The phrase is Daniel Dayan and Elihu Katz's – see their essay in Smith
     (1995: 185).
6   Corner (1995: 20–31) provides a good study of television reconstructions
     and 'micro dramas'.

Chapter 5

1 Baudrillard made this claim in 'The reality gulf', *Guardian*, 1 January 1991. See Norris (1992) for a discussion of this interesting but fundamentally outrageous notion.

2 See Winston (1995) for a detailed critique of Griersonian film, which he alleges is constantly 'running away from social meaning' (1995: 35ff).

3 Paul Rotha, for example, used the following formula as sub-title for his book *Documentary Film* (first published in 1936): 'The use of the film medium to interpret creatively and in social terms the life of the people as it exists in reality'.

4 See the entry on 'classic Hollywood cinema/classic narrative cinema' in Hayward (1996: 45–9). See also Nichols (1981: 70–92) on the effects of continuity editing.

5 Winston (1995) has many fascinating sections on the artfulness of the pre-war documentarians, but see especially pages 99–103 on Flaherty's 1922 *Nanook of the North*. See also Barnouw (1993: 33–51).

6 Watt used the first phrase in an interview for the BBC2 *Arena* programme (1983). The second phrase is taken from the notes on the Imperial War Museum's 1992 video version of *Target for Tonight*.

7 Eisenstein's film *The Battleship Potemkin* (1925) was a particularly influential film for Grierson and the documentary movement. Grierson also prepared the English sub-titles for the first US showing of the film in 1926 (see Aitken, 1990: 75).

8 American television, too, recruited documentary film personnel to its post-war news and current affairs departments.

9 In *Documentary Film*, Rotha stressed 'Documentary has always a purpose to fulfil and it is that purpose which is intended to be of first interest to the spectator' (1952: 123).

10 *The Documentary Conscience* is the eloquent title of Rosenthal's 1980 book.

11 Orson Welles' radio adaptation of *The War of the Worlds* in 1938 is the example most often quoted.

12 Caughie's article was reprinted in: Bennett *et al.* (1981) and Goodwin and Kerr (1983); it was first published in *Screen*, 21:3, 1980, 9–33.

13 The most useful sources for Brecht's theories are in two books edited by John Willett (1984; 1986).

14 He references the quotation to Edgar E. Willis (1951), *Foundations in Broadcasting*, New York, Oxford University Press, 101.

15 For more detail on Federal Theatre and the 'Living Newspaper', see O'Connor and Brown (1980).

16 See also Chapter 1. Edgar's essay began as a radio talk, 'Acting out facts' (BBC Radio 3, 28 December 1980), and has been much anthologised. It is most conveniently found in Edgar (1988). Interestingly, the headline of the version of his essay that appeared in the British entertainment trade

paper *The Stage* (16 April 1981) was 'Why we must save the documentary drama', even though Edgar consistently refers to 'drama-documentary' throughout his article.

17 An introductory guide to this particular literary theory is Freund (1987).

18 Interestingly, a study (in 1990) of the effects on an audience of Granada's 1990 *Who Bombed Birmingham?* found that seventy-six per cent of those questioned believed they had acquired fresh information through the dramadoc, but only fifty-nine per cent believed that most of the information offered was true (see Kilborn and Izod (1997: 236).

19 I spoke to Martin McKeand at the *'Médias: entre Fiction et Réalité'* conference in Dijon on 27 and 28 November 1992.

Chapter 6

1 See Briggs (1995) on the BBC; on European public service broadcasting, see Smith (1995: 62–91).

2 See Barnouw (1966 – three vols) on the history of American networks.

3 See Scannell (1986: 1–26).

4 Arthur Swinson gives an earlier date, citing two 1946 programmes: *Germany Under Control* (Robert Barr) and *I Want to Be an Actor* (Duncan Ross).

5 To be fair to Firth, he also remarked in an interview (*Elle* magazine, September 1992: 40): 'I know it always sounds terribly precious when an actor talks like this...But it gave me a clue. And you apply your imagination...'

6 Prior talks of the show emerging from 'the BBC's Drama Documentary Unit' (1996: 7). In the past it has usually been called the 'Documentary-Drama Group' (Goodwin and Kerr, 1983: 3); indeed, Corner argues a special significance in the slippage from the 'Dramatized Documentary Unit' of the early 1950s (1996:38).

7 See Laing (1986) for more on this period.

8 See Balio (1990: 3–40) on the effects of the Paramount Decree.

9 See Stott (1973) for more detail.

10 I have used the 1979 reprint of Bluem's book, but it first appeared in 1965. His important account of first-phase developments should be seen as the American equivalent of the British account offered by Swinson in the previous section.

11 In Newcomb (1997: 516), Janet Steiger uses the term 'documentary-drama' to describe *Cathy Come Home*.

12 I was able to view this television play on video at the Museum of Broadcast Communication in Chicago, which has an excellent archive of early network material. The *Armstrong Circle Theatre* programmes are part of the David Susskind Collection.

13 He made this remark on BBC2's *Face to Face* on 19 September 1994.

14 *Cathy Come Home* has been transmitted on British networks five times (1966, 1967, 1968, 1976 and 1993).

15 Sandford's 1973 article for *Theatre Quarterly* is reprinted in Goodwin and Kerr (1983). Sandford's early experience was in radio; *Cathy Come Home* was preceded by a radio feature, *Homeless Families*, which provided a research base for *Cathy*. I have interviewed Jeremy Sandford twice (on 24 November 1995 and 4 October 1996).

16 Interview with Tony Garnett (London, 7 November 1996).

17 Chapter 5 of Corner (1996) contains a detailed analysis of *Cathy Come Home*.

18 See, for example, Gomery (1983).

19 The writer called this film 'a "Theater of Fact" production' (Auster, 1990: 164).

20 For a recent account of Drew/Leacock's work, see Ellis (1989).

21 David Edgar remarked (at the 1996 'Reality Time' conference) that it was possible to chart the history of the form through the way in which captions have been used over the years.

22 Kilborn and Izod list six 'Iron Curtain' dramadocs that were transmitted between 1972 and 1980 (1997: 243).

23 In 1990 a special *World in Action* programme made in post-velvet revolution Czechoslovakia was able to show *Invasion* to Alexander Dubček. He was moved to embrace Julian Glover (his impersonator in the drama) at the end of the transmission.

24 Corner (1996: 40) classifies *The War Game* as 'imitation documentary'. It generated a large controversy, documented in, for example: C. Aubrey (1982), *Nukespeak: the Media and the Bomb*, London, Comedia. *Days of Hope* was debated extensively in *Screen* in 1979. *Death of a Princess* was broadcast on PBS in the USA in 1980. Accounts of the 'media events' surrounding all these films can be found in Goodwin and Kerr (1983) – see also Paget (1990: 97–105).

25 Cumings actually refers to this documentary drama as 'a documentary', saying PBS's screening of it was a 'highlight' of US television's 1979–80 'scrutiny' of Saudi Arabia (1992: 121).

Chapter 7

1 See *Screen International 978* (7–13 October 1994: 37–8, 40).

2 Interview with Ray Fitzwalter (Manchester, 14 March 1996). Quotations are from this interview unless stated otherwise.

3 See Chris Mullins (1986), *Error of Judgement*, London, Chatto and Windus.

4 In the sub-genre of dramadoc that has investigated recent miscarriages of justice the termination of the case in the real world often leads to repeat transmissions. In 1993 the BBC dramadoc *Bad Company* explored the 'Bridgewater case' convictions (four men convicted of murdering a newspaper delivery boy in 1978). After the release of the three living protagonists in this real-life drama in 1996 the film was transmitted again in 1997 with a final caption updating the story.

5 Readers might like to refer again to the material on the process of production at the beginning of Chapter 1.

6 McCarthy and Keenan have thus far been unsuccessful in brokering a deal for their own film version of their story. This bears out their agents' misgivings. David Aukin, to name one producer, discussed their projected film *Blind Flight* with the Channel 4 after *Hostages* was transmitted. Keenan was 'a natural script editor', he remarked. But Channel 4 did not go ahead with the project (see Aukin's article 'Farewell to Four', the *Guardian*, 3 November 1997).

7 This claim seems unfortunately to have been made by Thames Television in its trailer for the transmission, not by Granada itself.

8 In fact, the real publicity in September 1992 went to Lynda La Plante's new BBC drama series *Civvies*, about demobilised paratroopers. A 'based on fact' series, it provoked controversy because of the peculiar place the 'Paras' occupy in the British popular imagination (following 'Bloody Sunday' in Northern Ireland in 1972 and the 1982 Falklands War). *Civvies*' unusual focus on the emotional lives of these hyper-macho men caused widespread complaint from a variety of institutions (not least from the Paras themselves). In the tabloids especially, *Civvies* took precedence over *Hostages*.

Chapter 8

1 David Edgar used this phrase in a note to me of April 1997.

2 Quoted in the *Sunday Telegraph* on 2 January 1993.

3 Woodhead often emphasises the journalistic over the dramatic – Corner quotes another example (1996: 41).

4 Importantly, Gilligan says this does not 'represent a generalisation about either sex'.

5 Cowie also quotes this list. She then says: 'and, I would add, the law' (1997: 2). I strongly agree with this addition.

6 At least, this has been so until the determined theoretical assault of feminism, from around 1970 onwards, began to make a social impact.

7 Mulvey (1989) reprints the essay 'Visual pleasure and narrative cinema', which first appeared in 1975. See also Hayward on these matters (1996: 97–116) and on the Imaginary (185–90).

8 See 'What's up, docs?', *Guardian*, 6 October 1997, in which John Willis argues that 'small DVC cameras have reduced both crew sizes and costs, opening up the potential for greater intimacy as well as more flexibility'.

9 McFarlane bases his argument on structuralist theory (principally, Roland Barthes' 'cardinal' and 'catalyser', and Seymour Chatman's 'kernel' and

'satellite', narrative functions). For students of novel and film McFarlane's theory permits a non-judgmental means of comparison that can: 'establish some guidelines for exploring the different natures of the experiences of the two related texts' (1996: 197).

10 John Tulloch sees intertextuality as a key feature of television drama. He talks of its 'dynamic succession and synchrony [with] other texts, other social events' (1990: 130).

11 Nelson (1997) argues for 'both/and' critical approaches in a book which sees television drama as, significantly, 'in transition'.

12 The BBC attempted to formalise this idea in the early 1990s by creating a so-called 'Rapid-Response Unit' in television drama.

13 Jimmy McGovern was the writer of the hugely popular 1990s *Cracker* series, about a clinical psychologist who works for the Manchester police. *Hillsborough* was in part inspired by the reaction of Hillsborough families to a *Cracker* series which depicted a man so traumatised by Hillsborough that he became a serial killer. One of the strongest of McGovern's many strong suits is his ability to mine the psychological ramifications of guilt and blame.

14 On 1997 UK figures, it costs over £0.5 million to produce an hour of television drama, which is three or four times the cost of equivalent factual programming (*Guardian*, 18 February 1997). See also Willis (1997).

15 Vidal's claim poses many problems, of course, but the magic figure for large-scale success on British network television is ten million. The 'McLibel case' ended in June 1997 in a rather hollow legal victory for McDonalds (the publicity in particular being somewhat damaging).

Bibliography

Ableman, P. (1972), 'Edna and Sheila: two kinds of truth', *Theatre Quarterly*, 2:7, 45–8.

Aitken, I. (1990), *Film and Reform*, London, Routledge.

Anderson, M. *et al.* (1972), *A Handbook of Contemporary Drama*, New York, Pitman (entry on 'Documentary theater or theatre of fact', 125–6).

Aston, E., and G. Savona (1991), *Theatre as Sign-system*, London and New York, Routledge.

Aukin, D. (1997), 'Farewell to Four', *Guardian*, 3 November.

Auster, A. (1990), '*The Missiles of October:* A case history of television docudrama and modern memory', *Journal of Popular Film and Television*, 17:4, 164–72.

Baker, R. (1995), *Media Law: A User's Guide for Film and Programme Makers*, London, Blueprint.

Balio, T. (ed.) (1990), *Hollywood in the Age of Television*, Boston, Unwin Hyman.

Barnouw, E. (1966), *A History of Broadcasting in the United States*, New York and Oxford, Oxford University Press (3 volumes).

Barnouw, E. (1975), *Tube of Plenty: The Evolution of American Television*, New York and Oxford, Oxford University Press.

Barnouw, E. (1993), *Documentary: A History of the Non-Fiction Film*, New York and Oxford, Oxford University Press.

Barr, C. (ed.) (1986), *All Our Yesterdays: 90 Years of British Cinema*, London, British Film Institute.

Barsam, R. (1974), 'Defining nonfiction film', in G. Mast and M. Cohen (eds), *Film Theory and Criticism*, New York, Oxford University Press.

Barthes, R. (1993), *Camera Lucida*, London, Vintage.

Bell, E. (1986), 'The origins of British television documentary: the BBC 1945–55', in Corner (ed.), *Documentary and the Mass Media*, 65–80.

Bennett, T., S. Boyd-Bowman, C. Mercer, and J. Woollacott (eds) (1981), *Popular Television and Film*, London and Milton Keynes, British Film Institute/Open University Press.

Bluem, A. (1979), *Documentary in American Television: Form, Function, Method*, New York, Hastings House.

Bourdieu, P. (1984), *Distinction* (trans. R. Nice), London, Routledge.

Brandt, G. (ed.) (1981), *British Television Drama*, Cambridge, Cambridge University Press.

Brandt, G. (ed.) (1993), *British Television Drama in the 1980s*, Cambridge, Cambridge University Press.

Briggs, A. (1995), *The History of Broadcasting in the United Kingdom*, Oxford, Oxford University Press (5 volumes).

Brown, C. (1994), 'Box office bonanza', *Screen International 978*, 7–13 October 1994, 37.

Brown, L. (1992), *Encyclopaedia of Television*, Detroit and London, Gale Research.

Brown, L. (1995), 'The American networks', in Smith (ed.), *Television: An International History*, 259–84.

Carveth, R. (1993), 'Amy Fisher and the ethics of "Headline" docudramas', *Journal of Popular Film and Television*, 21:3, 121–7.

Caughie, J. (1981), 'Progressive television and documentary drama', in Bennett *et al.* (eds), *Popular Television and Film*, 327–52.

Chaney, D. (1993), *Fictions of Collective Life: Public Drama in Late Modern Culture*, New York and London, Routledge.

Chater, K. (1992), *The Television Researcher's Guide*, Borehamwood, BBC Training.

Corner, J. (ed.) (1986), *Documentary and the Mass Media*, London, Edward Arnold.

Corner, J. (ed.) (1991), *Popular Television in Britain: Studies in Cultural History*, London, British Film Institute.

Corner, J. (1995), *Television Form and Public Address*, London, Edward Arnold.

Corner, J. (1996), *The Art of Record: A Critical Introduction to Documentary*, Manchester and New York, Manchester University Press.

Corner, J. and S. Harvey (eds) (1996), *Television Times: A Reader*, London and New York, Arnold.

Corner, J. (1997), 'Television in theory', *Media, Culture and Society*, 19:2, 247–62.

Cowie, E. (1997), 'The spectacle of reality and documentary film', *Documentary Box 10*, Yamagata International Documentary Festival, Tokyo, 1–8.

Crowther, B. (1984), *Hollywood Faction: Reality and Myth in the Movies*, London, Columbus.

Cumings, B. (1992), *War and Television*, London and New York, Verso.

Custen, G. (1992), *Bio/pics: How Hollywood Constructed Public History*, New Brunswick, NJ, Rutgers University Press.

Dayan, D. and E. Katz (1995), 'Political ceremony and instant history', in Smith (ed.), *Television: An International History*, 169–88.

Doncaster, C. (1956), 'The story documentary', in Rotha (ed.), *Television in the Making*, 44–8.

Edgar, D. (1988), *The Second Time as Farce*, London, Lawrence and Wishart.

Edgar, D. (1989), 'Faction plan', *Listener*, 1 June, 13–14, 32.

Edgar, D. (1993), 'Seeing isn't believing', *Sunday Times*, 22 August.

Edgerton, G. (1985), 'The American made-for-TV movie', in Rose (ed.), *TV Genres: A Handbook and Reference Guide*.

Edgerton, G. (1991), 'High concept, small screen: reperceiving the industrial and stylistic origins of the American made-for-TV movie', *Journal of Popular Film and Television*, 19:3, 114–27.

Ellis, J. (1992), *Visible Fictions: Cinema, Television, Video*, London and New York, Routledge.

Ellis, J. C. (1989), *The Documentary Idea: A Critical History of English Language Documentary Film and Video*, New Jersey, Prentice Hall.

Erven, E. van (1988), *Radical People's Theatre*, Bloomington, Indiana University Press.

Erven, E. van (1992), *The Playful Revolution: Theatre and Liberation in Asia*, Bloomington, Indiana University Press.

Feuer, J. (1995), *Seeing Through the Eighties: Television and Reaganism*, London, British Film Institute.

Foley, B. (1986), *Telling the Truth: The Theory and Practice of Documentary Fiction*, Ithaca, NY, Cornell University Press.

Fowles, J. (1992), *Why Viewers Watch: A Reappraisal of Television's Effects*, London, Sage.

Freund, E. (1987), *The Return of the Reader: Reader-Response Criticism*, London, Methuen.

Garnham, N. (1972), 'TV documentary and ideology', *Screen* 13:2, 109–15.

Gilligan, C. (1982), *In a Different Voice: Psychological Theory and Women's Development*, Cambridge, Mass., Harvard University Press.

Gitlin, T. (1994), *Inside Prime Time*, London, Routledge.

Gomery, D. (1983), 'Television, Hollywood, and the development of movies made-for-TV', in Kaplan, E. (ed.), *Regarding Television: Critical Approaches – An Anthology*, Los Angeles, University Publications of America/American Film Institute.

Goodenough, O. (1989), 'Avoiding legal trouble in preparing docudramas', *New York Law Journal*, 24 November, 5 and 29.

Goodenough, O. and H. J. Blumenthal (1992), *This Business of Television*, New York, Billboard.

Goodwin, A. and P. Kerr (1983) *BFI Dossier 19: Drama-documentary*, London: British Film Institute.

Goodwin, A. (1986), *Teaching TV Drama-documentary*, London, British Film Institute.

Goodwin, A. and G. Whannel (eds) (1990), *Understanding Television*, London,

Routledge.

Grierson, J. (1933), 'The documentary producer', *Cinema Quarterly*, 2:1, 7–9.

Gunter, B. and C. McLaughlin (1992), *Television: The Public's View*, London, John Libbey.

Guynn, W. (1990), *A Cinema of Nonfiction*, Rutherford, NJ, Associated Universities Press.

Halliwell, L. and P. Purser (1986), *Halliwell's Television Companion*, London, Paladin.

Hardy, F. (ed.) (1979), *Grierson on Documentary*, London and Boston, Faber and Faber.

Hartley, J. (1992), *Tele-ology: Studies in Television*, London and New York, Routledge.

Hare, D. (1984), *The History Plays*, London, Faber and Faber.

Hayward, S. (1996), *Key Concepts in Cinema Studies*, London and New York, Routledge.

Higson, A. (1986), 'Britain's outstanding contribution to film', in Barr (ed.) *All Our Yesterdays*, 72–97.

Hodgson, T. (1988), *The Batsford Dictionary of Drama*, London, Batsford.

Hoffer, T., R. Musburger and R. Nelson (1980), 'Evolution of docudrama on American Television networks: a content analysis, 1966–1978', *Southern Speech Communication Journal*, Winter, 149–63.

Hoffer, T., R. Musburger and R. Nelson (1985), 'Docudrama', in Rose (ed.), *TV Genres*, 181–211.

Holland, P. (1997), *The Television Handbook*, London and New York, Routledge.

Hood, S. (ed.) (1994), *Behind the Screens: The Structure of British Television in the 90s*, London, Lawrence and Wishart.

Horenstein, M. A., B. Rigby, M. Flory and V. Gershwin (1994), *Reel Life Real Life*, New Jersey, Fourth Write Press.

Hutcheon, L. (1988), *A Poetics of Postmodernism: History, Theory, Fiction*, London and New York, Routledge.

Jacobs, L. (1971), *The Documentary Tradition*, New York, Hopkinson and Blake.

Jarvis, P. (1991), *Teletalk: A Dictionary of Broadcasting Terms*, Borehamwood, BBC Training.

Kearey, A. (n.d., *ca* 1958), *Emergency – Ward 10*, London, ATV.

Keenan, B. (1992a), *An Evil Cradling*, London, Vintage.

Keenan, B. (1992b), 'Introduction', in McGuinness, *Someone Who'll Watch Over Me*.

Keighron, P. and C. Walker (1994), 'Working in television: 5 interviews', in Hood (ed.), *Behind the Screens*, 184–212.

Kepley, V. Jr (1990), 'From "Frontal Lobes" to the "Bob-and-Bob" show: NBC management and programming strategies, 1949–65', in Balio (ed.), *Hollywood in the Age of Television*, 41–61.

Kerr, P. (1990), 'F for fake? Friction over faction', in Goodwin and Whannel (eds), *Understanding Television*, 74–87.

Kilborn, R. (1994), 'Drama over Lockerbie. A new look at the drama-documentary debate', *The Historical Journal of Film, Radio and Television*, 14:1, 59–76.

Kilborn, R. and J. Izod (1997), *An Introduction to Television Documentary: Confronting Reality*, Manchester, Manchester University Press.

Kuehl, J. (1978), 'The motives for making drama documentaries', *Vision*, 3:1, 3–7.

Kuehl, J. (1981), 'Truth claims', *Sight and Sound*, 50:4, 272–4.

Laing, S. (1986), *Representations of Working-class Life 1957–1964*, London, Methuen.

Lazere, D. (ed.) (1987), *American Media and Mass Culture: Left Perspectives*, Berkeley and Los Angeles, University of California Press.

Lewin, G. R. (1971), *Documentary Explorations*, Garden City, NY, Doubleday.

McArthur, C. (1980), *BFI Television Monograph 8: Television and History*, London, British Film Institute.

MacDonald, K. and M. Cousins (1996), *Imagining Reality: The Faber Book of Documentary*, London and Boston, Faber and Faber.

McCarthy, J. and J. Morrell (1994), *Some Other Rainbow*, London, Corgi Books.

McFarlane, B. (1996), *Novel to Film: An Introduction to the Theory of Adaptation*, Oxford, Clarendon Press.

McGuinness, F. (1992), *Someone Who'll Watch Over Me*, London and Boston, Faber and Faber.

McNeil, A. (1991), *Total Television: A Comprehensive Guide to Programming from 1948 to the Present Day*, New York, Penguin.

Mapplebeck, V. (1997), 'Spoofer's double exposure', *Guardian*, 1 September.

Marill, A. (1987), *Movies Made for Television: The Telefeature and the Mini-series 1964–1986*, New York, Baseline.

Marris, P. (ed.) (1982), *BFI Dossier 16: Paul Rotha*, London, British Film Institute.

Maxwell, R. (1992), *The Mysteries of Paris and London*, London, University Press of Virginia.

Mendelson, E. (ed.) (1977), *The English Auden*, London, Faber and Faber.

Monaco, J. (1977), *How to Read a Film: The Art, Technology, Language, History and Theory of Film and Media*, New York, Oxford University Press.

Mulvey, L. (1989), *Visual and Other Pleasures*, London, Macmillan.

Musburger, R. (1985), 'Setting the scene of the television docudrama', *Journal of Popular Film and Television*, 13:2, 92–101.

Nelson, R. (1997), *TV Drama in Transition: Forms, Values and Cultural Change*,

London and New York, Macmillan/St Martin's.

Newcomb, H. (ed.) (1997), *The Museum of Broadcast Communication Encyclopaedia of Television*, Chicago and London, Fitzroy Dearborn (3 volumes).

Nichols, B. (1981), *Ideology and the Image*, Bloomington, Indiana University Press.

Nichols, B. (1991), *Representing Reality: Issues and Concepts in Documentary*, Bloomington, Indiana University Press.

Nichols, B. (1994), *Blurred Boundaries: Questions of Meaning in Contemporary Culture*, Bloomington, Indiana University Press.

Norris, C. (1992) *Uncritical Theory: Postmodernism, Intellectuals and the Gulf War*, London, Lawrence and Wishart.

O'Connor, J. and L. Brown (1980), *The Federal Theatre Project*, London, Eyre Methuen.

O'Connor, J. E. (ed.) (1983), *American History American Television: Interpreting the Video Past*, New York, Frederick Ungar.

O'Sullivan, T., J. Hartley, D. Saunders, M. Montgomery and J. Fiske (1994), *Key Concepts in Cultural and Communication Studies*, London, Routledge.

Page, A. (ed.) (1992), *The Death of the Playwright: Modern British Drama and Literary Theory*, London, Macmillan.

Paget, D. (1990), *True Stories?: Documentary Drama on Radio, Stage and Screen*, Manchester and New York, Manchester University Press.

Paget, D. (1992), 'Oh what a lovely post-modern war: drama and the Falklands', in Holderness, G. (ed.), *The Politics of Theatre and Drama*, London, Macmillan.

Petley, J. (1996), 'Fact plus fiction equals friction', *Media, Culture and Society*, 18:1, 11–25.

Prior, A. (1996), *Script to Screen: The Story of Five Television Plays*, St. Albans, Ver Books.

Rabiger, M. (1987), *Directing the Documentary*, Boston and London, Focal Press.

Rabinowitz, P. (1994), *They Must Be Represented: The Politics of Documentary*, London and New York, Verso.

Rapping, E. (1987), *The Looking Glass World of Nonfiction TV*, Boston, South End Press.

Renov, M. (ed.) (1993), *Theorising Documentary*, London and New York, Routledge.

Robertson, G. and A. Nicol (1992), *Media Law*, London, Penguin.

Rose, B. (ed.) (1985), *TV Genres: A Handbook and Reference Guide*, Westport, Conn., Greenwood Press.

Rosenthal, A. (ed.) (1980), *The Documentary Conscience*, Berkeley and Los Angeles, University of California Press.

Rosenthal, A. (ed.) (1988), *New Challenges for Documentary*, Berkeley and Los

Angeles, University of California Press.

Rosenthal, A. (1995), *Writing Docudrama: Dramatizing Reality for Film and TV*, Boston and Oxford, Focal Press.

Rotha, P. (with S. Road and R. Griffith) (3rd edn, 1952), *Documentary Film*, London, Faber and Faber.

Rotha, P. (ed.) (1956), *Television in the Making*, London, Focal Press.

Sackett, S. (1993), *Prime-Time Hits: Television's Most Popular Network Programs*, New York, Billboard.

Sandford, J. (1973), 'Edna and Cathy: just huge commercials', *Theatre Quarterly*, 3:10, 79–85. Extract also in Goodwin and Kerr (eds), *BFI Dossier 19*, 16–19.

Sandford, J. (1976), *Cathy Come Home*, London, Marion Boyars.

Scannell, P. (1979), 'The social eye of television, 1946–1955', *Media, Culture and Society*, 1:1, 97–106.

Scannell, P. (1986), '"The stuff of radio": developments in radio features and documentaries before the war', in Corner (ed.) *Documentary and the Mass Media*, 1–26.

Scheibler, S. (1993), 'Constantly performing the documentary: the seductive promise of *Lightning Over Water*', in Renov (ed.), *Theorising Documentary*, 135–50.

Schulze, L. (1990), 'The made-for-TV movie: industrial practice, cultural form, popular reception', in Balio (ed.), *Hollywood in the Age of Television*, 351–76.

Self, D. (1984), *TV Drama: An Introduction*, London, Macmillan.

Sendall, B., and J. Potter (1982), *Independent Television in Britain*, London, Macmillan (4 volumes).

Silverstone, R. (1986), 'The agonistic narratives of television science, in Corner (ed.), *Documentary and the Mass Media*, 81–106.

Sklar, R. (1980), *Prime-Time America: Life On and Behind the Television Screen*, New York, Oxford University Press.

Smith, A. (ed.) (1995), *Television: An International History*, Oxford, Oxford University Press.

Sparkes, R. (1992), *Television and the Drama of Crime: Moral Tales and the Place of Crime in Public Life*, Milton Keynes, Open University Press.

Steiger, J. (1997), 'Docudrama', in Newcomb (ed.), *The Museum of Broadcast Communication Encyclopaedia of Television*, Chicago and London, Fitzroy Dearborn, vol. 1, 514–17.

Stott, W. (1973), *Documentary Expression and Thirties America*, Oxford and New York, Oxford University Press.

Styan, J. (1962), 'Television drama', in J. Russell Brown and B. Harris (eds), *Stratford-upon-Avon Studies 4: Contemporary Theatre*, London, Edward

Arnold, 185–204.

Sussex, E. (1975), *The Rise and Fall of British Documentary*, Berkeley and Los Angeles, University of California Press.

Sussex, E. (1981), 'Getting it right', *Sight and Sound*, 51:1, 10–15.

Swallow, N. (1956), 'Documentary TV journalism', in Rotha (ed.), *Television in the Making*, 49–55.

Swallow, N. (1966), *Factual Television*, London, Focal Press.

Swallow, N. (1982), 'Rotha and television', in Marris (ed.), *BFI Dossier 16: Paul Rotha*, 86–9.

Swinson, A. (1955, 2nd edn, 1960), *Writing for Television*, London, Adam and Charles Black.

Swinson, A. (1956), 'Writing for television', in Rotha (ed.), *Television in the Making*, 37–43.

Swinson, A. (1963), *Writing for Television Today*, London, Adam and Charles Black.

Tulloch, J. (1990), *Television Drama: Agency, Audience and Myth*, London and New York, Routledge.

Tunstall, J. (1993), *Television Producers*, London and New York, Routledge.

Vaughan, D. (1976), *Television Documentary Usage*, London, British Film Institute.

Vaughan, D. (1986), 'Notes on the ascent of a fictitious mountain', in Corner (ed.), *Documentary and the Mass Media*, 161–75).

Willett, J. (1984), *Brecht on Theatre*, London, Methuen.

Willett, J. (1986), *Brecht in Context*, London, Methuen.

Williams, R. (1992), *Television: Technology and Cultural Form*, London, Routledge.

Williams, R. (1976), *Keywords: A Vocabulary of Culture and Society*, London, Fontana.

Williams, S. (1994), 'Fiction and reality: the making of *Hostages*', in A. Piroelle, and J.-P. Durix, *Interfaces 6*, Dijon, Université de Bourgogne.

Williamson, J. (1986), *Consuming Passions: The Dynamics of Popular Culture*, London and New York, Marion Boyars.

Willis, J. (1997), 'What's up, docs?', *Guardian*, 6 October.

Winston, B. (1994), in Hood (ed.), *Behind the Screens*, 20–42.

Winston, B. (1995), *Claiming the Real*, London, British Film Institute.

Woolfe, H. B. (1933), 'Commercial documentary', *Cinema Quarterly*, 2:2, 96–100.

Wyver, J. (1983), 'Invasion', *Time Out*, 15–21 August 1980 (extracted in Goodwin and Kerr (eds), *BFI Dossier 19: Drama-documentary*, 31–3).

Index